OXFORD BIBLE SERIES

General Editors
P. R. Ackroyd and G. N. Stanton

There are many commentaries on individual books of the Bible but the reader who wishes to take a broader view has less choice. This series is intended to meet this need. Each volume embraces a number of biblical books. Four deal thematically with different kinds of material in the Old Testament: narrative, prophecy, poetry/psalmody, wisdom, and law. Three handle different aspects of the New Testament: from the Gospels, Paul and Pauline Christianity, to varieties of New Testament thought. An additional volume looks at the nature of biblical interpretation, covering both Testaments.

Discussion in detail of selected biblical passages provides examples of the ways in which the interpretation of the text makes possible deeper understanding of the wider issues, both theological and historical, with which the Bible is concerned.

OXFORD BIBLE SERIES

General Editors
P. R. Ackroyd and G. N. Stanton

The Poems and Psalms of the Hebrew Bible

S. E. GILLINGHAM

OXFORD

UNIVERSITY PRESS

OXFORD

UNIVERSITY PRESS

Great Clarendon Street, Oxford OX2 6DP

Oxford University Press is a department of the University of Oxford.
It furthers the University's objective of excellence in research, scholarship,
and education by publishing worldwide in

Oxford New York

Athens Auckland Bangkok Bogotá Buenos Aires Calcutta
Cape Town Chennai Dar es Salaam Delhi Florence Hong Kong Istanbul
Karachi Kuala Lumpur Madrid Melbourne Mexico City Mumbai
Nairobi Paris São Paulo Singapore Taipei Tokyo Toronto Warsaw

with associated companies in Berlin Ibadan

Oxford is a registered trade mark of Oxford University Press
in the UK and in certain other countries

Published in the United States
by Oxford University Press Inc., New York

British Library Cataloguing in Publication Data
Data available

Library of Congress Cataloging in Publication Data
The poems and psalms of the Hebrew Bible/S. E. Gillingham.
(Oxford Bible series)
Includes bibliographical references and index.
1. Hebrew poetry, Biblical—History and criticism.   2. Bible.
O.T. Psalms—Criticism, interpretation, etc.   I. Title.   II. Series.
BS1405.2G54   1994   892.4'11094221—dc20   94-152
ISBN 0-19-213243-1 (Pbk)

3 5 7 9 10 8 6 4

Printed and bound in Great Britain by
Selwood Printing Ltd. West Sussex

GENERAL EDITORS' PREFACE

There are many commentaries on individual books of the Bible, but the reader who wishes to take a broader view has less choice. This series is intended to meet this need. Its structure is thematic, with each volume embracing a number of biblical books. It is designed for use with any of the familiar translations of the Bible; quotations are normally from RSV, but the authors of the individual volumes also use other translations or make their own where this helps to bring out the particular meaning of a passage.

To provide general orientation, there are two volumes of a more introductory character: one considers the Old Testament in its cultural and historical context, examining ways of approach to its complex ancient material; the other, on the New Testament, discusses the origins of Christianity. These two volumes point forward to the four which deal with different kinds of material in the Old Testament: narrative, prophecy, poetry/psalmody, wisdom and law; and to the three which handle different aspects of the New Testament: the Gospels, Paul and Pauline Christianity, the varieties of New Testament thought. Another volume looks at the nature of biblical interpretation, covering both Testaments. This is designed both to draw together some of the many themes touched on elsewhere, and also to invite the reader to look further at the problems of understanding an ancient literature in the very different cultural context of the present time.

The authors of the individual volumes write for a general readership. Technical terms and Hebrew or Greek words are explained; the latter are used only when essential to the understanding of the text. The general introductory volumes are designed to stand on their own, providing a framework, but also to serve to raise some of the questions which the remaining volumes examine in closer detail. All the volumes, with the exception of the two general ones and that on biblical interpretation, include discussion of selected biblical passages in greater depth, thus providing examples of the ways in which the interpretation of the text makes possible deeper understanding of the wider issues, both historical and theological, with which the Bible is concerned. Select bibliographies in each volume point the way to further discussion of the many issues which remain open to fuller explanation.

P.R.A.
G.N.S.

PREFACE

To read a biblical poem as an ancient literary text is difficult enough; to understand its setting within the social and religious life of the Israelite people requires an even more complicated appraisal. This study seeks to integrate both the critical and imaginative ways of reading biblical poetry.

There is no need at this stage to outline further my method and its application to selected biblical poems: the table of contents should make my line of argument clear. The purpose of this Preface is rather to acknowledge those who have made possible the completion of this book. First and foremost I am grateful to Peter Ackroyd, who had initially intended to write it himself: he most graciously offered me his draft copy, from which I could then stake out my own territory according to my interests and preferences.

Three seminal studies on Hebrew poetry have influenced my work. I owe a debt to L. Alonso Schökel, whose book *A Manual of Hebrew Poetics* offered many fresh insights into the nature of biblical poetry and whose examples of biblical verse have shaped my own interpretation of the same issues. Similarly, W. G. E. Watson's *Classical Hebrew Poetry* has been an invaluable resource; so too has *The Art of Biblical Poetry* by R. Alter, whose writing on literary issues is always fresh and stimulating. There are of course many other scholars from whose work I have drawn in innumerable ways: their works are listed under the general bibliography at the end of the book.

My students at Worcester and Keble colleges have been an enormous source of encouragement, and I acknowledge here my gratitude to all of them. Deserving particular mention is Paula Gooder, who proof-read so patiently the Hebrew transliterations. Several colleagues in the Theology Faculty have been equally supportive: special thanks are due to Hugh Williamson, who offered some useful insights on my chapter on Hebrew metre; to Chris Rowland, who helped me to shape my thoughts about method in the earlier stages; and to Geoffrey Rowell, who has always helped me to see the power of poetry not only in the Hebrew scriptures, but beyond them.

This book was read in its earlier stages by three colleagues, each of whom has influenced its final form in different ways. I am indebted to Graham Stanton for his patience and thoroughness in enabling me to see how the book should be accommodated to the Oxford Bible Series; also to Br. Robert Atwell, OSB, of Burford Priory, who made many constructive suggestions about style and emphases. But I am especially beholden to John Barton, for he it was who encouraged me to rework Peter Ackroyd's book in the first place, and his constant support and scholarly advice have been an enormous influence on my theological reflection. It is fitting therefore that I dedicate this book to him—a mentor, colleague, and trusted friend.

S.G.

Worcester College, Oxford
January 1994

CONTENTS

ABBREVIATIONS

ABD	*Anchor Bible Dictionary* (New York, 1992)
AV	Authorized Version
Bib.	*Biblica*
BQ	*Biblical Quarterly*
CBQ	*Catholic Biblical Quarterly*
CTA	*Corpus des tablettes en cunéiformes alphabétiques* (A. Herdner: Paris, 1963)
EJ	*Encyclopaedia Judaica* (Jerusalem, 1972)
IBC	*Interpreter's Bible Commentary* (New York, Abingdon, Nashville, 1951)
IDB	*Interpreter's Dictionary of the Bible* (Nashville, Tenn., 1962)
Interp.	*Interpretation*
JBC	*Jerome Bible Commentary* (New York and London, 1968)
JBL	*Journal of Biblical Literature*
JETS	*Journal of the Evangelical Theological Society*
JQR	*Jewish Quarterly Review*
JSOT	*Journal for the Study of the Old Testament*
JSS	*Journal for Semitic Studies*
JTS	*Journal of Theological Studies*
NEB	New English Bible
NIV	New International Version
NJB	New Jerusalem Bible
NRSV	New Revised Standard Version
OTS	*Oudtestamentische Studien*
REB	Revised English Bible
RSV	Revised Standard Version
SBL	Society of Biblical Literature
SBL MS	Society of Biblical Literature Monograph Series
SDB	*Supplément au dictionnaire de la Bible* (Paris, 1947–)
SJTh	*Scottish Journal of Theology*
StTh	*Studies in Theology*

TB	*Tyndale Bulletin*
ThLZ	*Theologische Literaturzeitung*
UF	*Ugarit-Forschungen*
UT	*Ugaritic Textbook* (C. Gordon: Rome, 1965)
VT	*Vetus Testamentum*
ZAW	*Zeitschrift für die Alttestamentliche Wissenschaft*

PART I

Identifying Hebrew Poetry

I

Poets, Poems, and Performances

A. Interpreting Poetry: An Analogy from Music

It is not difficult to think of correspondences between reading poetry and listening to music. In his lecture on 'The Music of Poetry', delivered at Glasgow University in 1942, T. S. Eliot develops these as follows:

> I think that a poet may gain much from the study of music . . . I believe that the properties in which music concerns the poet most nearly, are the sense of rhythm and the sense of structure . . . possibilities of transitions in a poem comparable to the different movements of a symphony or a quartet . . . possibilities of contrapuntal arrangement of subject-matter . . . (*On Poetry and Poets*, 38.)

Within this particular context, Eliot is referring to the poet or musician as composer rather than to the audience as participators. In a more recent work called *The Art of Performance*, Frances Young uses an analogy from music which applies as much to those who participate in the performance as to those who compose the score. The analogy is apposite as an introduction to our discussion on the nature of biblical poetry.

Young speaks of two levels in our appreciation of music—first, the 'lexical level', whereby we focus primarily on the score, in terms of its interplay between accepted conventions and the creative imagination of the composer; and second, the 'performance level', when the musicians bring the score to life in the presence of practised listeners. These two levels represent two complementary approaches: the one, understanding music, and the other, appreciating it. The first is concerned with the more visible aspects in an analysis of the written score, and the second with a more auditory and receptive process, whereby nuances of a performance give the score new life and meaning.

It is possible to transpose Young's musical analogy into our considerations about poetry. The literary form of the poem is akin to the score, whilst the performance of the poem may be understood as the way poetry is received, by practised listeners. The two approaches of *understanding* (the lexical and intellectual level) and *appreciation* (the level which is as much concerned with the imagination as with the intellect) are two parts of the same process.

Understanding is necessary for academic study of and critical engagement with any poetic text. It involves discerning the structure, the form, and the conventions of language, and also (where possible) evaluating the setting of the poem in the life of the poet and the poet's culture. In this process, we, as readers, become the subjects of the exercise, and the poem and the poet are the objects. By contrast, an appreciation of poetry is a reversal of this process: the poem becomes the subject, so that as we allow ourselves to be addressed, the poetry is the active element and we are the recipients.

This twofold approach might also be described as *looking at* a poem and *looking through* it. The difference is more one of degree than of kind; to look at a poem has more to do with a process of detachment and analysis, whilst to look through it concerns more an attitude of engagement and receptivity. We need both in order to gain a more profound discernment of any poetry. To return to T. S. Eliot:

If in literary criticism, we place all the emphasis upon *understanding*, we are in danger of slipping from understanding to mere explanation. We are in danger even of pursuing criticism as if it was a science, which it can never be. If, on the other hand, we over-emphasise *enjoyment*, we will tend to fall into the subjective and impressionistic, and our enjoyment will profit us no more than mere amusement and pastime. ('The Frontiers of Criticism', in *On Poetry and Poets*, 117.)

B. Understanding and Appreciation of Hebrew Poetry

We might well question whether this twofold response to poetry is applicable to Hebrew verse in particular. It could be argued that our focus of attention should be on the former aspect only—that of understanding and analysis—and that we should be more concerned with the acquisition of technical knowledge than with the enjoyment of poetry. But if Eliot's observations are correct, then to read poetry even from an ancient culture requires not only explanation and understanding, but also enjoyment and appreciation. There is also one other reason supporting this approach, and this relates to biblical poetry in particular.

No one with any literary sensitivity can read Hebrew poetry without realizing that its very process of transmission has been through the art of performance. Whether discussing the tribal blessings buried in the early stories of the patriarchs, or the victory songs celebrating Israel's origins as a nation, or the carefully constructed laments used by the people at times of national loss— whatever the example of Hebrew poetry we may use, we soon become aware that this 'text' has been repeated and performed countless times, either through popular activities of folk-religion, or within the more formal liturgy of the Temple community. Hebrew poetry has been preserved not simply because it became accepted as good literature; it has been remembered and repeated because of its evocative power in performance—a performance which created both a memory and identity in the history of the people. Thus, to understand Hebrew poetry at all, we have to participate imaginatively in its performative power.

This observation is especially pertinent with regard to the psalms. These are ancient liturgical poems: not only is it important to read a psalm as one would any ancient poetic text, but it is also possible to receive it as a liturgical prayer. The psalms have an evocative power: they communicate beyond the boundaries of ancient Israel, and continuously testify to a capacity to perform from their one 'score'.

Two critical issues arise out of this understanding of biblical poetry in general and the psalms in particular. The first is the theological issue of *inspiration*: because Hebrew verse emanates from a Judaeo-Christian tradition which gives it a special religious authority, how do we integrate into our ordinary reading the claims from that tradition that it has both divine and human inspiration? The second issue is the more technical one of *translation*: because our study is concerned with English readers who have relatively little—if any—familiarity with the Hebrew originals, is it possible to appreciate fully the 'score' of Hebrew poetry in a translated form?

C. Inspiration and Biblical Poetry

The issue of inspiration is important not only because we are look-ing at the poetry of the Hebrew Scriptures, but also because we need to assess the quality of a poem and the creative ability of the poet. It is certainly true that with biblical poetry, the issue is more defined: how are we to judge the human inspiration of a poet when the verse is set within a broader framework of literature which many would claim was divinely inspired? In brief, whence comes the poet's inspiration?

Robert Lowth has been a formative influence for an understand-ing of inspiration and Hebrew verse. He first delivered lectures on this subject in 1741, as Praelector of Poetry for the University of Oxford, and these were published in Latin in 1753 and in English in 1839. Lowth accepted unreservedly that the Hebrew poets were inspired not only by natural means, but also by a supernatural activity. In his view (following, for example, earlier writers such as Philip Sidney), Hebrew verse was a form of *prophetic* utterance. Of his thirty-four lectures, he included the five on the poetry of the psalms under a main title 'Prophetic Poetry': the psalmists, being inspired, utter their poetry as the word of God in human form, just as the prophets did. Lowth's later work on the poetic forms of the prophet Isaiah made the same point in reverse: the prophetic oracles are poetic in form (even though the Hebrew text presents them as prose) because poetry is the most appropriate medium for divine inspiration, and the prophets were inspired by the word of God. According to Lowth, therefore, biblical poetry must be prophetic in its origin, and prophecy must be poetic in its form.

The basic understanding here (and one which has influenced much writing on Hebrew poetry since Lowth) is that the source and the goal of the poet's inspiration—whether prophet or psalmist—was from God and for God.

The last two hundred and fifty years have progressed in a somewhat different direction. Scholars today prefer to view the inspiration of both prophets and psalmists in a more mundane and human way. For example, the modern liturgical translations of the Psalter (from the 1928 Prayer Book to *The Liturgical Psalter* adapted by the Anglican Church for inclusion in *The Alternative Service Book* (1980)) actually marginalize verses they consider to be less than inspired: those verses, deemed 'unsuitable for use in public worship', are printed in square brackets. Perhaps the best-known example is from Ps. 137:

> [happy shall be he who takes your little ones:
> and dashes them against the stones.]   (v. 9)

The idea of selective inspiration cuts both ways: who might claim divine inspiration for such sentiments? Or who might claim divine inspiration for deleting them?

But the issue of inspiration is obviously relevant in a context beyond that of Scripture alone. Not only is it possible to question the inspiration of particular verses of biblical poems, but it is also possible to encounter an inspired quality in other poetry which is not in the Bible. Just as Scripture is now seen to contain less-than-inspired poetry (whether in divine or human terms), so too in other literary works, both ancient and modern, there is ample evidence of verse which is equally inspired. No longer can we follow Lowth and use biblical poetry as the highest expression of inspired poetry, so that it becomes the measuring-line in determining the artistic merit and profundity of meaning of other poetry.

Below is a selection of poems which have some clear correspondences with poems from Scripture—indeed they are derivatives of the poetry of the prophets and psalms. Together they illustrate the difficulty of finding adequate criteria for establishing distinctive inspiration for a biblical poem.

The first examples are both poems of protest against God. The biblical poem is from the book of Jeremiah, written in about the seventh century BCE, a prayer which remonstrates with God's justice on account of the prophet's isolation because of his people's rejection of his message of divine judgement. The non-biblical example is a poem of Gerard Manley Hopkins, written in 1889, the last year of his life—a poem which also questions divine justice and which has clearly been influenced by the lament in Jeremiah 12. Both poems suggest a quality of inspiration in terms of their outward form and evocation of meaning. We may note the attention given by each poet to the overall structure, for whilst Jeremiah's prayer follows the typical style of Hebrew lament in its initial cry for divine help, leading to a description of distress, and ending with a note of confidence in the protection and provision of God, Hopkins's poem develops creatively the fourteen-line sonnet form. Each poem has a certain artistry: in Jeremiah 12, this is evidenced in the use of the paired line-forms, whilst in Hopkins, the form is found in the familiar 'sprung rhythm' and the use of 'inscape' in the heart of the poem, whereby the meaning of the poem is as much in the sensuous shaping of the language as in the concepts conveyed through it. So too in each example we perceive the richness of imagery and interconnection of words which evoke a certain response in the reader. How, then, do we determine the nature of inspiration within each of these poems?

> Righteous art thou, O LORD,
>> when I complain to thee;
>> yet I would plead my cause before thee.
> Why does the way of the wicked prosper?
> Why do all who are treacherous thrive?
>
> Thou plantest them, and they take root;
>> they grow and bring forth fruit;
> thou art near in their mouth
>> and far from their heart.
>
> But thou, O LORD, knowest me;
>> thou seest me, and triest my mind toward thee.
> Pull them out like sheep for the slaughter,
>> and set them apart for the day of slaughter.

How long will the land mourn,
  and the grass of every field wither?
For the wickedness of those who dwell in it
  the birds and beasts are swept away,
    because men said, 'He will not see our latter end.'

'If you have raced with men on foot,
  and they have wearied you,
    how will you compete with horses?
And if in a safe land you fall down,
  how will you do in the jungle of the Jordan?

For even your brothers and the house of your father,
  even they have dealt treacherously with you;
    they are in full cry after you;
believe them not,
  even though they speak fair words to you.'

                                (Jer. 12: 1–6)

Justus quidem tu es, Domine

Thou art indeed just, Lord, if I contend
With thee; but, sir, so what I plead is just.
Why do sinners' ways prosper? and why must
Disappointment all I endeavour end?

Wert thou my enemy, O thou my friend,
How wouldst thou worse, I wonder, than thou dost
Defeat, thwart me? Oh, the sots and thralls of lust
Do in spare hours more thrive than I that spend,

Sir, life upon thy cause. See, banks and brakes
Now, leavèd how thick! lacèd they are again
With fretty chervil, look, and fresh wind shakes

Them; birds build—but not I build; no, but strain,
Time's eunuch, and not breed one work that wakes.
Mine, O thou lord of life, send my roots rain.

It is quite clear that we cannot make special pleading for the inspiration of poetry on the grounds that it is found in Scripture. We read poetry whether within or outside the Bible as literature and for enjoyment; we cannot affirm a particular inspiration for one poem, yet deny it for another.

This issue is further illustrated in the following pairs of poems. They contrast well with the examples from Jeremiah 12 and Hopkins. Instead of prayers of protest, these are hymns of praise. In each case, the second popular example has been influenced by the biblical poem, and is an adaptation of it, albeit making use of the stanza form and the rhyming couplet, which are more in tune with English conventions of poetry than anything from the Hebrew. Nevertheless, it is again impossible to pronounce particular inspiration for the 'original' and to deny it for the 'copy'.

1.

> Make a joyful noise to the LORD, all the lands!
>   Serve the LORD with gladness!
>   Come into his presence with singing!
> Know that the LORD is God!
>   It is he that made us, and we are his;
>   we are his people, and the sheep of his pasture.

> (Psalm 100: 1–3)

.   .   .   .

> All people that on earth do dwell,
>   Sing to the Lord with cheerful voice;
> Him serve with fear, his praise forth tell,
>   Come ye before him, and rejoice.
> The Lord, ye know, is God indeed,
>   Without our aid he did us make;
> We are his folk, he doth us feed,
>   And for his sheep he doth us take.

> William Kethe (d. 1594)

2.

> O give thanks to the Lord of lords,
>   for his steadfast love endures for ever;
> to him who alone does great wonders,
>   for his steadfast love endures for ever;
> to him who by understanding made the heavens,
>   for his steadfast love endures for ever;

to him who spread out the earth upon the waters,
for his steadfast love endures for ever;

(Psalm 136: 3–6)

. . . .

Let us with a gladsome mind,
Praise the Lord for he is kind:
For his mercies aye endure,
Ever faithful, ever sure.

Let us blaze his name abroad,
For of gods he is the God:
For his mercies aye endure,
Ever faithful, ever sure.

He with all-commanding might
Filled the new-made world with light:
For his mercies aye endure,
Ever faithful, ever sure.

John Milton (1608–74)

3.

I will bless the LORD at all times;
his praise shall continually be in my mouth.
My soul makes its boast in the LORD;
let the afflicted hear and be glad.
O magnify the LORD with me,
and let us exalt his name together!
I sought the LORD, and he answered me,
and delivered me from all my fears.

(Psalm 34: 1–4)

. . . .

Through all the changing scenes of life,
In trouble and in joy,
The praises of my God shall still
My heart and tongue employ.

O magnify the LORD with me,
With me exalt his name;

When in distress to him I called,
He to my rescue came.

Nahum Tate (1652–1715) and
Nicholas Brady (1659–1726)

4.

Bless the LORD, O my soul,
and all that is within me,
bless his holy name!
Bless the LORD, O my soul,
and forget not his benefits,
who forgives all your iniquity,
who heals all your diseases

.   .   .   .   .

Bless the LORD, all his works,
in all places of his dominion.
Bless the LORD, O my soul!

(Psalm 103: 1–3, 22)

.   .   .   .   .

Praise, my soul, the King of heaven;
To his feet thy tribute bring.
Ransomed, healed, restored, forgiven,
Who like thee his praise should sing?
Praise him! Praise him!
Praise the everlasting King.

Henry Francis Lyte (1793–1847)

These extracts cumulatively offer an important observation with respect to the nature of their poetic inspiration. The theological content and the poetic expression are evident in each pair, so that it is invariably a matter of personal literary taste to prefer one over and against another. It could be argued that the second example in each case is derivative, in so far as it has been inspired by the Hebrew original, and thus could be seen as an imitation. On this account the biblical example is the source of the inspiration of the non-biblical verse. In this way, special pleading for the biblical example usually has little to do with a literary appraisal: it rests on an entirely different theological argument about the nature of Scripture, rather than on one about the nature of biblical poetry.

A musical analogy might be helpful in recognizing this distinction. The poetry within Scripture could be said to pertain to a particular (albeit diverse) tradition in the same way that we might discern vast yet distinctive traditions of music (for example, from Austria, or Italy, or France, or Russia). Innumerable imitations and musical variations have developed out of these different cultural styles, which each have their own distinctive source of inspiration, different in degree although not necessarily in kind from the inspiration of the earlier creative source from which they are derived. The same observation might apply to biblical poetry and its adaptations: the evaluation of inspiration is very much bound up with the religio-historical tradition in which the poetry finds its voice.

D. Poetry, Culture, and Language

We now turn to the issue of whether it is possible to understand and appreciate a text which has come to us as a 'translated score'. Here again, Hebrew possesses an interesting distinctive feature: its poetic form consists mainly of balanced expressions of thought which make it relatively easy to translate into line-forms, thus allowing its inner coherence to remain intact. As C. S. Lewis rather laconically puts it: 'It is (according to one's point of view) either a wonderful piece of luck or a wise provision of God's, that poetry which was to be turned into all languages should have as its formal characteristic one that does not disappear (as mere metre does) in translation' (*Reflections on the Psalms*, 12).

Certainly Robert Lowth would have agreed with this observation. For different reasons, Lowth wished Hebrew poetry to reflect a distinctive quality on its own merits; this was in reaction to the legacy of the Renaissance writers on poetry, such as Wyatt, Surrey, Sidney, Donne, and Milton, who, albeit also wishing to affirm the artistry and creativity of the biblical poetry, supposed that this was because it followed the same poetic conventions as did Greek and Roman classical poetry. In Lowth's view, Hebrew poetry had a commendable quality *of its own*—summarized by the terseness of expression in its balanced pairing of ideas:

> For the Greek, beyond every other language (and the Latin next to it), is copious, flowing and harmonious, possessed of a great variety of measures, of which the impression is so definite, the effects so striking, that if you should recite some lame and imperfect portion of a verse . . . the numbers would nevertheless be clearly discernible . . . But in the Hebrew language the whole economy is different. Its form is simple, above every other; the words are uniform, and resemble each other almost exactly . . . so that possibly they found it necessary to distinguish the extent of the verse by the conclusion of the sentence, lest the lines by running into each other, should become altogether implicated and confused. (From Lecture III, 'The Hebrew Poetry is Metrical', p. 35.)

Does this, then, mean that we can understand the essence of Hebrew poetry without having to refer to the original text? Luis Alonso Schökel, writing in *A Manual of Hebrew Poetics*, believes not. Hebrew poetry, he observes, also consists in 'a conscious, clever and varied use of sound'. Thus, although one might be able to transpose the *balance of ideas* from the original language, it is impossible to reproduce the *sonority* from the original as well, for a translator is constrained by the poetic capabilities of his or her own language when seeking to imitate it. The repetitions of sounds and the plays on words are poetic ploys integral to the Hebrew, and thus although we may be able to preserve some of the essence in the terseness and brevity of balanced ideas, we will gain better insights into the full artistic impact with some understanding of Hebrew. (On this account, the following chapters will, where necessary, offer the transliterated form of the Hebrew, so that it is possible for non-Hebraists to perceive some of these subtleties.)

Schökel's point is well illustrated in a verse from Isaiah 5: 7. This completes a poem of judgement against Israel—a poem taking up the form and language of an ancient vintage song—indicating to the people that they will be pruned and purged as one would a vineyard which has grown wild. The song ends:

A   and he looked for justice,
B   but behold, bloodshed:

A   for righteousness,
B   but behold, a cry!

What is preserved in translation is the balance of the words in lines A ('justice' and 'righteousness') and in lines B ('bloodshed' and 'cry'). Similarly preserved is the climactic ascent of the verse, within the implication that the cry of those suffering the bloodshed will one day be avenged, and justice will be seen to have been done. The balancing of ideas and images is thus retained in spite of the translation.

However, what *is* missed in translation is a different effect—not just the balance of sense, but also the balance of sound, which in turn offers us further insights into the sense on account of the sound. A transliteration of the Hebrew runs as follows:

wayqaw leˁmišpāṭ	and-he-looked for-justice
weḥinnēh miśpāḥ	but-behold bloodshed
liṣdāqâ	for-righteousness
weḥinnēh ṣeˁāqâ	but-behold a-cry!

In this rendering, the balance of sound is between justice (mišpāṭ) and bloodshed (miśpāḥ) and between righteousness (ṣeˁdāqâ) and cry (ṣeˁāqâ). A deeper meaning thus becomes evident in perceiving the balance of sound alongside the balance of sense: when justice is replaced (i.e. covered) by bloodshed, then the cry must be replaced (i.e. vindicated) by righteousness. A good appreciation of the poetry can obviously be attained in translation; but by having some knowledge of the Hebrew, we are better equipped to understand the subtleties of poetic effect.

E. Conclusions: The Art of Hebrew Poetry

Further observations relevant to our discussion may be found in two very different scholars who have lectured a good deal on the relationship between theology and poetry. John Keble held the Chair of Poetry at Oxford between 1832 and 1841; his *Praelectiones Academicae* were (like those of Lowth) given during his time as professor. In these, Keble develops the idea that the art of poetry is to *conceal* as much as it is to *reveal*. Poetry starts with what is known and from this reaches out to convey the unknown, being 'a universal description of a particular detail' (Lecture XXXIII). This idea is also found in Keble's Preface to his *Psalter in English Verse*:

the rule which He who spake by the Prophets [is] to disclose, rather than exhibit, His dealings and His will; to keep Himself, to the generality, under a veil of reserve . . . Considering the Psalms as divine *Poems*, this surely is a quality which we should expect to find in them: a certain combination of reserve with openness being of the very essence of poetry. (xli.)

Good poetry evokes a response as much by what is not truly expressed, as by what is given explicit expression. We may also recall Tennyson in 'In Memoriam V':

> For words, like Nature, half reveal
> And half conceal the Soul within.

Paradoxically, poetry (like music) can often be appreciated best when it is least perfectly understood. Ancient biblical poetry in particular has a power to evoke a response in us, because (on account of its antiquity) it has a capacity both to stir our memories with things which are strangely familiar, and also to challenge our vision with its depiction of things which will always remain strangely unknown: anyone familiar with reading the psalms will understand this paradox. This is not to deny scholarly reading its proper place, but it is to delineate its limits, especially where ancient poetic texts are concerned.

C. S. Lewis was a Fellow and Tutor in English Literature at Magdalen College, Oxford, from 1925, and held the Chair in English Medieval and Renaissance Literature at Cambridge from 1954. Lewis frequently developed the idea that the purpose of good poetry was to be an 'artistic imitation of reality'. This is very much akin to Keble's view: concealing and revealing, poetry becomes a particular embodiment of universal realities: 'For poetry too is a little incarnation, giving body to what had been before invisible and inaudible' (C. S. Lewis, *Reflections on the Psalms*, 12). This model of the incarnation is in fact the converse of Keble's observations. Poetry takes things from our experience to point us to things outside our experience; it reveals, yet it also conceals. A verse from a poem by Lewis, entitled 'The Birth of Language', depicts this well:

> So dim below these symbols show,
> Bony and abstract every one.
> Yet if true verse but lift the curse,
> They feel in dreams their native Sun.

(Poems, 11)

This is akin to what Eliot calls 'a raid on the inarticulate', for it offers us a sense of the mysterious and the inexplicable. Herein is our challenge: there is always the need to appreciate all good verse with our intellect, but at the same time such verse strains at the limits of intellect alone. A study of biblical poetry cannot be the preserve of the expertise of academic scholars, for there is a danger that, using the mind alone, the text would be dissected and controlled as if it were a mathematical equation. Yet nor can a reading be left entirely at the mercy of amateur interpreters, for then there is the danger of gross subjectivity and superficiality: in intuiting and spiritualizing the inner meaning of a text, it is similarly reduced, this time to little more than a magical incantation. Understanding and appreciation, intellect and imagination need to work together for balanced reading: and the following chapters are written with this tension very much in mind.

Poetry and Prose

It is usually assumed that there are clear distinctions between poetry and prose. For example, in *The Poetry of the Old Testament*, T. H. Robinson states on the first page:

Most of us know the difference between poetry and prose. When we hear or see a passage we have no difficulty in deciding to which class of literature it belongs. Conventionally and very conveniently, poetry is written in definite lines, each of which is, as it were, a complete whole, and in one way or another stands apart from what precedes and what follows. (p. 11.)

Robinson is, of course, referring to English poetry, and the principles he assumes include the use of syllable stress and a certain regularity of rhythm. But because there are certain conventions for delineating poetry in our own language, this need not offer a framework of reference for similarly ascertaining Hebrew poetry.

Robinson wrote in 1947. Studies since have suggested that the resemblance between the two languages is indeed less straightforward. As we have seen, one feature of Hebrew poetry is the way its essence (the binary balancing of ideas) can be retained in translation. Yet curiously enough, this essence is still retained when the Hebrew is presented in English in prose style. For example, in *The Penguin Book of Hebrew Verse*, T. Carmi renders the verse in prose in English, on the grounds that there are too many differences between English and Hebrew poetry to permit the presenting of a particular medium of the one in the same medium of the other. Carmi's approach highlights the distinctiveness of *Hebrew* poetry, but it nevertheless diminishes the contrast between *prose* and *poetry*.

Various implications follow from this. Not least, we have to ask whether our attempt to make a division between Hebrew poetry and prose is our own imposition on the text, a result in part of our assumptions about how poetry works from what we know of Greek and Latin verse. Because we supposedly know how to determine a poem in our tongue, are we assuming that Semitic poetry follows the same conventions too? Did the Hebrews even have the same perception as we have regarding the boundaries between poetry and prose?

Three factors together suggest that there are in fact no clear-cut distinctions between prose and poetry in Hebrew. First, the Masoretes, who between the eighth and tenth centuries CE copied the ancient Hebrew texts, giving them their pointing, vocalization, and stress, seemed to have had little regard for any consistent division of poetry and prose. Psalms, Proverbs, Song of Solomon, Job, Lamentations, and some of the twelve minor prophets are presented in entirety in poetic form, but there is no specific literary category called 'Poetic Books'; rather, the threefold division is that of Law, Prophets, and Writings. (This is in clear contrast to the threefold division in the Greek translation of the Scriptures, which subdivides the biblical books into categories of History, Prophecy, and Poetry.)

Second, in our own language as well as in Hebrew, recent literary critical studies of the biblical material have directed our attention to the 'poetics' of biblical *narratives* in terms of style, form, and structure, and so have broadened our own understanding of what counts as 'poetic'. (On this issue, see D. M. Gunn and D. Fewell, *Narrative in the Hebrew Bible*, also in the Oxford Bible Series, 147 ff.)

A third example of the blurred distinctions between prose and poetry is illustrated in the following selection of so-called poetic texts in the Bible as presented in the various modern translations. The several variations of what counts as a poetic line-form and what reads as prose demonstrate the uncertainty of scholarly opinion in this matter.

Genesis 1: 27:

AV   So God created man in his own image, in the image of God
          created he him; male and female created he them.

NEB   So God created man in his own image; in the image of God he
          created him; male and female he created them.

REB   God created human beings in his own image;
              in the image of God he created them;
              male and female he created them.

RSV   So God created man in his own image, in the image of God he
          created him; male and female he created them.

NRSV   So God created humankind in his image,
              in the image of God he created them;
              male and female he created them.

NJB   God created man in the image of himself,
              in the image of God he created them;
              male and female he created them.

NIV   So God created man
                  in his own image
              in the image of God
                  he created them
              male and female
                  he created them.

Jeremiah 15: 10:

AV   Woe is me, my mother, that thou hast borne me a man of
          strife and a man of contemption to the whole earth! I
          have neither lent on usury, nor men have lent to me on
          usury; yet every one of them doth curse me.

NEB   Alas, alas, my mother, that you ever gave me birth!
              a man doomed to strife, with the whole world against me.
              I have borrowed from no one, I have lent to no one,
                  yet all men abuse me.

REB   Alas, my mother, that ever you gave birth to me,
              a man doomed to strife
              with the whole world against me!
              I have borrowed from no one

> I have lent to no one
> yet everyone abuses me.

RSV   Woe is me, my mother, that you bore me, a man of strife and contention to the whole land! I have not lent, nor have I borrowed, yet all of them curse me.

NRSV   Woe is me, my mother, that you bore me, a man of strife and contention to the whole land! I have not lent, nor have I borrowed, yet all of them curse me.

NJB   A disaster for me, mother, that you bore me
  to be a man of strife and dissension for the whole country
  I neither lend nor borrow,
  yet all of them curse me.

NIV   Alas, my mother, that you gave me birth,
    a man with whom the whole land strives and contends!
  I have not lent nor borrowed,
    yet everyone curses me.

This selection speaks for itself: it shows the very different judgement of scholars in their own assessment of what counts as poetry and prose, both in Hebrew and in English.

So what might be the criteria for ascertaining Hebrew poetry? The following two sections will seek to outline some of them, starting with more general features and moving on to more specific characteristics.

A. Criteria Suggesting Hebrew Verse: General Observations

We may note four more general features of Hebrew verse:

1. *A terseness of style*, whereby a maximum of four Hebrew words serves each clause: a good example is in Exod. 15: 12–13:

> Thou-dost-stretch-out   thy-right-hand,
>   (the-)earth   swallowed-them.
> Thou-hast-led   in-thy-steadfast-love   (a-)people
>   whom   thou-hast-redeemed.

2. *Figurative language*, which takes the reader/listener away from a particular and time-centred focus of attention towards a more

typical and timeless world-view. Psalm 46: 1–3 is a good example, for in its concern for God's protection of Zion, the imagery has a more far-reaching and timeless appeal than would a piece of narrative writing:

> God is our refuge and strength,
> a very present help in trouble.
> Therefore we will not fear though the earth should change,
>   though the mountains shake in the heart of the sea;
> though its waters roar and foam,
>   though the mountains tremble with its tumult.

3. *An ambiguity of meaning*, which is linked to the use of figurative language, which gives the text its capacity both to 'conceal' and to 'reveal'. The first of the following two examples is from an individual prayer of complaint, the second from a psalm of praise:

When I declared not my sin, [lit.: When I kept silence]
    my body wasted away
    through my groaning all day long.
For day and night thy hand was heavy upon me;
    my strength was dried up [Hebrew obscure; lit.: my moisture was dry]
    as by the heat of summer [lit.: as by the summer droughts].

(Ps. 32: 3–4)

The context appears to be a severe fever which the poet attributed to unconfessed sin; but to state this in the more stark, prosaic form would mean losing its impact on the reader's empathy.

Similarly, if the following congregational hymn of praise were offered in prose style, a certain impact would be lost:

> Let the heavens be glad, and let the earth rejoice;
>   let the sea roar, and all that fills it;
>   let the field exult, and everything in it!
> Then shall the trees of the wood sing for joy
>   Before the LORD, for he comes,
>   for he comes to judge the earth.

(Ps. 96: 11–13)

In this case, the description is of the whole of the created order finding harmony in the Creator's care. A prose form can achieve the same meaning; but its impact on the imagination is entirely different.

4. *Evocation of a response*, which is of course, intrinsic to all poetry, regardless of culture and language. The inclusion of this feature is not intended to deny that prose forms also evoke a response from the reader/listener, but rather to affirm that poetry does so in a different way. Much of our discussion in the previous chapter, using comparisons between a performance of music and a performance of poetry, was an illustration of the peculiar evocation of poetry: it is indeed a 'raid on the inarticulate', with an open-endedness which calls for a response from the reader or listener.

B. Criteria for Hebrew Verse: Some Specific Features

We may note the following twelve more particular characteristics which define further the boundaries between poetry and prose, especially in Hebrew:

1. *The omission of certain particles* which are used more pre-dominantly in so-called Hebrew prose, the most frequent including the definite article *h-*, the relative pronoun *ᵃšer*, and the sign of the definite object *et*. This feature is a more specific example of the general characteristic of terseness of style. In these two examples, the words in square brackets are those which have been omitted in Hebrew:

> What is-man that thou-art-mindful-of-him
> and [what-is] [the] son-of-man that thou-dost-care-for him?
>
> (Ps. 8: 4)
>
> [The-]stone [which] the builders rejected
> has become [the-]head [of-the-]corner.
>
> (Ps. 118: 22)

2. *The use of ellipsis*, or the omission of a word in a second phrase when it is the same as the one used in the first. Again this is related

to poetry's terseness of style. W. G. E. Watson (*Classical Hebrew Poetry*) cites the following example from Amos 5: 12:

> For I know how many are your transgressions
> and [   ] how great are your sins

3. *The organization of the material into line-forms*, whereby within certain variables each line conforms to various grammatical constraints. T. Collins (*Line-Forms in Hebrew Poetry*) proposes that one standard verse-line consists of a subject (NP1), an object (NP2), a verb (V), and modifiers of the verb (M), within which norm the Hebrew poet can create various configurations. One example cited by Collins is from Jer. 12: 6, noted previously:

For even your brothers and the house of your father	
even they have dealt treacherously with you;	NP1 V M
they are in full cry after you;	NP1 V M NP2
believe them not	V M
though they speak fair words to you.	V M NP2

4. *An unusual word-order*, when instead of the normal verb–subject–object sequence, the verb occurs in the middle or at the end of a clause. An interesting example is from the first line of an ancient poem, known as the oracle of Balaam. This may be translated literally (noting the ellipsis in the square bracket):

> From-Aram   has-brought-me Balak,
> the-king-of-Moab [   ] from-the-mountains-in-the-east
>
> (Num. 23: 7)

5. *Word-pairs*, such as evening/morning, light/dark, land/sea, bread/meat. Although these also occur often in the narrative forms, they are far more frequent in poetry, being an obvious way of expressing ideas in some balanced binary form. A typical example is in Ps. 54, which is full of such pairing. A more concise example in one verse would be Ps. 30: 5:

> For *his anger* is but for *a moment*
> and *his favour* is for *a lifetime*.

Weeping may tarry for *the night*,
but *joy* comes with *the morning*.

6. *Phonic word-pairs*, or words coupled which are onomatopoeic in the Hebrew. Two examples are tōhû/bōhû = waste and void (as in Gen. 1: 2 and in Jer. 4: 23) and mᵉbûsâ/mᵉbûkâ = trampling and confusion (see Isa. 22: 5).

7. *Gender-matched word-pairs*, whereby the pairing is a deliberate interplay of masculine and feminine nouns. Isaiah 11: 4 is one example, where the interconnections are the instruments and the recipients of judgement:

> and he shall smite the earth [f.]
> with the rod [m.] of his mouth [m.]
> and with the breath [f.] of his lips [f.]
> he shall slay the wicked [m.]

Watson cites several examples of this feature, noting that sometimes these words occur in alternate forms, at others in symmetrical pairs, echoing each other. Several examples occur in Genesis 1 (which hence suggests a reading of poetry, not prose)—for example, Gen. 1: 10:

God called the-dry-land [f. sing.] earth [f. sing.]
and the-gathering-together of-the-waters [m. pl.] he called seas [m. pl.]

Another example is from Prov. 3: 22, a maxim about following the tenets of wisdom and discretion:

> They-will-be life [m.] to-your-soul [f.]
> and-adornment [m.] for-your-neck [f.]

8. *Rhyming*. Although less frequent in Hebrew, this is usually achieved by the use of suffixes. Examples include the third-person feminine plural -nâ, the first person plural -nû, and the repeated use of the first person singular -î. Schökel offers examples from Jer. 9: 18 and Jer. 12: 7:

> For a sound of wailing is heard from Zion:
> 'How we-are-ruined (ʾêk šuddādᵉnû)

We-are-utterly-ashamed (bōšnû mᵉˀōd̠),
because we-have-left-the-land (kî-ʿāzab̠nû ˀāreṣ)
  because they-have-cast-down our-dwellings (kî-hišlîk̠û
  miškᵉnôt̠ēnû)
'I-have-forsaken my-house (ʿāzab̠tî et̠-bêtî)
  I-have-abandoned my-heritage (nāṭaštî et̠-naḥᵃlātî)
  I-have-given the-beloved of-my-soul (nāt̠atî et̠-yᵉd̠id̠ût̠ nap̠šî)
  into-the-hands of-her-enemies.'

9. *Repetition*, by way of a similar phrase acting as an 'envelope
figure' at the beginning or ending of a sequence, or by the use of
refrains at the end of a stanza. Within larger poems, the refrain in
Isa. 5: 25, 9: 12, 17, 21, and 10: 4 serves as an interesting example,
because it creates a clear poetic unit. So too the refrain in Pss. 42: 5,
11 and 43: 5 brings together the two psalms as one whole poem. A
more concise example is from Jer. 15: 2:

> Those who are for pestilence, to pestilence,
> and those who are for the sword, to the sword;
> those who are for famine, to famine,
> and those who are for captivity, to captivity.

10. *Unusual vocabulary and archaisms*, more apparent to those with
a knowledge of Hebrew. It is evidenced, for example, in what is
known as the 'enclitic *mêm*' (used for emphasis), the 'vocative
lāmed̠' (used in address), and the 'emphatic *wāw*' ('but' . . .).
Another example is the variation of tenses within two balancing
lines: the imperfect (incompleted) tense—called the *yiqtôl*—may
occur in one colon, whilst the perfect (completed) tense—called the
qātal—may occur in the other colon. Psalm 38: 11 is a good example
of this. Another example is the change of voice, from the passive to
active, as in Ps. 24: 7:

My friends and companions stand (yaʿᵃmōd̠û) aloof from my plague
and my kinsmen stand (ʿāmād̠û) afar off.

(Ps. 38: 11)

Lift up (śᵉˀû) your heads, O gates!
  and be lifted up (wᵉhinnāśᵉˀû), O ancient doors!

(Ps. 24: 7)

11. *Chiasmus*, where each of the lines leads up to one climactic point and recedes back down again; in a larger unit, this is sometimes achieved by way of a refrain, but in a smaller unit, it is suggested more by the balance of ideas. One typical pattern might be ABCDCBA. Psalm 46 is thought to have this chiasmus overall, with the central focus in vv. 5 and 6, regarding God's presence in the city. So too has Ps. 56, where the chiasmus is developed between God, the 'I' who speaks, and the enemies, interspersed with the refrain in vv. 5 and 11–12. Other examples include Isa. 1: 21–6; Jer. 2: 5–9; Amos 9: 1–4; Ps. 136: 10–15; Job 32: 6–10; and Eccles. 3: 2–8.

12. *The use of tricola*, whereby three similar phrases occur one after the other. There are several examples in the psalms:

> Wait for the LORD;
> be strong, and let your heart take courage;
> yea, wait for the LORD!

(Ps. 27: 14)

> Lift up your heads, O gates!
> and be lifted up, O ancient doors!
> that the King of glory may come in.

(Ps. 24: 7, 9)

Whether we look at the more general features or at the more technical, specific characteristics, one question should be evident: are not many of these details still to be found in other passages usually identified as prose?

The answer must be in the affirmative. All of the four more general criteria suggesting Hebrew verse can be found in Hebrew prose narrative: terseness of style, figurative language, ambiguity of meaning, and the expectation of a response from the listener/ reader are all in evidence in many narrative forms.

Furthermore, prose passages also make use of some of the specific features listed above. Word-pairs, for example, are found in Genesis 1 (e.g. light and darkness; sea and dry land; earth and heaven); repetition occurs, for instance in the speeches of Moses in Deuteronomy (see Deut. 7–11) and in the narratives of Samuel and

Kings (see 2 Sam. 7, 1 Kgs. 18, and 2 Kgs. 17). Chiasmus is found in many narrative passages, both in Genesis (e.g. chapters 6–9, concerning the Flood) and in Exodus (e.g. chapters 12–15, on the crossing of the Red Sea). And tricola are also used for stylistic emphasis in prose passages (e.g. 1 Sam. 8: 3).

This sort of fluidity between poetry and prose may be demonstrated in two other ways. On the one hand, there are several prose texts which could be read as poetry, and on the other, several so-called poetic texts could also be written as prose.

C. Prose Which Might Be Read as Poetry

A few scholars have attempted (unsuccessfully) to show that the entire Old Testament, properly accented, could be written in verse. Two notable studies have been by E. Sievers, a German writing at the beginning of the twentieth century, and P. Kraus, a Semitic scholar writing in the 1930s. Rather than selecting several examples at random, a more productive exercise would be to take one particular genre, against which this issue of determining prose and poetry might be more consistently tested. The genre of prose prayers is a good test case.

Prose prayers occur throughout the various literary sources of the Old Testament. They are found in the Yahwistic account of the Pentateuch, for example in Gen. 4: 13–14 (Cain); Gen. 15: 2–3 (Abraham); Gen. 32: 9–12 (Jacob); and Exod. 3: 11, 13; 4: 1, 10, 13; 5: 22–3; 17: 4 (Moses). They also occur in the Priestly account, for example Gen. 17: 18 (Abraham) and Exod. 6: 12, 30 (Moses). They are also used in the Deuteronomistic literature, including Deut. 3: 24–5 (Moses); Judg. 6: 36–7, 39 (Gideon); Judg. 11: 30–1 (Jephthah); Judg. 13: 8 (Manoah); Judg. 15: 18, 16: 28, 30 (Samson); 1 Sam. 1: 11 (Hannah); 1 Sam. 3: 10, 16: 2 (Samuel); 2 Sam. 5: 19, 15: 31 (David); 1 Kgs. 3: 6–9 (Solomon); 1 Kgs. 17: 20, 21, 18: 36–7, 19: 4, 10, 14 (Elijah); and 2 Kgs. 20: 3 (Hezekiah). The prophetic literature uses prose prayers occasionally, for example: Isa. 6: 5, 8 (Isaiah); Jer. 1: 6, 14: 13, 15: 10–12, and 45: 3 (all Jeremiah except the last, which is Baruch); Amos 7: 2, 5; Jonah 1: 14 (pagan sailors); and Jonah 4: 2–3, 8–9 (Jonah).

Like the poetic material, especially in the psalms, prose prayers are cast sometimes in the form of petition and reproach (in content not unlike Jeremiah 12) and at other times in the form of thanksgiving or praise. In this way they are conscious imitations of poetic prayer forms. Yet their literary context is unmistakably prose-narrative: they form an intrinsic part of their story, and the characters are invariably introduced in the third person. Their poetic features include generally a terse style and figurative language, and more specifically ellipsis, changes in the word-order, word-pairing, word-plays, chiasmus, and repetition. A close analysis of just two of these examples should illustrate this more clearly.

(I) GENESIS 4: 13–14

The prayer reads in prose (RSV) as follows:

And Cain said to the Lord, My punishment is greater than I can bear. Lo, today you have driven me from the face of the earth, and I shall be hidden from you; and I shall be a vagabond and fugitive in the land. And then anyone who finds me will kill me.

It may, however, be set out as follows (using the word-units as in the Hebrew):

(*a*) Greater [is] my-punishment than-I-can-bear
(*b*) Lo, you-have-driven me this-day from [the] face of-the-earth
(*c*) And-from-your-face I-shall-be-hidden
(*d*) And-I-shall-become a vagabond and a fugitive in-the-land.
(*e*) And-then whoever-finds-me will-kill-me.

A relationship exists between Gen. 4: 1–16 and Gen. 3: 1–23, not least in their structure. In both, the theme moves from the offence (Gen. 3: 6 / 4: 8) to God's question (Gen. 3: 9*b* / 4: 9*a*) to man's reply (Gen. 3: 10 / 4: 9*b*) to God's second question (Gen. 3: 11, 13*a* / 4: 10) to God's sentence (3: 17*b* / 4: 11–12). In this sequence, the above prayer in 4: 13–14 stands out: the guilty (Cain) has the right to appeal, whereas Adam and Eve are silenced. Cain's prayer is thus important in the way that it shows a 'softening' of the purposes of God, for Yahweh offers mercy whilst still upholding justice: Cain is removed from God's presence, but he is granted protection—and all this on account of this particular dialogue whereby God hears Cain's cry.

The prayer has a discernible form—one which has echoes of the form within the psalms of complaint. It starts with a reproach to God (line (*a*)), followed by the reasons for the reproach (line (*b*)), then the consequences of God's sentence (lines (*c*), (*d*)), with the last line (*e*) as the climax to the prayer. The prayer fits several of the characteristics of poetry: in line (*a*), the verb no longer stands at the beginning of the clause; both lines (*a*) and (*b*) echo the figurative language used in psalmody (for line (*a*), see Pss. 22: 6–7; 31: 10; 38: 3–4; and for line (*b*), see Pss. 13: 1; 27: 9; 30: 7; 44: 24; 69: 17; 88: 14; 102: 2; 143: 7); and lines (*b*) and (*c*) suggest a certain parallelism in the balance of 'driven' 'from the face of the earth' and 'hidden' 'from the face of God'; furthermore, in line (*d*) there is evidence of word-pairing and ellipsis. It has a distinctive terse style, demonstrated in the number of Hebrew words per line, and the speech itself offers the reader a poignant reminder of the issue of justice in the context of Cain's murder of Abel and God's curse on Cain. The editor (whom many scholars would term the 'Yahwist') depicts Cain using ordinary human speech-patterns, in order to signify an element of spontaneity, yet also so casts the speech with a deliberate artistry and progression of ideas that it creates its own dramatic impact. Prayer of this nature has been called 'common speech on its best behaviour': it is neither simple conversational form, nor is it at first sight an obvious poem; but, if the above observations hold, Cain's prayer could certainly be termed 'poetic'.

(II) JUDGES 15: 18

The RSV prose reading is as follows:

And he was very thirsty, and cried to the Lord and said, By the hand of your servant you have provided this great deliverance, and now I am dying of thirst, and will fall into the hands of the uncircumcised.

The words of the prayer could be set out like this:

(*a*) You, you-have-provided by-the-hand-of-your-servant
(*b*) This great deliverance

(*c*) And-now I-die from-thirst
(*d*) And-I-shall-fall into-[the]-hand(s) of-the-uncircumcised.

The purpose of this prayer is to show the frailty of the hero Samson, in his thirst and fear of death, and thus his ultimate dependence upon God, despite his previous clear lack of fear when faced with his enemies. The prayer and its answer serve also as an explanation for the place-name En-hakkore (v. 19) and the naming of the spring water at Lehi. But our focus of attention is on the form of the prayer.

Its structure has correspondences with the psalms, for although the prayer starts without the usual invocation, the protest in lines (*a*) and (*b*) is clearly addressed to God; lines (*c*) and (*d*) continue with the typical description of distress found in several psalms on this theme. The terseness of expression is evident throughout. Basically, two longer cola ((*a*) + (*b*); (*c*) + (*d*)) may be seen, with a longer first half in lines (*a*)–(*b*), and a longer second half in lines (*c*)–(*d*). If we look at this prayer by way of line-forms, a certain chiasmus is also evident: line (*a*) 'you have provided' / 'the hand of your servant' is matched by line (*d*) 'I shall fall' / 'the hands of the uncircumcised'; and line (*b*) 'this great deliverance' is matched by line (*c*) 'now I die of thirst'. The chiasmus thus runs as ABBA. Interesting too is the feature of *qātal / yiqtōl* in lines (*c*) and (*d*). Perhaps the most significant characteristic of artistry is the word-play: the correspondences of ʾattâ (you) in line (*a*) and wᵉᶜattâ (and now) in line (*c*), and of bᵉyad- ᶜabdᵉqā (by the hand of your servant) in line (*a*) with bᵉyad-hāᶜªrēlîm (by the hand of the uncircumcised) in line (*d*). We may note too the imagery-plays between the physical needs of Samson (thirst and death), and the more metaphorical expressions of thirsting for God and loss of fullness of life given by God, which are frequently found in the psalms (e.g. Pss. 22: 15 and 69: 21, on thirst, and Pss. 35: 4 and 39: 4–6, on death).

Again we may conclude that this is a crafted speech form, and its deliberate design and heightened effect suggest that, like Cain's prayer, Samson's prayer also displays what Alter has termed a 'poetic trembling'; illustrations from the earlier list of prose prayers would repeatedly make the same point.

D. Poetry Which Could Be Read as Prose

If Hebrew prose can be divided into line-forms and read as poetry, then the reverse should be the case. The suggestion that Hebrew verse is simply a developed prose style with rhetorical tendencies has been made by James Kugel in *The Idea of Biblical Poetry*. Kugel's theory is in part convincing. For the sake of consistency and precision, we shall again limit our discussion to one genre alone—that of the psalms.

A clear illustration of prosaic tendencies is found in the historical psalms which rehearse the story of God's dealings with his people from past to present. For example, Ps. 106 is a confession of God's saving work through the people's history, ending with an acknowledgement of sin and a prayer for God's grace. However, another way of reading Ps. 106 could also suggest a narrative passage, set in a credal form like that found in Exod. 13: 14–16; Deut. 6: 20–5; and particularly in Deut. 26: 5–10.

Other psalmic examples (also used by Kugel) also lack the compact style of poetry. The most convincing are Pss. 103: 17–18 and 136: 5. In both cases the verses are exceptionally long; the rhythm and pattern of the psalm are broken, as if the actual contents were more important than the vehicle of presentation:

> But the steadfast love of the LORD is from everlasting to everlasting
>   upon those who fear him,
>   and his righteousness to children's children,
> to those who keep his covenant and remember to do his commandments.

(Ps. 103: 17–18)

Here the terse style is nowhere evident. Apart from some indication of parallel ideas earlier in the psalm, the use of our other listed poetic devices is hardly apparent. As with Ps. 106, it would be relatively easy to interpret this as prose, and to assign it to Deuteronomistic style (cf. Deut. 5: 10; 7: 9). Another example is Ps. 87: 1 ff., whose prose-like tendencies are increased by its several textual dislocations:

On the holy mount stands the city he founded;
the LORD loves the gates of Zion
more than all the dwelling-places of Jacob.

Glorious things are spoken of you,
  O city of God.

Among those who know me I mention Rahab and Babylon;
  behold, Philistia and Tyre, with Ethiopia—
'This one was born there,' they say . . .

Several ancient manuscripts actually present the psalms in prose form. In the findings among the Dead Sea Scrolls at Qumran, of the thirty-one copies of the Psalter which were found (mainly copies from Ps. 101 onwards in Cave 11, named 11 QPs^a) several scrolls contained psalms written in a continuous script, running on from one psalm to another, the prose format (even in its fragmentary form on the parchment) being clear and uninterrupted. Similar examples from Cave 4 at Qumran (4 QPs^a), probably dating from the Hasmonean period (104–37 BCE), also show selected psalms (Pss. 6–7, 31, 32, 35–6, 38, 71, 53–4, 66–7, 69) in a similar continuous script—with Ps. 71 inexplicably following 38. This is all the more remarkable when it is evident that another find in Cave 4 of Qumran (called 4 QPs^b), probably from the Herodian period (37 BCE–?100 CE), also containing several psalms (e.g. Pss. 91–4, 99–100, 102–3, 112–16, 118) shows by contrast an arrangement of clear verse form, in eight short and narrow columns of eighteen lines. The reasons for this different presentation may well have been as much the aesthetic interest in stichography and in different techniques in spacing the material; but whatever the motivation, these Qumran findings, even in a supposedly established poetic genre such as psalmody, suggest that poetic and prosaic traditions existed alongside one another.

Prose presentation of later psalmody occurs also in the extra-biblical material such as the *Hymns* of the Hekhalôt literature. These date from some time after the third century CE: as hymns of heavenly visions, composed by the *Merkāvâ* mystics in Palestine and Babylon, almost every edition presents them not as poetry, but as prose.

Another example is found in the Aleppo Codex (tenth century

CE), an ancient manuscript in which the book of Psalms follows straight on after Chronicles, and Ps. 1 is written in the same prose style as 2 Chr. 36, even though Ps. 2 is set in line-forms.

We also have evidence of psalms written in prose on manuscripts of translations from Hebrew into Greek: for example, the Bodmer Papyrus XXIV, found in Egypt and dating from between the second and fourth centuries CE, has copies of the psalms arranged in prose, giving no attention to line-forms and versification. All this points to the same conclusion: even Hebrew psalmody can be perceived as prose, a feature which again suggests that the over-compartmentalizing of prose and poetry is not a Semitic phenomenon.

So are there no distinctions at all between prose and poetry? Perhaps one has to conclude that understanding the difference has more to do with appreciation and less to do with knowledge: in other words, the distinction is a subtle one, and requires a more intuitive and aesthetic approach. This is best illustrated by way of examples from the biblical text. Below are two sets of depictions of the same event, one set throughout in poetry, the other in prose. In each case, the poetic account is probably much older than that in prose, and the different effect of each upon the reader is all too clear.

The first example is the narrative of the escape from the Red Sea in Exod. 14; this is followed in Exod. 15 by a poetic celebration of the same event:

Then the LORD said to Moses, 'Stretch out your hand over the sea, that the water may come back upon the Egyptians, upon their chariots, and upon their horsemen.' So Moses stretched forth his hand over the sea, and the sea returned to its wonted flow when the morning appeared; and the Egyptians fled into it, and the LORD routed the Egyptians in the midst of the sea. The waters returned and covered the chariots and the horsemen and all the host of Pharaoh that had followed them into the sea; not so much as one of them remained. But the people of Israel walked on dry ground through the sea, the waters being a wall to them on their right hand and on their left. (Exod. 14: 26–9.)

Then Moses and the people of Israel sang this song to the LORD, saying,

> I will sing to the LORD, for he has triumphed gloriously;
> the horse and his rider he has thrown into the sea
> .   .   .   .
> Pharaoh's chariots and his host he cast into the sea;
> and his picked officers are sunk in the Red Sea.
> The floods cover them;
>   they went down into the depths like a stone.
> Thy right hand, O LORD,
>   glorious in power,
> The right hand, O LORD,
>   shatters the enemy . . .

(Exod. 15: 1, 4–6)

The second example is taken from the narrative of Deborah's and Barak's victory over Sisera in Judg. 4, followed by the poetic account of the same event in Judg. 5.

But Sisera fled away on foot to the tent of Jael, the wife of Heber the Kenite; for there was peace between Jabin the king of Hazor and the house of Heber the Kenite. And Jael came out to meet Sisera, and said to him, 'Turn aside, my lord, turn aside to me; have no fear.' And he said to her, 'Pray, give me a little water to drink; for I am thirsty.' So she opened a skin of milk and gave him a drink and covered him. And he said to her, 'Stand at the door of the tent, and if any man comes and asks you, "Is any one here?" say, "No."' But Jael the wife of Heber took a tent peg, and took a hammer in her hand, and went softly to him, and drove the peg into his temple, till it went down into the ground, as he was lying fast asleep from weariness. So he died. (Judg. 4: 18–21.)

> Most blessed of women be Jael,
> the wife of Heber the Kenite,
> of tent-dwelling women most blessed.
> He asked water and she gave him milk,
>   she brought him curds in a lordly bowl.
> She put her hand to the tent peg
>   and her right hand to the workmen's mallet;
> she struck Sisera a blow,
>   she crushed his head,
>   she shattered and pierced his temple.

> He sank, he fell,
>   he lay still at her feet;
> at her feet he sank, he fell;
>   where he sank, there he fell dead . . .

(Judg. 5: 24–7)

Each of these examples reveals the nuances between the two styles of writing. The biblical 'prose' is written in what has been called a 'poetic trembling'; and biblical poetry reveals a prosaic style in its recitation. In the two examples above, the prose is believed to have been composed after the poetic version, possibly as a means of expanding the details whilst retaining the drama of the poetic rhetoric. Although the boundaries are unclear, there is some distinction between the prosaic and poetic accounts. The prose is more preoccupied with details of time and context; the poetry celebrates the occasion with a sense of timelessness. The prose suggests a distancing from the reader, explaining, rather than letting the events speak for themselves; the poetry invites the reader to participate in the events, following the mood of the poem. To this effect, even in the English translation, the reader cannot help but note the heightened rhetorical style and different rhythmic quality of the poetic material.

Ultimately, the difference between Hebrew prose and poetry is more one of degree than of kind, and the distinction does not imply a value-judgement of one over the other. Nevertheless, any sensitive reader must be persuaded that we respond differently to composition in line-forms, which depicts a visible balance of ideas transposed through a heightened use of imagery.

E. Hebrew Verse in its Cultural Context

An entirely different way of ascertaining whether Hebrew poetry can be distinguished from prose is to compare the literature of the Old Testament with that of the other cultures of the ancient Near East.

Comparisons with other ancient Near Eastern poetry reveal an interesting feature: an element lacking in Hebrew poetry, but evident elsewhere, is the continuous narrative presented through a poetic medium—what might be called 'epic poetry'. Hebrew poetry uses a great variety of forms—including laments, songs of praise, prophetic oracles, proverbial sayings, liturgical fragments—and thus it is most significant that the genre of epic poetry is absent. The story forms in the books from Genesis to 2 Kings (for example, the 'epic' of Noah and the Flood, or the exploits of the judges) are narratives, and can hardly be read as epic poetry, even though the poetic devices noted earlier are evidenced occasionally within the accounts. Conversely, as we saw in the examples from Exod. 15 and Judg. 5, and also in earlier examples from Pss. 103 and 106, poetry 'rehearses' aspects of a story, without relating the story itself. There is a certain 'narrativity'—what Robert Alter, who has written several literary works which discuss the issue of poetry and prose, calls 'a steady progression of image or theme, a sort of mounting semantic pressure, which is to say, a structure of intensification' (*The Art of Biblical Poetry*, 61). This is not, however, epic poetry, for there is no characterization and interplay of story and dialogue, no background detail, no playing on human curiosity through the art of narration.

Indeed, such psalms as 103 and 106 seem to assume that the audience already knows the story, and so they use this knowledge for a different purpose—normally celebrating a victory and attributing the glory to God. It is apparent that whereas in other cultures, epic poetry was used as a means of telling stories *about* the names and attributes of their deities, Israel's poetry was composed more as a means of encouraging the people to respond directly *to* their God. This liturgical and performative context for Israelite poetry may suggest one reason why Israel possessed no epic poetry as such.

By contrast, there are many epic accounts told through the medium of poetry in ancient Near Eastern cultures outside Israel. We could refer to examples from Mesopotamia (in both Sumerian and Akkadian), from the Hittites, or from the Egyptians; but perhaps the most helpful examples are from Ras Shamra, an ancient trading city on the Mediterranean coast of Syria. Since the late 1920s, a team headed by French scholars has been deciphering alphabetical cuneiform tablets, written in Ugaritic and in

Akkadian, dating from between the fourteenth and twelfth centuries BCE—at least three centuries before the poetry of the Old Testament was popularized.

Some of these tablets could be termed 'prose'. They include letters, royal grants, legal texts, financial and administrative lists. Nevertheless, the bulk of the material in Ugaritic is in poetry, and the greatest proportion of the poetry deals with religious and mythological themes. These epic poems feature both story and dialogue, describe feasts and fights, and depict various characters, human and divine; they reveal a poetic art quite different from that found in the victory songs of Moses and Deborah. The best known of the Ugaritic epics include *The Ba'l and 'Anat Cycle*, *The Legend of Krt*, *The Legend of Aqht*, *The Birth of the Good Gods of Fertility*, and *The Marriage of Yariḥ and Nikkal*. (Various classifications of these texts have been made, but two referred to in the excerpts below are from A. Herdner's *Corpus des tablettes en cunéiformes alphabétiques*, published in Paris in 1963, known as *CTA*, and from C. Gordon's *Ugaritic Textbook*, published in Rome in 1965, known as *UT*.)

It is possible that these epics are poetic accounts of the survival of an early dynasty at Ugarit, elaborated with mythical elements. However, in the present texts, the interest is focused rather upon a pantheon of deities; the historical theme of kingship is evident only within the legend of Keret, an ancient king of Ugarit, who (like the biblical Job) loses his possessions and family, to be healed and restored by the most high god, El. Normally the leading role is ascribed to Ba'l, the rain- and fertility-god, whose consort is the warrior-goddess, 'Anat. In these epics, written in cuneiform on clay tablets, often in continuous script because of the lack of space (a feature similar to that of the findings at Qumran), poetic devices such as word-pairs, chiasmus, and refrains are repeatedly used. In contrast to those of Israel, the stories of the ancient heroes and deities of Ugarit have been written not through the medium of prose, but through poetry.

The clearest correspondence to these epics in Hebrew poetry is found in victory songs celebrating the nation's military success. Examples include God's control of chaos by the slaying of the dragon monster of the sea, as in Pss. 74: 13–14 and 89: 10–11, and in

Isa. 51: 9–10; God's power and glory associated with his dwelling and/or appearing on sacred mountains, as in Pss. 48: 1–3; 68: 7–10; and Hab. 3: 2–3; God's control over nature, whereby he is heard through the elements of thunder and lightning, as in Pss. 29: 3–9 and 93: 3–4; God's world rule, established from an ancient throne from time immemorial, as in Pss. 44: 1–4; 47: 8–9; and 93: 1–2. But this is still not epic poetry; they are basically songs, performed in the cult, even though, like the poetry of Ugarit, they go beyond history and utilize various motifs from ancient mythological tales. The difference is that in the Hebrew songs, the story element and character portrayal are entirely absent. Even the mythical motifs are developed more in metaphorical terms—a style which is poetic, but hardly has epic dimensions. It is as if the biblical writers needed to use mythological motifs in order to explain the mysteries of life before human time, but they only borrowed the vestiges of the myths: to depict a mythical story normally associated with a pantheon of deities and display it in epic and poetic form would have been too much of a theological compromise for an essentially monotheistic faith. We are brought back to our earlier observations that Hebrew poetry was a means of encouraging the people to *encounter* their God, rather than a way of relating stories about him.

But it is important that we nevertheless recognize several similarities between Hebrew and Ugaritic verse. This is significant, because Ugarit had ceased to exist before Israel's own literary output developed. The poems of Ras Shamra give us good evidence of a more distinctive *poetic* tradition out of which other Semitic poetry developed, including that of the Hebrews.

The best examples are found in the word-pairing. The example below is a clear illustration of this: in this case, the balance of ideas, set in alternate lines, is interspersed with a refrain. The example is from a description of a fight between Ba'l and Mot, the god of death.

yt'n kgmrm	they shake each other like gmr-animals;
mt 'z b'l 'z	Mot is strong, Ba'l is strong;
ynghn krumm	they gore like buffaloes;
mt 'z b'l 'z	Mot is strong, Ba'l is strong;

yntkn kbtnm   they bite like serpents;
mt ʿz bʾl ʿz   Mot is strong, Baʿl is strong;

(*Baʾl and ʿAnat Cycle*: UT 134; CTA 6. v. 16–22)

A corresponding example from the Old Testament would be Ps. 136, for example verses 4–6:

lᵉ ʿōśēh niplāʾōt gᵉdōlōt lᵉbadô
  kî lᵉʿôlām ḥasdô
lᵉ ʿōśēh haššāmayim biṯbûnâ
  kî lᵉʿôlām ḥasdô
lᵉ rôqaʿ hāʾāreṣ ʿal-hammāyim
  kî lᵉʿôlām ḥasdô

to him who alone does great wonders,
  for his steadfast love endures for ever;
to him who by understanding made the heavens,
  for his steadfast love endures for ever;
to him who spread out the earth upon the waters,
  for his steadfast love endures for ever

The clear balance of ideas from the use of word-pairs often results in the selection of particular stressed words to combine with a certain balance of sound. This feature is used also in Hebrew, albeit with less frequency. One form is of a line with two words and two stresses, as in the following example of alternating pairs:

yprsḥ ym   Yam sprawls
yql larṣ   falls to earth
tnġṣn pnth   his joints shake
wydlp tmnh   and his frame collapses.

(*Baʾl and ʿAnat Cycle*: UT 133;
CTA 2. iv. 25–6)

A good example in Hebrew is from Isa. 1: 16–17:

hiḏlû hārēaʿ	Cease	to-do-evil,
limdû hêṭēb	Learn	to-do-good;
diršû mišpāṭ	Seek	justice
ʾaššᵉrû ḥāmôṣ	Correct	oppression
šipṭû yāṯôm	Defend	(the) fatherless
rîbû ʾalᵉmānâ	Plead-for	(the) widow.

Another poetic form in Ugaritic is of a cola with three words and three stresses:

| wng | mlk | lbty | and depart, king, from my house; |
| rḫq | krt | lḫzry | be distant, Krt, from my court! |

(*Krt*: *UT* 132; *CTA* 14. iii. 131–3)

Or again:

| ydn | dn | almnt | he judges the cause of the widow |
| ytpṭ | ṭpṭ | ytm | and adjudicates the cause of the fatherless |

(2 *Aqht*: *UT* 119; *CTA* 17. v. 7–8)

This three/three rhythm is more popular in Hebrew, occurring not only in the prophets, but also in the psalms, in Proverbs, and in the book of Job.

Another example of the way that stress and line-forms work together in Ugaritic is in the use of tricola:

ht	ibk	bʿlm	now, thine enemies O Baʿl
ht	ibk	tmḫṣ	now, thine enemies thou shalt smite,
ht	tṣmt	ṣrtk	now, thou shalt destroy thy foes . . .

(*Baʿl and ʿAnat Cycle*: *UT* 144; *CTA* 2. iv. 8–9)

Here we may note also the word-pair enemies (ʾêḇîm) and evildoers (ṣarîm), which is found repeatedly in Hebrew poetic texts, especially the psalms—for example, Pss. 13: 4; 27: 2; 42: 9–10; 69: 18–19; 74: 10; 81: 14; and 143: 12; also Isa. 1: 24; 9: 11; Mic. 5: 9 and Lam. 2: 4, 17; 4: 12. An interesting correspondence of the same word-pair is found in Ps. 92: 9 (with lengthier line-forms than in the corresponding Ugaritic example above):

kî	hinnēh	ʾōyḇêkā	ʾaḏōnay	For, lo, thy enemies, o LORD,
kî	hinnēh	ʾōyḇêkā	yōʾḇēḏû	for, lo, thy enemies shall perish
yiṯpārḏû		kol-poʿalê ʾāwen		all evildoers shall be scattered.

Word-pairing is, in fact, the most obvious correspondence between Ugaritic and Hebrew poetry. Scholars claim to have found over one hundred such examples, not only in the use of nouns (e.g. light/darkness; sea/river; earth/deep; thunder/lightning; laughter/joy; death/life; silver/gold; tent/dwelling; strength/might; justice/

righteousness), but also in the use of verbs (e.g. smite/destroy; build/raise; eat/consume; reign/sit enthroned). In Ugaritic poetry, unlike Hebrew, this feature is found almost entirely in the epic poems; it is hardly evident in the prose tablets. This again highlights the sharper differences between prose and poetry in Ugaritic. By contrast, in the biblical literature word-pairs are found throughout both the poetic and prose material. For example, 'earth and the deep' (see *CTA* 3. iii. 21–2, iv. 60–1) is found not only in Pss. 42: 6–7; 71: 20; 135: 6; 148: 7; and Prov. 3: 19–20, but also in Gen. 1: 2; 'death and life' (see *CTA* 16. i. 22–3) is found not only in Ps. 56: 13 and Prov. 13: 14, but also in Deut. 30: 15, 19; Jer. 21: 8; and Ezek. 18: 13, 17, 32; 'tent and dwelling' (see *CTA* 15. iii. 17–18 and 17. v. 31–3) is found in Ps. 78: 60, but also in Exod. 39: 32; 40: 34; Num. 24: 5; Isa. 54: 2; and Jer. 30: 18.

Thus, although there is a clear demarcation between prose and poetry in Ugaritic, on account of the word-pairing which occurs predominantly in the poetry, this differentiation cannot be applied to Hebrew poetry in the same way. Hebrew literature contains a far greater percentage of prose material anyway, and because of this, much of the peculiar poetic diction is spread also throughout the prose of Hebrew. In Ugaritic, prose was used mainly for political and economical and informative purposes; poetry, mainly for religious and sacral activities. In Hebrew, the prose form was, of course, also used for legal, fiscal, diplomatic, and annalistic purposes; but, unlike Ugaritic, much of the religious and sacral material is found as much in prose as it is in poetry, because the religious and sacral stories (the narratives, which, in Ugaritic, are epic poetry) were expressed mainly in prose. It is not surprising that the word-pairs listed above (and one could list at least forty other such examples) occur within Hebrew prose material as much as within Hebrew poetry. It seems that every attempt to classify poetry in Hebrew fails on account of the lack of clear boundaries.

We may therefore conclude this chapter by referring back to our first quotation by Robinson. It would appear that the over-categorizing of Hebrew poetry and prose is a result of our modern assumptions about poetry in general. If we examine the material as much as is possible from the Semitic context itself, we are left with more questions than answers concerning whether there are distinctive forms of prose and poetry in the biblical literature. What we have overall are 'poetic components' within the prose accounts, and 'prose-like tendencies' within the poetry. The distinction is more quantitative than qualitative, more of degree than of kind. This is all the more evident when we compare and contrast the supposedly different poetic tendencies which the biblical literature transcribed in the Hebrew as poetry—Proverbs, psalmody, the dialogues in Job—for even within this so-called poetic 'category', a great diversity of style and content is to be found. We may think we know that there are two forms of literature, labelled prose and poetry—two languages, two ways of communicating experience and reality—but we cannot help but suspect that the labelling never arose in Hebrew, because questions were not asked about form, language, and intention in the way we ask them, and so the answers we should like to receive are rarely given.

With this observation in mind, we turn now in the following two chapters to the much-debated issues of metre and parallelism, for these have been used as the two key criteria in determining the borderlines between prose and poetry in biblical literature.

3

Metre

An assessment of the metrical quality of poetry is very much related to its 'performative' nature. Whether biblical poetry was composed and recited for didactic and reflective purposes, or whether it was composed and sung (perhaps antiphonally) for particular liturgical and musical occasions, it served the same purpose: biblical verse was heard as much as it was read.

The musical quality of biblical poetry, not least the psalms, is most significant in any discussion of metre. Just as the libretto of an opera becomes 'sung speech' when adapted to a musical score, so too, the poetry of the psalms becomes sung speech when adapted to the music of Israel's worship. A musical appreciation shows clearly how the two senses of sight and sound are brought together in dynamic tension. The visual element—looking at the text as the score—plays upon the imagination and its ability to 'word-paint', by way of the rich use of imagery and the order and balance of ideas. The auditory aspect—listening to the performance of the poem—offers a different sort of enjoyment, on account of the resonance and sonority within its rhythm and tone. In his work on *The Early Poetry of Israel in its Physical and Social Origins*, G. A. Smith describes poetry as 'primitively the art of saying the same beautiful things over and over again . . . which rhymed and sang back to each other not in sound only but in sense as well' (p. 16).

Seeing and hearing are brought together in an appreciation both of music and of poetry. The sound brings the sense to life, and vice versa. The appeal of the poetry is both to our inner vision and to our outer hearing, and there is usually a complex and somewhat mysterious relationship between the two.

The purpose of this and the following chapter is to examine

further this relationship between the sound and sense in some of the clearest examples of Hebrew poetry. The sound is, of course, related to the issue of metre; the sense, to that of parallelism. In this chapter we shall first consider the issue of metre in the context of the musicality in the poetry, as expressed in the liturgies of the Jewish and Christian traditions; this will provide a framework in which we are then able to consider the merits and demerits of recent theories about metre in biblical poetry.

A. Poetry, Liturgy, and Music

We do not have to look far within the biblical texts to be persuaded of the close relationship between poetry and music in Israelite culture. The case is clearest within the psalms. The noun *šîr* ('song') is found in its various forms nearly forty times in the psalms, and the verb *zāmar* ('to accompany the singing', possibly on a stringed instrument) occurs over forty times. The Greek word for a psalm is *psalmós*, a translation of *mizmôr*, from the root *zāmar*, and meaning 'a song to a stringed instrument'. The Greek for the book of Psalms is *psaltérion*, from which we derive our terms 'psaltery' and Psalter. It is, in brief, a book of praises to be sung to an instrumental accompaniment. (The Hebrew word *t^ehillâ*, found in Ps. 145, means 'song of praise', and the plural form, *t^ehillîm*, denotes the entire book of Psalms in Hebrew).

The term 'choirmaster' is prefixed to fifty-five psalms (e.g. Pss. 4, 5, 6, 8, 9, 11, 12, 13, 14, 18, 19, 20, 21, 22). The superscriptions concerning the choir-guilds of Asaph (Pss. 50, 73–83) and of Korah (Pss. 42, 44–9, 84–5, 87–8), as well as references to the Alamoth (Ps. 46—possibly referring to women's voices), to Ethan the Ezrahite (Ps. 89), to Heman the Ezrahite (Ps. 88), and to Jeduthun (Pss. 39, 62, 77) all probably point to the use of psalms by various groups of Levitical musicians in the second Temple.

Various hymn-tunes are also suggested in the superscriptions— 'Do Not Destroy' in Pss. 57–9 and 75 (see Isa. 65: 8); 'Dove of the Far-off Terebinths' in Ps. 56; 'Hind of the Dawn' in Ps. 22; 'Mahalath' in Pss. 53 and 88; the 'Lilies' in Pss. 45, 69, and 80; the 'Gittith' in Pss. 8, 81, and 84 (possibly a vintage tune), and 'Shushan

Eduth' in Ps. 60. An interesting question is whether the psalm was composed to fit with a popular tune, or whether the tune was super-imposed upon a psalm: in several cases two or three psalms coincide with the same tune, and either option is possible. It is more probable that the words inspired the music, as is the case with the compositions of hymns, liturgies, and oratorios today.

Several musical instruments also feature both in psalm-headings and in the psalm itself: the 'flutes' in the superscription to Ps. 5; 'pipes' in Ps. 150: 4; ? 'trumpet', for example, in Ps. 47: 5; the 'sheminith' (? an eight-stringed instrument) in the superscriptions to Pss. 6 and 12; 'stringed instruments' in psalm-headings 4, 6, 54, 55, 67, and 76 ? also Ps. 61; 'lyre' (? harp), for example in Ps. 33: 2; 'harp' in Pss. 57: 8; 150: 3; 'cymbals' in Ps. 150: 5 and 'timbrels' in Pss. 81: 2; 149: 3; and 150: 4.

Obviously it is far from clear *how* such music was used. We possess no Hebrew musical score, and although attempts have been made to reconstruct (on cassette tape!) Hurrian music from the findings at Ras Shamra, similar attempts have so far failed with biblical poetry. Scholars such as L. Haupt and L. Arends in the mid-nineteenth century tried to do so by means of the Hebraic accentual signs, but the only result was a westernized (occidental) form of music, using four-part harmony, key signatures, and major and minor keys—a gross misunderstanding of the different conventions within an ancient (oriental) musical tradition.

Nevertheless, the previous survey demonstrates that musical accompaniment to psalmody was essentially rhythmic and accentual. Another indication of this may be seen in the use of the sigla known as *ṭe'amîm*: these may originally have been an accentual form of punctuation, but according to scholars such as Suzanne Haik-Vantoura, they could have been developed by the Masoretes by the ninth century CE as some form of musical notation, indicating different tones and different pitches for singing. Initially they served as pauses written into the text—a way of learning the sense by listening to the sound—for the purpose of reading aloud and learning by heart. It could have been partly to enable children to learn the sacred text of Scripture. (An obvious contemporary analogy is the way nursery rhymes are taught to children.)

What is clear from the tradition of the Masoretes is that whatever the initial reason behind the use of the *ṭe'amîm*, the signs and accents developed in an increasingly complicated way which went far beyond the needs of parsing and understanding: it is more than plausible that they eventually produced a musical system. The fact that the *ṭe'amîm* were used in different ways in the book of Psalms, in Proverbs, and in Job from how they were in the prose sections of the rest of the Bible indicates at the very least some distinctive features of this poetry. The system was applied most rigorously, so that poetic texts which occur in the prose narratives have different *ṭe'amîm* from the poetry of the psalms: for example, Ps. 18 has a different system from its counterpart in 2 Sam. 22, and Ps. 105: 1–15 is different from its parallel text in 1 Chr. 16: 8–22.

The *ṭe'amîm* illustrate that 'hearing' Hebrew poetry with its accentual rhythm is as important as 'seeing' it through the word-pictures. Sound and sense belong together: they became a means of bringing audible order and visible harmony into a chaotic world. We might even press the case further and suggest that (on account of the prohibition regarding graven images) the cultural and artistic worlds of poetry and music were the most appropriate media for permissible creativity. 'Art' in its narrower, representational sense was, of course, not a feature of early Judaism. Instead of art, we find the sacred text becoming the focus for cultural creativity, not only in terms of reading (through the various interpretations of the text, which the rabbis called *midrašîm*) but also through poetic recitation and through singing.

From the fourth century CE, an interesting development took place among some Jewish groups of poets in Palestine. Some time after the Roman Emperor Justinian (CE 483–565) passed a law forbidding Jews any kind of scriptural exegesis in their synagogues, the *piyyutîm* (liturgical poets), recognizing the distinctive inspiration of the sacred text, produced an alternative form of poetry. Partly in an attempt to circumvent the law with different 'poetic' forms of exegesis, partly in response to the drying-up of the creative aspects of the poetry and liturgy within Rabbinic Judaism itself, and partly as a way of demonstrating that the Hebrew tongue could express itself in the acclaimed inspirational poetic modes of the Greeks, these poets (also called *paytanîm*) and singers (*ḥazannîm*) wrote poetry which could be sung or chanted to music. The tunes were probably based upon the ancient traditions, and the melodies and rhythms still survive today, particularly among Yemenite and Bukharan Jews. The most creative period in this respect was between the fourth and sixth centuries CE, under Byzantine rule. The purpose of the *piyyutîm* was initially liturgical, providing new prayers and hymns for sabbaths and holy days. By the medieval period their influence had spread through Italy into central and eastern Europe, and had developed into a most complicated system of metre, line-forms, and end-rhymes. Although this developed into 'art for art's sake', with metre, parallelism, rhyme, and strophic formations becoming techniques in themselves, it is nevertheless self-evident that there always had been a close link between poetry and music within the Jewish tradition.

Within the Christian tradition we find a similar relationship between biblical poetry and musical interpretation. The best example is to be found in what is most commonly known as *plain-song*—a form of melodic and tonic singing of the psalms and other canticles from Scripture. This form of singing also had antecedents in the second century CE, being refined and popularized under Pope Gregory the Great (590–604) so that it became known as Gregorian plainchant. Although the linguistic medium was Latin, not Hebrew, the formative musical influence was more that of the East than the West. Today many scholars agree that the roots of plainsong lie in the Jewish tradition of singing poetry. (For example, A. Sendrey, in *Music in Ancient Israel* (pp. 230 ff.), offers several comparisons between extant Gregorian chants and ancient Jewish songs from the psalms, Lamentations, and priestly blessings.) Its free but regular rhythm places plainsong more within an oriental than an occidental culture: in both Hebrew poetry and Latin plainsong the accent is natural, and the rhythm flows easily with the speech forms in such a way that the words are brought to life through the resonance of the rhythm and the purity of the melody. Although in Latin the stress is obviously different, falling usually on the penultimate or the prepenultimate syllable, the word-accents in plainsong follow a similar pattern to the Hebrew: there is no evidence of a predetermined qualitative metre, for the rhythm is varied and flexible, being more like 'singing-speech'.

This differentiates plainsong entirely from Greek poetry in the Western tradition, where the sound and sense conventions are more rigid. Plainsong not only follows more closely the free rhythm of speech, but several other characteristics also confirm that it has a stronger affinity to the music of the East than to that of the West. There is no time signature; this would predetermine the beat and might force the words into unacceptable accents. There is no harmony; the tonic chant is found only in the one melodic line, to bring out the sense of the words as 'plainly' (or 'purely') as possible. Instead of modern notation, the form is of square notes on a *four-line* stave, and there is no key signature as such: the placing of the doh-clef (♩) and the fah-clef (♩) freely on the stave causes the pitch to be relative rather than absolute, in order to suit a range of voices. The music falls into an eight-tonal pattern which has many correspondences with the melodic modes in Hebrew (some would see evidence of this, for example, in the eight-line stanzas in Ps. 119, or the sevenfold 'voice of God' with the eighth as a response in Ps. 29). Furthermore, the balanced formation which is evident in Hebrew verse, in the binary presentation of the ideas, is one of the characteristic features in plainsong: the first half of the verse is the 'ascent' (the first recit and cadence), leading to the pause between the two halves (the mediant), and the second half of the verse is the 'descent' (the second recit and cadence). All is for simplicity and flexibility, with the concern being for a complete balance between sense and sound. In *The Interpretation of Plainchant*, A. Robertson writes:

Now plainchant, like prose, knows of a regularly recurring and divisible beat as does measured music, for the beat in the chant, represented by the quaver-unit, is indivisible, though it may be lengthened; and the binary and ternary groups are mixed at will, producing the free rhythm which alone can make long stretches of unaccompanied melody acceptable to the ear. With accents occurring at absolutely regular intervals, as in measured music, plainchant would become as square as its notation and intolerable to listen to. (p. 16.)

To illustrate this balance not only in the rhythm of the words but also in the rhythm of the music, Robertson gives an example of binary and ternary mixing of rhythms where plainsong is used in

English, and where it is clear that both freedom and order are found together:

Thóu art the / Kíng of / Glóry O / Chríst

Thóu art the / éver / lásting / Són of the / Fáther.

This is a good example of the use of plainsong in our vernacular. For like Latin, with its *legato* accent, the English language has also been found to be an appropriate vehicle for plainsong. (Contemporary *Gelineau* music, from the 1950s in France, has provided the same enhancement of biblical poetry through the use of what has been called 'sprung rhythm'—a feature which has been developed more recently in English, using a type of tonic chant which is distinctive from but related to plainsong; see, for example, A. Robertson, *Music of the Catholic Church*, 51 ff.).

These observations of Jewish and Christian musical renderings of biblical poetry offer important implications not only for our studies of Hebrew metre and parallelism, but also for our earlier observations concerning the boundaries between poetry and prose. Firstly, they confirm that the balance of sound (in the rhythm) and the balance of sense (in the presentation of ideas in a bipartite form) are interdependent. On this basis, it is more difficult (though not impossible) to sing continuous prose than it is poetry, for the latter has the more distinctive potential of being broken into corresponding lines with some audible rhythm. This is why the psalms are most appropriate for singing, not least antiphonally. We might also note the 'fourteen canticles' which are sung in the Christian tradition in this way (Exod. 15; Deut. 32; 1 Sam. 2; Hab. 3; Isa. 26; Jonah 2; Dan. 3, with the two apocryphal additions of the Prayer of Azariah and the Song of the Three Young Men; Isa. 38, and the apocryphal Prayer of Manasseh; Luke 1: 68–79 and 46–55; Luke 2: 29–32 and the Gloria).

Second, these observations also confirm our earlier conclusion that sound and sense are intended to complement one another. Thus the definition of Hebrew poetry is not about rhythm on its own, let alone the more rigid form of rhythm, namely metre; nor is it about balance of ideas on its own, least of all a prescribed system of this, namely parallelism. It is about both working together, and yet about much more as well, for the essence of Hebrew poetry which we have discovered through seeing its interpretation through music is as much in its freedom and flexibility as in tight conventions and ordered systems. The following comment by Sendrey concerning Hebrew and Greek music in the ancient world, even if overstated, is pertinent:

The preponderantly philosophical disposition of the Greeks brought forth an important musical system, showing, however, unmistakable signs of purely intellectual construction . . . It stems from reflection, and not from emotion . . . With the Jewish notion of God as the unique and supreme creative power, with the moral approach of the Jews to all phenomena of life, the thinking, feeling . . . underwent eventually a profound transformation . . . Jewish music is highly emotional, and in this respect quite contrary to Greek music, the basic principle of which is intellectuality . . . For the Hellenes, music was a rigid theoretic discipline, while the Hebrews have discovered a new and purely spiritual approach to tonal art. (*Music in Ancient Israel*, 550–2.)

Much of this has an echo in the observations of Robert Lowth, writing some three centuries earlier. Although Sendrey's stark contrasts between Judaism and Hellenism raise many questions about the nuances in cultural influences, his observations regarding the essence of Jewish music and poetry still stand. Furthermore, the West has inherited the Greek way of thinking about music and poetry to a far greater extent than it has imbibed Jewish creativity; it is therefore no surprise that we impose on to Hebrew poetry categories which are foreign to it. The following section on metre and Hebrew poetry will illustrate the truth of this point.

B. Metrical Theories and Hebrew Poetry

As we have seen, rhythm, stress, and sonority are vital components of Hebrew poetry. Yet none of these is identical to metre. Each can be found where there is no metre, although obviously the reverse cannot hold: metre is dependent on rhythm for its conventions. The model of 'sung speech' is as appropriate a one for Hebrew poetry as it is for Latin plainsong.

It is remarkable that so many of the Church Fathers assumed that Hebrew poetry was not only rhythmic but also metrical. For example, Origen of Alexandria (*c.*185–*c.*254 CE) was influenced both by Hellenistic philosophy and by Rabbinical interpretation of Scripture, and gave detailed attention to the Greek and Hebrew versions of the Old Testament; hence his belief that Hebrew poetry was metrical in essence. In his *Hexapla*, in which he cited the Greek Septuagint version, Origen was convinced that the psalms were trimeter and tetrameter, and believed that the Greek translators were mistaken to create two metrical lines from one single verse, broken only by a caesura. Similarly, Eusebius of Caesarea (*c.*260–*c.*340 CE) upheld the view that the psalms adhered consistently to a regular metre. Eusebius was concerned to defend and promote the Christian faith in a pagan world, and in so doing, he became the first scholar to write a systematic history of the Christian Church. Because psalmists were far from inferior to the Greek sophists and orators, they too were therefore inspired, he believed, to write in heroic metre—'hexameters … and also verses in trimeter and tetrameter lines'. The same point is made by John Chrysostom of Antioch (*c.*347–407 CE), a great Christian preacher and exegete of the Greek Bible, later to become Bishop of Constantinople. David, moved by the Spirit, composed in metric form the book of 150 psalms, 'according to the metre of his own language, and sang them with melody, with rhythm'. This view was upheld also by Jerome (*c.*342–420 CE), a scholar who was commissioned by the Pope to make an improved Latin translation of the Scriptures, using not only the Greek but also the Hebrew 'original'. Jerome observed that, on the whole, Hebrew poetry was usually composed in a quantitative metre, mainly of hexameters, with dactyls (a metrical foot comprising one long and two short syllables) and spondees (a metrical foot with two long syllables), but also with interpolations of other verse-feet.

The reason for this affirmation of the metrical nature of Hebrew poetry becomes clearer when one reads the views of other Church Fathers who opposed this position. Gregory of Nyssa (*c.*335–94 CE), one of the Cappadocian fathers in the Eastern Church, offers us a clue: his view was that Hebrew poetry had no resemblance to classical Hellenistic metre because its source of inspiration was qualitatively different. Either it was assumed that Greek (metrical) poetry was of the highest worth, and it was thus held that Hebrew poetry had appropriated the same conventions (including metre), with the consequence that its poetic inspiration was of the same high worth; or, alternatively, one believed that Hebrew poetry was distinctive, since its source of inspiration was different, and it was necessarily independent of Hellenistic poetic conventions. On this basis, Hebrew poetry possessed instead a free accentual rhythm which was more dynamic than mechanical.

One cannot help noting that the two contrasting opinions expressed in the patristic period linger in a different guise today. Either Hebrew poetry is very like that of cultures whose literature contemporary scholarship holds in respect, in which case it is assumed that it has utilized some of these conventions; or Hebrew poetry is *sui generis*, in which case it is free to follow its own conventions, which need not include those of clear metrical arrangement.

Scholars who support a pro-metrical theory today of course offer other reasons for doing so as well. It should not be surprising that much of the debate concerning the metric classification of poetry developed near the end of the nineteenth century in Germany. For example, in the late 1870s, J. Ley proposed that a stress accent was evident in the parallel line-forms, and scanned the lines with assumptions that they would follow hexameters, tetrameters, pentameters, and so on. (We may note the observations of Origen and Eusebius here.) In the 1880s this was developed further by K. Budde: working through the book of Lamentations, he observed that the first 'parallel line' was longer than the second line; the first line usually had three stresses (occasionally four), and the second line had two stresses (sometimes three). This produced a somewhat 'limping' sound, and because it was used in the prayers of lament, Budde called this 3:2 line a lament-like metre (Hebrew: *qinâ*). (A subsequent problem has been that this 3:2 metre has since been found in many other texts which offer no suggestion of a lament form, and many lament forms do not use the 3:2 but rather a 3:3 stress.)

Budde's views were developed in the 1890s by another German, E. Sievers, who was already an expert in the metrics of Old English and German poetry. Sievers proposed a more detailed metrical system which used primary and secondary accents in each line-form, and concluded (partly as a result of his assessment of the stress system in *Beowulf*) that the line-form in Hebrew consisted basically of two unstressed syllables followed by one stressed syllable. This system—called *anapaestic metre*—Sievers found wherever the text allowed a division of line-forms on the basis of some evidence of a bipartite arrangement in the sense. Sievers' stress system bears some resemblance to the dactyl, being transliterated as ∪ ∪ – or – – ⁄ or ♪♪ ♩ (two short syllables and one long, stressed syllable). According to Sievers, anapaestic metre is the key criterion for determining Hebrew poetry.

By contrast, G. Bickell, also writing in German in the 1890s, proposed a system influenced by his particular research on Syriac poetry. This was simply the alternation of a stressed and then unstressed syllable within one 'metrical foot'. The usual form was ∪ – | ∪ – | ∪ –, or – ⁄ | – ⁄ – ⁄ or ♪♩ ♪♩ , with the stress falling on the second syllable. This system was known as *iambic metre*. (If the stress was instead on the first of the two syllables, namely – ∪ | – ∪ | – ∪ or ⁄ – | ⁄ – | ⁄ –, then this would be *trochaic metre*, but this was a less consistent feature in Hebrew verse.)

Bickell's view has been developed in the twentieth century by G. Hölscher and S. Mowinckel. Using the *iambic metre* as their basic guide, they noted that this was found throughout Hebrew poetry, albeit with some flexibility—for example, where two stressed syllables occur side by side. But Hölscher and Mowinckel were convinced that Hebrew poetry was composed in iambic metre: the line-forms were classified in terms of iambic hexameters, iambic pentameters, and so on—depending on the number of times so-called 'metrical feet', employing unstress/stress, occurred in one line.

In this way, Hebrew poetry became understood as a professional technique: only those with a good knowledge of how Hebrew metre worked could properly understand how to divide the poetry into phonetically balanced line-forms. Mowinckel held that the poets consciously chose one primary formula, namely the 4:4 or 3:3 stress over two line-forms. For scholars like Mowinckel, this numerical classification was essential because it supported further the theory that Hebrew poetry was composed by professional liturgical experts:

Poetry is originally connected with singing, and characteristic of the rhythm of singing are more fixed rules for the alternation of long and short—or accented and unaccented—syllables. It tends towards expression in a lucid numerical formula, it is rational. (*The Psalms in Israel's Worship*, ii. 159.)

This could not contrast more starkly with our earlier discussion on the nature of plainsong and the conclusions on oriental music and poetry offered by Sendrey.

Several scholars still affirm the iambic and anapaestic views of Hebrew metre. Others by contrast emphasize not so much the *phonetic* element as the *quantitative* features of the 'lucid numerical formulae'. (In that this disregards the phonetic element, many scholars would question whether it is strictly a metrical system at all.) Most scholars who focus on the quantitative features have been influenced by Ugaritic poetry. Assuming that the ideal in Ugaritic poetry was an equal number of syllables in each line, forming half of a parallel pair (a feature which was certainly used in our examples from Ugaritic in the last chapter), scholars have proposed that the same method could apply to Hebrew poetry as well. Thus, instead of counting the *accents* in each line-form, which requires first determining which stress system is correct, each *syllable* is counted instead. The main problem is that when the second line does not produce an identical number of syllables to the first, one is left with all sorts of questions about irregularities. A further difficulty is that Ugaritic scholars (such as de Moor) have argued convincingly that Ugaritic poetry has no regular metre at all—the balanced lines being not so much concerned with the sound as with the sense. The problem here is that we know very little about the vocalization of Ugaritic, which makes any fixed opinion difficult to maintain.

An enthusiast for syllable-counting is D. N. Freedman, who also affirms the 'symmetry-sensitivity' in Ugaritic poetry. In contrast to de Moor, Freedman (for example in *Pottery, Poetry and Prophecy*) concludes that this symmetry suggests that the poetry can be measured in quantitative and phonetic terms—namely by counting the number of syllables in each line-form. This is not to say that the poets numbered their words and syllables into hundreds and thousands to determine the shape of their poems—they wrote with an intuition which was already deeply ingrained in their poetic consciousness. (Hence Freedman also side-steps the issue of irregularities, for this is part of the poet's creative and flexible use of regular poetic conventions.) This view is also applied in some detail by M. Dahood, another Ugaritic scholar, in his three-volume commentary on the book of Psalms. The interest in symmetry and word-pairs (an interest which we have already noted in Ugaritic poetry) is everywhere apparent.

The problem with symmetry, as with any metrical theory, is that it is apt to become too rigid a system. This is all too evident in further attempts to count words rather than accented syllables (so, Kosmala). The difficulty lies in ascertaining exactly what constitutes a 'word' in Hebrew—do words joined together by the *maqqēp* (rather like our hyphen) make up one word or two? Do the monosyllables such as *lo'* ('not') and *kî* ('for', 'because') serve as one isolated word, or are they connected with what follows them? The decisions on word-counting again require a number of assumptions before one starts. The difficulties seem to be compounded when instead of counting 'words', one counts letters to ascertain some quantitative uniformity (so, Loretz). Overall, it would appear that much of this search for a clear classification system on the basis of metrics raises questions about the so-called 'lucid, numerical formula' (so, Mowinckel) with which the Hebrew poets supposedly worked. The problem is compounded when one notes the appeal to the emendation of poetic texts for metrical (rather than syntactical) reasons. Such reductivism often wipes out features which could add to the richness of the poetic content if they were taken in a more metaphorical and theological sense.

It is for this reason that other scholars have abandoned altogether the search for a consistent metrical system. Two scholars in particular have popularized this more negative view—the one

(J. Kugel) following a phonetic and semantic approach, and the other (M. O'Connor) a grammatical and syntactic one.

For O'Connor, 'No consensus has ever been reached in the matter of Hebrew meter because there is none' (*Hebrew Verse Structure*, 138). O'Connor offers six *constraints* for the determining of Hebrew poetry, none of which is metrical: these consist mainly of the number of verbs and dependent clauses in each line-form. These constraints are based more upon syntax and sense than upon rhythm and sound.

Kugel's basic objection to metrical theories is the lack of regularity in Hebrew poetry:

All metrical theories suffer from the same syndrome. It starts with the observation that 'lines', or sentences, units of thought, major pauses, 'periods' or whatever, are roughly equal in length in a given passage of poetry . . . the approximate regularity of biblical songs does not correspond to any metrical system. (*The Idea of Biblical Poetry*, 297–8.)

For Kugel, the regularity can only be understood in terms of the sense—the balance of ideas, expressed in the parallelism—and he notes that this encourages more flexibility than anything predetermined in the rhythm.

Thus far we have assessed two extreme positions regarding Hebrew metre: it is a clearly developed system; it does not exist. There are, of course, other scholars who attempt a *via media*. Watson, for example, notes: 'Confusion arises because scholars fail to distinguish between metre as actually present in verse, and *regular* metre. There is metre, yes, but not regular metre, since metrical patterns are never maintained for more than a few verses at a stretch, if even that' (*Classical Hebrew Poetry*, 92). It would seem that Watson's view accords well with the evidence. On the one hand, it is clearly very difficult to determine Hebrew metre precisely. We no longer know the exact pronunciation, nor even where the accents fell when the poem was first composed and used; we still do not know enough about Ugaritic poetry to use this as a precise model for Hebrew verse—in fact, our own examples from Ugarit drew attention to the differences as well as to the similarities; we cannot presume that Hebrew poetry followed the Greek and Latin system of alternating long and short syllables; and from what we have previously discussed about the nature of the oriental music which would have accompanied much of the Hebrew poetry in the liturgical festivals, it would appear that fluidity and flexibility are more important than any rigid system.

Nevertheless, the musicality of the poetry indicates that by no means everything in Hebrew poetry is fluid and flexible. The musical analogy cuts both ways: it would be extremely difficult to set to music a text which followed no conventions whatsoever. The following survey within the Psalter shows that we have to account for some regular tonic accent or rhythmic stress in Hebrew poetry in many instances.

C. Applying Metrical Theories to the Texts

Here the problem is that of deciding what metrical theory to apply to a given text. The method I have used here is as flexible as possible: first, to seek out line-forms, usually on the basis of some parallelism or of some bipartite or tripartite components; second, to determine where syllable-stresses are most likely to fall in each composite word-unit in the Hebrew; third, to count how many of these syllable-stresses are found in one line-form. The appropriation of this method yields some interesting results, even working with the English translation.

For example, for Psalm 117, the shortest psalm in the Psalter, the English translation is set out so that it follows as closely as possible Hebrew construct-words (often called 'units'); it is clear that each unit has some sort of primary stress, usually on the ultimate, but often on the penultimate syllable in the unit, as is indicated below:

> Praise the-Lord   all-nations!
>
> hallû et-ʾᵃdōnáy kol-góyim
>
> Extol-him all-peoples!
>
> šabbᵉḥûhû kol-hāʾummîm   (v. 1)
>
> For great towards-us [is] his-steadfast-love
>
> kî gābár ʿālênû   ḥasdô

and-the-faithfulness-of-the-Lórd [endures] for éver
we'ᵉmet-'ᵃḏōnay   lᵉʿôlám   (v. 2)

Despite the very different placing of stress in Hebrew and in English, it is nevertheless possible in both languages to count three primary stresses in each line-form: each of the verses could thus be presented as having a 3:3 pattern. The fact that this 3:3 pattern could be seen as *six* accents for each verse is why scholars have called this hexameter; however, the uneven distribution of the accents should at the very least raise a question about this term.

This 3:3 accentual rhythm is used frequently in the psalms, particularly in psalms of praise, such as Ps. 117 above. The most consistent evidence is found, for example, in Pss. 33, 103, 114, 147, 148, 149, and 150. It may also be observed with some regularity in parts of Gen. 49: 1–28 (Jacob's blessing, parts of which possibly come from the time of David); in Num. 21: 14–15 (described as ancient 'war poetry'); in Num. 21: 16–17 (possibly from a 'drinking-song'), and also in parts of Deut. 32: 1–47 and 33: 1–29. The 3:3 pattern is also frequently used in the wisdom literature—for example, in Proverbs, and in much of the poetry in Job:

(Shall)-mán	than-Gód	be-[more]-ríghteous
ha'ᵉnôš	mᵉlôáh	yiṣdáq
or-than-his-máker	be-[more]-púre	a-mán?
im-mēʿōśēhû	yiṭhár	gāḇer

                                          (Job 4: 17)

It is possible to ascertain this same rhythm even in some of the narrative literature—for example, in the prose prayers. The 3:3 rhythm was undoubtedly a flexible poetic device used widely throughout the literature of ancient Israel.

Another common pattern is 4:4. Psalm 46 is interesting, not least because vv. 3, 7, and 11 (two of which form a refrain) are in the 3:3 stress, and by contrast vv. 1–2, 4–6, and 8–10 are in 4:4. For example:

God   is-in-her-mídst   she-shall-nót-be-sháken

ᵉlohím   bᵉqirbāh   bal-timmôṭ
He-will-hélp-her God   at-the-bréak-of the-mórning
ya ᶜzᵉreá   ᵉlohím   lipnōt   bōqer

(Ps. 46: 6)

Outside the Psalter, poetry with a 4:4 pattern is found in parts of
Exodus 15 and in many of the sayings in Proverbs.

A rhythm related to this, and often difficult to distinguish from it,
is 2:2. When set out in line-forms, it is more brisk—what some
scholars have called a 'marching rhythm'. It is not surprising that it
occurs in the ancient war poetry of Israel (cf. Judg. 5 and 1 Sam.
1: 19ff.), because it has a simple and dramatic binary form. It is a
frequent device used by the prophets, often interspersed with the
3:2 rhythm for dramatic effect. We have already used Isa. 1: 16–17
in another context, but the terse 2:2 beat is evident even in the
English:

Céase	to-do-évil
ḥídlû	hārēᶜa
leárn	to-do-góod
límdû	hêṭeḇ
seék	jústice
díršû	mišpāṭ
corréct	oppréssion
ʾaššᵉrû	ḥāmôṣ
defénd	the-fátherless
šípṭû	yāṯôm
pleád	for-the-wídow
ríḇû	ʾalᵉmānâ

It is possible to lengthen the above line-forms in such a way as to
effect a 2 × 4:4 instead of an 8 × 2:2 pattern of stress. The classification is perhaps more intuitive than objective; the staccato and
terse style fits the contents better than a lengthier, more rounded

4:4 metre. Nowhere could this be more evident than in Ps. 29, where the brevity of the repetition seems to echo the 'voice of the Lord' in its sevenfold cry in vv. 3–9, almost imitating the claps of thunder:

v. 3: The-voíce-of-the-LÓRD
qôl-'ᵃdónay
[is] upón-the-waters
'ál-hammáyım
The-Gód-of-glóry
él-hākābôd
thúndeŕs
hír'îm
The LÓRD [is] abóve-
'ᵃdônay 'ál-
mány waters
máyim rábîm

v. 4: The-voíce-of-the-LÓRD
qôl-'ᵃdónay
(is) fúll-of-pówer
bákoáḥ
The-vóice-of-the-LÓRD
qôl-'ᵃdónay
(is) fúll-of-májesty
béhādár

(Ps. 29: 3–4)

Some of these lines admittedly would scan better according to a 4:4 stress, although verse 3 works well as a tripartite 2:2:2 (as opposed to a bipartite 2:2) which would be impossible to effect with 4:4. Several psalms use this 2:2:2 pattern. Some of these, like Ps. 29, suggest the influence of Canaanite culture—for example, Ps. 68 (cf. vv. 7–8, again describing God's coming in the storm). A 2:2:2

pattern is also found in Ps. 91: 3 (concerning the threat of a deadly pestilence). It is found several times in the prophets (often in the so-called prose sections, for example in 2 Sam. 7 and in Isa. 8: 14, the Immanuel saying.) The 2:2 rhythm is by no means an inflexible pattern.

Similarly, the 3:3 pattern is also developed into a 3:3:3 rhythm. We have noted Ps. 24: 7 in another context:

> Lift-up O-gates your-heads,
> and-be-lifted-up, O-doors ancient
> and-shall-come-in [the]-King of-glory.

Pss. 60: 8; 77: 16–19; 103: 20; and much of Pss. 99 and 100 use this 3:3:3 pattern. All these examples celebrate (in one way or another) the rule of God in history, a tenet which almost certainly would have been celebrated in liturgy. It may be that this 3:3:3 pattern was used at a cultic festival which celebrated God's kingship over the entire earth.

Reference has been made to Budde's observation of the 3:2 rhythm throughout much of Lamentations. There is little doubt that this rhythm was used (although not exclusively) to echo the mood of lament, whereby the lack of a third matching accent in the second line brought out a sense of unfulfilled hopes. Amos 5: 2 gives us a good example of this in the prophets:

> Fallen, no-more to-rise
> nāpᵉlâ loʾ-tôsîp qûm
> (is)-the-virgin Israel
> bᵉtûlat yiśrāʾēl

This 3:2 rhythm is a common motif in the psalms of lament, a clear example being Ps. 5: 1–2:

> my-words give-ear-to, O LORD
> ʾᵃmāray haʾᵃzînâ ʾᵃdōnay
> give-heed-to my-groaning.
> bînâ hᵃgîgî

> Heárken to-the-soúnd-of my-crý
> haqšíbâ   lᵉqól   šawʿí
> my-kíng and-my-Gód.
> malkí   weʾlohȧ́y

Other 3:2 verses in the Psalter occur in many of the individual lament psalms, the clearest examples being Pss. 28, 35, 36, 40, 57, and 70. Interestingly, this 3:2 pattern is found in some part of every psalm in one particular collection, namely Pss. 120–34, the Psalms of Ascent—with the exception of Ps. 132. Psalm 23 provides another interesting example, in that its metre varies between 3:2 (vv. 1–3) and 2:2 (v. 4) and 3:2 (vv. 5–6). Psalm 55 offers a similar pattern, being mainly in 3:2, with v. 6 in 2:2, as does Ps. 84, also mainly in 3:2, with v. 3 as 2:2 and v. 12 as 2:3.

It is at this point, where the stress-patterns change and take on more unusual and less regular emphases, that the strict metrical theories are most vulnerable. We may also note the occurrences of a 4:3 pattern (e.g. Ps. 141: 4) and a 3:4 pattern (e.g. Pss. 4: 3; 17: 3; 18: 7). So too the 2:3 pattern in Ps. 84 also occurs frequently elsewhere; Isa. 40: 3*b* offers a good example.

On the one hand, it is clear that there are many consistent regular patterns, and these usually feature a 2:2, 3:3, 4:4, and 3:2 stress, and furthermore offer indications of having a particular liturgical (and, in some cases, musical) setting: the celebration of victory in war-songs, the haunting lament rhythm in times of individual or communal distress, and the commemoration of God's kingly rule over the entire cosmos are three possible examples.

But on the other hand, we are left with a good deal which we cannot know. Even our counting of tonal accents in the Hebrew is fraught with difficulties; for example, we cannot be sure every time whether the vowel-less letter (called the *šᵉwā*, transliterated as a vowel above the line) is vocal or silent, thus causing the stress to fall at another point in a word; we cannot always be sure whether compound word-units, expanded by prefixes and suffixes, suggest two accents rather than one; we cannot be sure whether the *maqqēp* (the hyphen-line) always causes the accent to fall later in a word-unit; nor can we be sure whether the monosyllables count as a separate accent on their own, or whether they allow the stress to fall on the following word. Furthermore, other evidence which weighs against over-systematizing is the paucity of strophic forms (whereby line-forms have a consistent enough regularity, due to a rhythmic pattern, to create a grouping which some might call a 'stanza'). Only very rarely is there clear evidence of strophes, and these are usually created by the use of refrains (e.g. Pss. 42–3, 57) or by the use of an alphabetic/acrostic device (as in parts of Lamentations) rather than by the build-up of regular metrical units. It would appear that there are few clear strophic formations because repeated line-forms which create strophes simply do not extend clearly throughout the whole of a poem.

Taken together, the difficulty of method in assessing tonal accents, as well as the small number of strophes evident in biblical verse, further suggest that where metrical classification is concerned, there is much of which we are still ignorant.

D. Metre and Psalmody

The following survey is the result of an analysis of the entire Psalter, which attempts to ascertain whether the above observations are in fact correct when the evidence is brought together. The psalms provide a good model for such a survey because they form one manageable, composite collection, through which some statistical analysis is possible. It will be seen that the results reveal more about the irregularities than about the consistencies of metrical design. For the sake of clarity, the presentation assesses the psalms in their various categories of form—such as hymns, laments, thanksgivings, and so on. (As yet, we have not discussed the purpose and extent of the forms of biblical poetry: a chart is to be found in the appendix at the end of Chapter 10, for those who may at this stage be unclear about this process of classification.)

Of the general hymns, Pss. 33, 103, 114, 117, 147, 148, 149, and 150 reflect a consistent 3:3 pattern. (There are exceptions, such as Pss. 33: 10, 12; 114: 7; 148: 8, 149: 1, 9, and 150: 6.) So too overall Pss. 100, 104, 111, 136, and 146 follow some similar pattern. This leaves Ps. 8 (which has some 2:2 and 3:3 patterns), much of Ps. 29 (which as we have seen follows a 2:2 and 2:2:2 pattern, but also has many textual corruptions), 113 and 135 (which borrow widely from other psalms), and 145 (which has two halves and two different rhythms). The kingship hymns offer some evidence of the 3:3 pattern. Psalms 97 and 98 offer the best examples (although even here 97: 1, 2, 8, and 10 and 98: 1–3 are different). By contrast, Ps. 93 has a 2:2 pattern in four short lines, then 3:3 in a single line; Ps. 47 has many variations, probably for liturgical effect; Ps. 96 is irregular and full of stylized forms used in other hymns, and Ps. 99 has irregularities due to textual disorders.

The Zion hymns offer little consistency in their patterns. Psalm 48 has a 3:3 rhythm (except for vv. 1–2) and Ps. 76 follows overall a 3:2 pattern (apart from vv. 4–5 and 11). Psalm 46 has no regular metre. Psalm 87 is irregular due to various textual dislocations. Psalm 122 is irregular, with some evidence of 3:2, vv. 1, 8, 9, vv. 2, 3, 4, and vv. 5, 6, 7 all being different.

The two historical psalms (Pss. 78 and 105) interestingly conform overall to a 3:3 pattern. Variations are found in Ps. 78: 21, 31, and 55, with 3:3:3, and in vv. 6, 7, 8, 20, 28, and 45, which are altogether different, and in Ps. 105: 1, 11, and 15.

The liturgies are full of different patterns, probably because they served some dramatic purpose within the rituals of the cult. Psalm 15 offers a 3:2 pattern in the antiphonal sections, but the rest is variable. Psalm 24: 1–6 is quite different from 24: 7–10. Psalm 134 is variable and it is likely to be composite, with different metres in the introductory exhortations and the following response.

Within the prophetic exhortations, Pss. 14, 52, and 53 have overall a 3:2 metre, and Pss. 50, 91, and 95 follow mainly a 3:3 pattern. Psalm 58 has many variations, suggesting overall a 4:3 rhythm, but with variations (in vv. 4 and 8). Psalm 81 has some 3:3 metre, but with many textual difficulties (e.g. vv. 5c–6; 10c–11). Psalm 75 follows overall a 3:3 pattern, apart from vv. 1, 7, and 8b.

Not all the communal laments reflect the expected 3:2 pattern. Psalms 44, 60, 80, 82, 83, 85, 90, 94, and 106 are mainly 3:3, although several verses in each of these break the pattern (cf. Pss. 44: 21; 60: 6–8, 9; 80: 9; 82: 5, 8; 83: 6, 17; 90: 2; 94: 9, 12, 17, and 23). Psalm 77 is in 3:3 overall in vv. 1–15, and in 3:3:3 in vv. 16–20. Psalm 108, which borrows from Ps. 57: 7–11 in vv. 1–5, is in 3:2 metre, whilst

vv. 6–13, borrowed from Ps. 60: 5–12, are mainly in 3:3 metre. Psalm 123 is mainly in 3:2; Ps. 74 is in 2:2 (except for vv. 6–7 and 20) and Ps. 126 is mainly in 2:2:2, with some 3:2. Psalm 79 does not sustain any pattern for more than three verses; and so too, Ps. 137 seems to deny any pattern at all.

The communal psalms of confidence are also irregular. Psalm 129 is the most regular, mainly in 3:2; Ps. 115 is roughly in 3:3; Ps. 133, despite its brevity, is different in vv. 1 and 2. Psalm 125 is the most irregular.

The communal thanksgivings also have irregularities. Only Ps. 107 has some predictable 3:3 metre (although the refrains in vv. 6, 13, 19, and 28 are different). Psalm 65 changes between 3:2 and 3:3. Psalms 66 and 67 have some evidence of 3:3, but with exceptions. Psalm 68 is hard to classify because of its textual corruptions and its fragmentary quotations. Psalms 118 and 124 are mainly irregular.

The royal psalms are similarly variable. Psalms 18, 20, and 132 all suggest some overall 3:3 pattern. Psalm 102 fits overall a 3:2. Psalm 2 is more variable—3:3 is evident, but with many variations (vv. 5, 7, 8, and 12). Psalm 21 follows 2:2 in vv. 1–6 and 3:3 in 7–13, with other variations. Psalm 45 has an unusual 4:4:4 pattern overall. Psalm 89 suggests a basic 4:4 pattern in the first half, and 3:3 in the second part, although vv. 38 ff. in the third part are irregular. Psalms 72 and 144 offer no regular pattern whatsoever.

Within the wisdom psalms, Ps. 119, with its preference for structure, follows overall a 3:2 metre, with several changes, often due to scribal emendations. Psalm 37 is 3:3, with variations. Psalm 19 suggests overall 4:4 in vv. 1–6, and 3:2 in vv. 7–14, although there are exceptions (vv. 4 and 6 appear to be 3:3). Psalm 127 reflects 3:3 in vv. 1–2 and 3:2 in vv. 3–5, and Ps. 128 suggests 3:2 in vv. 1–4, although v. 5 is 3:3:2. Psalm 49 has a basic 3:3 pattern, broken by textual difficulties and abrupt changes in subject-matter. Neither Ps. 1 nor Ps. 139 has a recognizably regular rhythm.

Within the individual laments, again many irregularities are evident, and again the 3:2 pattern is by no means always used. The 3:3 pattern is evident overall in Pss. 6 (except vv. 2, 4, 8), 25 (except vv. 1, 15), 26 (except v. 1), 38, 59 (except vv. 6, 12, 13, 14), 88 (except v. 5), 51 (except vv. 1, 11 particularly), and 56 (except for the refrain in vv. 4, 10–11), 63, 69, 102, and 142 (except v. 6). 3:2 is mainly evident in Pss. 5, 28 (except v. 9), 36 (although the second part is 3:3), 57 (vv. 1–5 being 3:3), and Ps. 70 (also 40: 13ff.). Psalm 12 is in 4:4 overall. Several other laments do show a 3:2 rhythm, but there are irregularities due to textual dislocations: these are Pss. 7, 17, 35, 64, 71, 140, and 141. Of the remaining laments, no discernible pattern overall can be found—sometimes this is because of their composite nature, perhaps in other cases because of textual problems, although another rather more mundane and obvious reason could be the troubled mind of the suppliant. These psalms are 13, 22, 31, 39, 42–3, 54, 61, 73, 86, 109, 120, 130, and 143, where only two or three verses together suggest any pattern.

Of the individual thanksgivings, the 3:3 pattern is found in Pss. 34, 92 (except v. 9, in 3:3:3), and 138 (with some uncertainties in some verses). Ps. 30 suggests 2:2 and 3:3 together. Psalms 9–10 have variable patterns; they may be composite, and there are dislocations in the text. Psalm 32 also shows little pattern, with textual difficulties. Psalms 40 and 41 are irregular for similar reasons to Pss. 9–10. Psalm 116 has no one pattern throughout, and several textual problems occur in vv. 10–19.

Of the individual psalms of confidence, Ps. 33 offers a 3:3 pattern (apart from vv. 3, 7, 8) and Ps. 4 a 4:4 pattern (apart from v. 1). Psalm 23 has a 3:2 and 2:2 pattern; and Ps. 131 has also a 3:2 (except for v. 2). Psalm 11 suggests overall a 2:2 pattern, and 84 overall a 3:2 rhythm. Psalm 16 is difficult to analyse, because of additional half-lines which break up what could be a 2:2 pattern. Psalm 27 is a composite psalm, with a corrupt text in its second part, and no regular metre throughout. Psalm 62 appears to be similarly composite, and again with no regularity, and Ps. 121 also offers no consistent pattern, changing every two verses.

In summary, it is evident that the hypothesis regarding the fixed nature of the metre of the psalms (for example, Mowinckel's 4:4 claim) does not fit the evidence from the psalms themselves. Even an entirely different method of assessment, such as determining different tonic accents, or counting syllables rather than accents, produces problems: the textual dislocations, the liturgically composite psalms, the changing moods of certain psalmists, and the phonetic irregularities cumulatively suggest that any system of metre needs to be appraised with a good deal of caution.

These conclusions are similar to those of G. B. Gray in *The Forms of Hebrew Poetry*. Gray was also cautious about actual metre, and saw that something other than a metrical system was required in order to understand the nature of a biblical poem. That something other for Gray was parallelism, whereby a line-form still retained some symmetry even when the metrical value was unclear or apparently non-existent. Gray emphasized that the symmetry was dependent not so much on the *sound*, as on the *sense* of the poetry: 'Parallelism is unmistakeable, metre in Hebrew literature is obscure: the laws of Hebrew metre have been and are matters of dispute, and at times the very existence of metre in the Old Testament has been questioned' (ibid. 47).

We may conclude that although there is clearly a discernible *rhythm* in many psalms, it is not a sufficiently clear guide to call it *metre*. To speak of 'rhythm' is to suggest something more dynamic, partly by way of its use of tonic accents, whilst to speak of 'metre' implies a more mechanical counting technique. 'Rhythm' implies discernible patterns, used with fluidity and flexibility throughout a poem; 'metre' implies a system imposed upon the poem from outside. The musical associations within the poetry would indicate a situation closer to rhythm than to metre. Just as in music, a musical score brings to life the meaning of what is said, transforming it into 'sung speech' without intrusion or distortion, so in Hebrew poetry the rhythm brings to life the meaning of the poem, but as another form of 'sung speech' which again neither intrudes nor distorts. As Gray observed, the sound of the verse is important, but the sense is more so. The purpose of the following chapter is to assess further the nature and use of this 'balance of sense'—the parallelism—in order to ascertain the extent to which this comprises the essence of Hebrew poetry.

4

Parallelism

Robert Alter makes an interesting comparison between the use of parallelism in Hebrew poetry and the ways in which images are thrown on to the cinema screen. Just as the screen enhances and reinforces an association of ideas in our imagination by the repetition of a particular image, so parallelism achieves the same effect by the ordering of words rather than pictures. By creating similar images with different words, the intensification of meaning is achieved.

Given our conclusions concerning the metre and musicality of biblical poetry, the associations between parallelism and cinema art are most appropriate; again we have an analogy which suggests an intuitive and creative process rather than a fixed technique. Just as the tonal characteristics of metre require the same sensitivities that one would expect in the composition of music, so the visual characteristics of parallelism require the same sensibilities expected in the world of screenplay. The purpose of this chapter is to demonstrate that the adaptation of parallelism in Hebrew verse is no more a rigid convention than is the use of metre.

There is no doubt that line-forms in Hebrew poetry are often of a repetitive nature. Instead of moving from the subordinate clause to the main clause, the poet repeats the subordinate clause twice, and similarly twice repeats the main idea. Psalm 114 is a good example. The formula would be AA BB:

A   When Israel went forth from Egypt,
A   the house of Jacob from a people of strange language,
B   Judah became his sanctuary,
B   Israel his dominion.   (vv. 1–2)

The sense is delayed, and consequently the emphasis is placed on the last of the four cola. Alonso Schökel describes this feature, saying that it is 'as if when walking one were to go two steps forward with the right foot and then two steps forward with the left' (*A Manual of Hebrew Poetics*, 48).

Another way of achieving a similar effect of delay is to interrupt the movement of thought by repeating the subordinate-clause-main-clause formula twice; if one were rewriting Ps. 114: 1–2 accordingly, the formula would be AB AB and would read as follows:

A   When Israel went forth from Egypt,
B   Judah became his sanctuary;
A   the house of Jacob from a people of strange language,
B   Israel became his dominion.

In both cases, we may note the 'binary sense' of two well-balanced ideas creating an overall symmetry by setting up a tension (A) and a resolution (B).

The above verse offers a clear example of parallelism. However, there are many other instances where the cola do not suggest this sort of clear patterning, and where it is not clear that the poet is using parallelism as a particular device.

Psalm 31 offers several good examples of the diversity evident in one poem. For instance, in v. 1 we may note that in the three cries of petition, there is no suggestion of any binary connection between them:

> In thee, O LORD, do I seek refuge;
>   let me never be put to shame;
>   in thy righteousness deliver me!

By contrast, v. 10 follows very clearly the form AA BB, as in Ps. 114:

> For my life is spent with sorrow,
>   and my years with sighing;
> my strength fails because of my misery,
>   and my bones waste away.

Verse 11 is again different; the first three clauses each echo the same idea. The last clause, albeit creating the emphasis, stands in a less close parallel relation to the other three, and might be seen to be outside the sequence (AAA B):

> I am the scorn of all my adversaries
> a horror to all my neighbours
> an object of dread to all my acquaintances
> those who see me in the street flee from me.

Verse 13 (which has affinities with Jer. 20: 3, 10) has another pattern. The first two clauses run together (the technical term would be 'enjambment') so that the first idea is completed in the second, whilst the final two clauses repeat each other in characteristic parallelism (A + B CC):

> Yea, I hear the whispering of many—
> terror on every side!—
> as they scheme together against me,
> as they plot to take my life.

Finally, v. 24 offers another pattern: this is more like AA B, with the clauses so short that AA appears as one colon within the whole couplet. The emphasis is on the final clause B—which, being in the vocative, would normally come first:

> Be strong, / and let your heart take courage
> all you who wait for the LORD!

One poet (or the compiler of a poem, if it is a composite work) is capable of using a variety of poetic designs, one example of which may be a specific use of parallelism. These variations are not unique to the psalmists: they are evident throughout the wisdom and prophetic literature as well. Of the prophets, second Isaiah (chapters 40–55) is the most intriguing in the way poetic forms are appropriated for dramatic effect. For example, the following illustration (from the prologue to the book) is a complex development of parallelism which might be classified as AABC; AAD:

> A   The grass withers
> A   the flower fades
> B   when the breath of the LORD blows upon it;
> C   surely the people is grass.

```
A    The grass withers
A    the flower fades
D        but the word of our God will stand for ever.
```

(Isa. 40: 7–8)

The parallelism is used in order to create a suspension of meaning, so that the two stresses caused by the emphasis (i.e. C and D) stand in contrast to each other: 'surely the people is grass' . . . 'but the word of our God will stand for ever'.

Another example from second Isaiah shows the same skill of creating tension; here this is by repeating three times the same idea in short, terse clauses (ABBB; CDCC):

```
A    For a long time
B                    I have held my peace
B                    I have kept still
B                    and restrained myself.
C    Now             I will cry out
D    like a woman in travail
C                    I will gasp
C                    I will pant.
```

(Isa. 42: 14)

Even from this limited selection, it is clear that although parallelism is an important poetic device, it is a creative art, with many variations, and hence is as difficult to classify consistently as is metre. Like metre, parallelism alone is not a sufficiently distinctive criterion to determine what is 'poetic style' and what is 'prose style'. Schökel's conclusions on the nature of Hebrew parallelism are most pertinent in this respect:

In all these examples we have had a view of parallelism as a flexible technique, with a variety of formulations and arrangements according to the different situations. This is where we come across the scholar's determination to divide, subdivide, classify and give a name to each variety . . . The important thing is to develop sensitivity to be able to appreciate the variations in their poetic function. (*A Manual of Hebrew Poetics*, 57.)

A. Theories about Parallelism and Hebrew Poetry

The following comparison of the different views of scholars demonstrates that many scholars do in fact claim that parallelism is as consistent a poetic technique as metre.

One of the key figures in promoting this understanding of parallelism in Hebrew poetry is Robert Lowth. We have already observed how Lowth perceived that Hebrew poetry was different from Greek or Latin poetry, with a quality of its own: it had a different economy, a simpler form, a uniformity of expression—a quality Lowth understood as parallelism. This particular and distinctively Semitic way of thinking was a feature which (as we have seen) enabled Hebrew poetry to be translated into other languages, without destroying its essence; it also influenced the use of binary forms in poetry in other languages (as we shall see below). Stephen Prickett summarizes Lowth's position as follows:

Whereas contemporary European verse, which relied heavily on the essentially untranslatable auditory effects of alliteration, assonance, rhyme, and metre, was extremely difficult to render in another language with any real equivalence of tone and feeling, Hebrew poetry was almost all translatable. (*Words and the Word*, 42.)

Lowth proposed that in Hebrew poetry there are three different types of parallelism: *synonymous parallelism*, where the same idea is repeated in a different way; *antithetic parallelism*, where the idea is presented in a contrasting way; and *synthetic parallelism*, where two ideas together comprise one greater idea—without the repetition of 'A' and 'B'. The first two types are fairly obvious; Psalm 114: 1–2 was discussed at the beginning of this chapter as illustrating these two possibilities. The third type (which Lowth broke up into a further five categories) is more difficult to determine. Because Lowth viewed parallelism in such a pervasive way throughout Hebrew thinking, he found it in prose texts as well, although he upheld that its most inspired form was in poetry.

Lowth may well have been right in noting that the use of parallelism in biblical poetry has influenced a good deal of thinking about English poetry as well. For example, Wordsworth and Coleridge wrote about poetic diction in terms of 'dialectical thinking', expressed with an intensity of feeling. Similarly, Gerard Manley Hopkins's essay on poetic diction (which he wrote as an undergraduate at Oxford in 1865) affirms the value of parallelism in all types of poetry, not only in Hebrew. He writes that it is a repetitive pattern which reflects a binary way of expressing thought and feeling, whether (in Hopkins's terms) in 'marked distinctive forms', or in 'transitional and chromatic' forms. (Hopkins's interest in 'sprung rhythm' was in part related to these observations.)

As with the theories concerning metre and poetry, we are brought back to the need for clear definitions, for parallelism can too easily be seen as a catch-all device used by the Hebrew poets. Most of the work on parallelism by scholars this century still belongs within the basic framework laid down by Lowth.

T. H. Robinson's book *The Poetry of the Old Testament* is a clear development of Lowth's views. Robinson also assumed that the sense expressed through the parallelism is of more importance than is the sound expressed through the rhythm, and he gave further attention to Lowth's more vague third category of 'synthetic parallelism':

If we consider a piece of Hebrew narrative prose, we observe that it is normally a continuous stream of co-ordinate sentences linked together by conjunctions—in the Hebrew by 'Waw Consecutives'. It allows the thought of the reader, then, to pursue a straight and unbroken course . . . But when a statement is made in poetry, the expectation that has been roused in our minds must be satisfied as soon as possible; a series of ideas has been put before us, and we require that it shall be repeated . . . We thus discover a fundamental principle of Hebrew verse form: Every verse must consist of at least two 'members', the second of which must, more or less completely, satisfy the expectation raised by the first. (p. 21.)

Stephen Geller (*Parallelism in Early Biblical Poetry*) also accepts Lowth's basic categorization; his only qualification is that rhythm and strophic structures are also critical criteria in determining poetic line-forms.

However, several scholars have questioned parallelism as a

reliable criterion at all. David Freedman, to whom reference was made earlier for his analysis of metre in terms of syllable-counting, is one such example. His book *Pottery, Poetry and Prophecy* (1980) starts with a prolegomenon to Gray's work which, having outlined, he then in part rejects. Affirming with Gray (and Lowth) that the dividing line between prose and poetry is a thin one, Freedman's alternative is his supposedly more rigorous, objective, and statistical method in identifying Hebrew poetry—that of counting syllables to determine patterns between one line-form and another.

The most sustained critique of parallelism as a criterion for determining poetry is that of James Kugel. His observation in *The Idea of Biblical Poetry*, that 'Biblical parallelism is of one sort, "A, and what's more, B", or a hundred sorts; but it is not three' (p. 58) is frequently quoted as a way of showing up the inconsistencies in Lowth's theory. There is little doubt that the creating of poetic images is an art, not a science, and frequently involves a flexibility (for example, the use of just one line, or of three and four, rather than two) which results in as many exceptions as there are conventions. Kugel is probably right to see parallelism less as one particular method used by Hebrew poets than as an adaptable rhetorical device used for 'seconding' or 'closing' poetic units. Consequently, in some instances parallelism may be of 'one' kind—reflecting an almost perfect echo or symmetry; yet in other cases it may be of 'a hundred' kinds—with 'B' following 'A', but otherwise providing little evidence that the poet was constrained by particular binary thought-patterns.

One of the most convincing aspects of Kugel's arguments is his illustration from various texts. The most interesting example, because it is so familiar, is Psalm 23. Although clear parallelism is apparent in verse 2, the other verses have less convincing evidence of the repetition or the contrasting ideas we noted earlier:

1. The LORD is my shepherd, /
   I shall not want;
2. he makes me lie down in green pastures. /
   He leads me beside still waters
3. He restores my soul. /
   He leads me in paths of righteousness for his name's sake.

4. Even though I walk through the valley of the shadow of death /
     I fear no evil;
   For thou art with me; /
     thy rod and thy staff, they comfort me.
5. Thou preparest a table before me in the presence of my enemies; /
     thou anointest my head with oil, my cup overflows.
6. Surely goodness and mercy shall follow me all the days of my life; /
     and I shall dwell in the house of the LORD for ever.

Interestingly, adaptations of this psalm (for example, the version in the Scottish Psalter) have tried to create a sense of parallelism where there is none, as seen in the extract below:

> The Lord's my shepherd, I'll not want;
>   He makes me down to lie
> In pastures green; he leadeth me
>   The quiet waters by.
>
> My soul he doth restore again,
>   And me to walk doth make
> Within the paths of righteousness
>   E'en for his own name's sake.
>
> Yea, though I walk in death's dark vale,
>   Yet will I fear none ill,
> For thou art with me, and thy rod
>   And staff me comfort still.

If one refers back to a literal rendering of the Hebrew, it is, however, apparent how little parallelism there really is. The unequal length of the lines, thus creating an irregularity in the sound as well as the sense, and the difficulty in knowing whether the lines should be divided further to make tricola (e.g. vv. 2, 3, 5) further confuse the issue.

Kugel offers similar illustrations from other psalms. Psalm 122 is a good example, and shows how the versification (itself a classification dating from after the time of the Masoretes, and not therefore an intrinsic part of the poetry) often runs counter to the division on the basis of parallelism:

1. I was glad when they said to me, /
     'Let us go to the house of the LORD!'

2. Our feet have been standing within your gates, O Jerusalem! /
3. Jerusalem, built as a city /
   which is bound firmly together,
4. to which the tribes go up /
   the tribes of the LORD /
   as was decreed for Israel, to give thanks to the name of the LORD.
5. There thrones of judgement were set, /
   the thrones of the house of David.

Only verse 5 offers the clear repetition of ideas identified with parallelism. Like Ps. 23, Ps. 122 reflects irregular lengths of lines, best seen by comparing verse 2 (one colon) with verse 4 (three cola, possibly four). The psalm simply does not conform to the conventional repetition or contrast of ideas which typify parallelism.

As well as refuting parallelism as a clear criterion of poetry, Kugel shows how confused the issue is by offering several examples from prose accounts which suggest it. For example, he renders Genesis 21: 1, 6, and 22: 17 as follows:

> The LORD visited Sarah as he had said, /
>   and the LORD did to Sarah as he had promised;
>
> 'God has made laughter for me; /
>   every one who hears will laugh over me.'
>
> 'I will indeed bless you, /
>   and I will multiply your descendants
> as the stars of heaven /
>   and as the sand which is on the seashore.'

A similar 'poem' written in parallel lines could be adapted from narrative and legal material—Kugel uses examples from the story of Moses in the bulrushes in Exod. 2: 1–7 and the law on adultery in Num. 5: 12–15.

We might add to Kugel's observations our own list from Chapter 3 of the parallelisms in the prose prayers (see Gen. 4: 13–14 (Cain) and Judg. 15: 18 (Samson)). The case is clear: if parallelism is to be used as a device to identify poetry, we have to broaden our understanding of what Hebrew poetry is. The debate about parallelism is not only about symmetry, but about a general pattern. By emphasizing a general pattern rather than a specific technique, the dividing line between what is prose and what is poetry yet again becomes blurred: parallelism is as common a feature in prose as it is an inconsistent feature in poetry. It is no surprise that Kugel concludes that all that can be said about parallelism is that it pertains to a seconding, or an intensifying, of the meaning, which does not create a clear criterion for identifying poetry.

Because we do not have access to the literary conventions, Kugel is correct in his contention that we do not have the literary competence to read the biblical text with rigid presuppositions. And when we add to this the likelihood that the Hebrew poet (as any poet) is most probably seeking to achieve new possibilities within the bounds of formal conventions, we can be less confident still in assuming we know how to define Hebrew verse. It could even be argued that the term 'parallelism', in describing the sense of all Hebrew poetry, is as misleading as is the term 'metre' in describing the sound of it.

B. Applying Theories of Parallelism to the Texts

As with our discussion about metre and poetry, there is a need for a precise (although not rigid) definition of parallelism which goes beyond Kugel but not as far as Lowth. The following assessment attempts to achieve this balance. On the one hand, it will be seen that *the structure of parallelism is of one type only*–a seconding of two lines A and B, used either in terms of straightforward repetition (Lowth's synonymous parallelism) or contrasting opposites (Lowth's antithetical parallelism). In this sense, a general definition of parallelism is established which avoids Lowth's third and more vague category of synthetic (or incomplete) parallelism. On the other hand, there are nuances within this one structure which suggest at least *three variations of thought*. These are developed below, and it will be seen that they establish a particularity within the broader pattern of things.

1. The *first variation* of parallelism is where 'A' is interchangeable with 'B' [A = B]—either positively in terms of an echo, or negatively in terms of a contrast. We noted this feature in Ps. 114.

Within this variation we are thus able to include both synonymous parallelism (A is the same as B) and antithetic parallelism (A is the opposite of B). In some instances the matching is most precise, to the extent that symmetry in the word-pairing affects even the genders of the nouns in each colon. Watson offers several illustrations of this—for example, of two masculine nouns (A) followed by two feminine nouns (B), as in Job 10: 12:

> Thou hast granted me life (m.) and steadfast love (m.)
> and thy care (f.) has preserved my spirit (f.)

Another illustration is of a feminine then masculine noun (A) followed by a feminine then masculine noun (B), as in Isa. 62: 1:

> For Zion's sake I will not keep silent,
> and for Jerusalem's sake I will not rest,
> until her vindication (f.) goes forth as brightness (m.),
> and her salvation (f.) as a burning torch (m.)

There are several permutations of this pairing—for example, a chiasmic symmetry whereby the masculine and feminine/ masculine and feminine, or the masculine and feminine/feminine and masculine are set in pairs.

As well as the gender-pairing, there are other less specific examples of word-pairs, chosen more on account of their balance of sense than on account of gender. As we have seen, word-pairing was a common practice in other ancient Near Eastern poetry, not least that of Ugarit. The word-pairs can occur both in nouns and in verbs:

> Though they dig into Sheol,
>
> from there shall my hand take them;
> Though they climb up to heaven,
>
> from there I will bring them down.
>
> (Amos 9: 2)

Psalm 33 offers several different examples, including the following:

By the word of the LORD the heavens were made,

and all their host by the breath of his mouth.

He gathered the waters of the sea as in a bottle;

he puts the deeps in storehouses.

(Ps. 33: 6–7)

2. The *second variation* is where A is expressed as the most important idea, and B is a qualification of it [A > B], completing more fully the thought expressed in the preceding line. Again, this is achieved either by repetition and echo, or by comparison and contrast, and is a modification of the category of so-called synthetic or incomplete parallelism. It is sometimes a movement from the general (colon A) to the specific (colon B); at other times it may be a movement from the literal (A) to the figurative (B). An intriguing example is the use of numbers:

If Cain is avenged sevenfold,
    truly Lamech seventy-sevenfold.

(Gen. 4: 24)

Three things are too wonderful for me;
    four I do not understand.

(Prov. 30: 18)

Mostly this variation is achieved by a heightening or focusing of phrases, giving the impression of greater precision:

I made the earth,

and created man upon it:

it was my hands that stretched out the heavens,

and I commanded all their host.

(Isa. 45: 12)

They have made his land a waste:

his cities are in ruins, without inhabitant.

(Jer. 2: 15)

3. The *third variation* is where A is expressed as the introductory idea, but is still open to further expansion, and so B is seen not only to complement but also to complete A. B is thus given more importance than A [A < B]. This can again be achieved either by way of repetition or contrast. It is thus the converse of our second variation, and so it too is a modification of synthetic/incomplete parallelism. An interesting example is from Isaiah 40: 3:

In the wilderness prepare the way of the LORD,

make straight in the desert a highway for our God.

Psalm 29, a hymn describing the presence of God in a thunderstorm, uses this device with dramatic effect:

Ascribe to the LORD, O heavenly beings,
    ascribe to the LORD *glory and strength*.
The LORD sits enthroned over the flood;
    the LORD sits enthroned as *king for ever*.

Within this variation there is some evidence of what has been called 'staircase parallelism', whereby the ideas proceed in steps. Jeremiah 31: 21 ('Return, O Virgin Israel, return to these your cities') and Psalm 77: 17 ('When the waters saw you, God, when the waters saw you they trembled') are illustrations of this device. A more developed example is found in Judges 5, the song of war attributed to Deborah, referred to earlier (see pp. 35–6).

LORD, when thou didst go forth from Se'ir,
    when thou didst march from the region of Edom,
the earth trembled,
    and the heavens dropped,
    yea, the clouds dropped water.

> The mountains quaked before the LORD,
>   yon Sinai before the LORD,
>   the God of Israel.
>
> .   .   .   .
>
> She put her hand to the tent peg
>   and her right hand to the workmen's mallet;
> she struck Sisera a blow,
>   she crushed his head,
>   she shattered and pierced his temple.
> He sank, he fell,
>   he lay still at her feet;
> at her feet he sank, he fell;
>   where he sank, there he fell dead.
>
>   (Judg. 5: 4–5; 26–7)

In this way, a threefold categorization of parallelism may be proposed. This is by no means an inflexible system; on the one hand, the convention of 'seconding' is clear, whilst on the other hand, the many variations within this pattern are also given due attention. The constraint has been to limit the categories to the smallest units of two or three cola within the line-forms of Hebrew verse; by limiting the 'seconding' to between two and four cola, or line-forms, rather than trying to find parallelism in complete stanzas or whole strophes (what some scholars term 'external' or 'structural' parallelism) it is possible to maintain a definition which is neither too general nor too specific.

These conclusions regarding parallelism as a poetic technique are similar to those regarding metre. In each case it can be seen that neither metre nor parallelism creates the *essence* of Hebrew verse, which somehow still defies neat categories and tidy definitions.

C. Parallelism in Semitic Poetry Using New Testament Examples

In the previous chapter it was seen that an interpretation of metre had to take into account its musical tradition. But in addition to this, any reading of parallelism must take into account an oral tradition. This observation is important; if the most significant influences on Hebrew poetry comprise both its musicality and its oral nature, this raises significant questions about the limits of an exclusively literary approach to Hebrew verse.

It is self-evident that Hebrew poetry belongs to a rich oral tradition. Several biblical examples reveal that it was probably composed to be heard rather than to be read. This issue will be developed with respect to the Old Testament in the following three chapters; at this point, examples from the New Testament may also be found useful, for they too illustrate the oral dimension of Semitic poetry.

One particular genre of the New Testament is especially appropriate. Not only does it confirm our observations about the oral nature of the poetry, but it also shows how the 'three-in-one' definition of parallelism holds good, and indicates the way in which parallelism can be studied better in short sayings (of between two and four line-forms) rather than in lengthy passages. This genre may be termed *the poetic aphorisms attributed to Jesus*. It is a complex genre, in that it concerns critical questions regarding the relationship, if any, of these traditions to the historical Jesus. (On this account, to avoid complicating the issue further, only the Synoptic Gospels have been used, and not the Gospel of John.) However, the most significant feature of these aphorisms for our purposes concerns not so much their origin (whether in the words of Jesus or in the confession of faith of the early Church) as their significance as examples of poetic parallelism recited and remembered within the Christian community: in this way, they pertain first to an oral tradition and only later to a literary one.

Many of the following poetic sayings, expressed in concise and pithy form, were probably spoken first in Aramaic, not Hebrew. (The two languages are closely related as part of the Semitic family; furthermore, the feature of 'seconding' is translatable into the Greek of the New Testament and so through to our English translation, thus providing a good example of the way that parallelism, in its simplest form, transcends language.) Their purpose is didactic, and the balancing of ideas suggests that parallelism was used as an aid to the memory by easy recitation.

(I) SAYINGS WHICH CAN BE CLASSIFIED AS A = B (straight-forward repetition or contrast)

> Give to him who begs from you,
>   and do not refuse him who would borrow from you.
>
> > (Matt. 5: 42 (Luke 6: 30))

> Are you able to drink the cup that I drink,
>   or to be baptised with the baptism with which I am baptised?
>
> > (Mark 10: 38 (Matt. 20: 22))

> My yoke is easy,
>   and my burden is light.
>
> > (Matt. 11: 30)

> If a kingdom is against itself,
>   that kingdom cannot stand.
> And if a house is divided against itself,
>   that house will not be able to stand.
>
> > (Mark 3: 24–25 (Matt. 12: 25;
> > > Luke 11: 17))

> The sun will be darkened,
>   and the moon will not give its light,
> And the stars will be falling from the heavens,
>   and the powers in the heavens will be shaken.
>
> > (Mark 13: 24–5 (Matt. 24: 29))

> Love your enemies,
>   do good to those who hate you,
> bless those who curse you,
>   pray for those who abuse you.
>
> > (Luke 6: 27)

> Judge not, and you will not be judged;
>   condemn not, and you will not be condemned;
> Forgive, and you will be forgiven;
>   give, and it will be given to you.
>
> > (Luke 6: 37–8 (Matt. 7: 1–2))

For this your brother was dead and is alive,
    he was lost and is found.

                  (Luke 15: 32)

He who is faithful in a very little
    is faithful also in much;
and he who is dishonest in a very little
    is dishonest also in much.

                  (Luke 16: 10)

(II) SAYINGS WHICH CAN BE CLASSIFIED AS A > B (where A is the dominant thought and B fills it out)

And forgive us our debts,
    as we also forgive our debtors.
        (Matt. 6: 12 (Luke 11: 4))

Ask, and it will be given you;
    seek, and you will find;
    knock, and it will be opened to you.
For everyone who asks receives
    and he who seeks finds,
    and to him who knocks it will be opened.
        (Matt. 7: 7–8 (Luke 11: 9–10))

So, every sound tree bears good fruit,
    but the bad tree bears evil fruit.
              (Matt. 7: 17)

The sabbath was made for man,
    not man for the sabbath.
              (Mark 2: 27)

I came to cast fire upon the earth;
    and would that it were already kindled!
I have a baptism to be baptised with;
    and how I am constrained until it is accomplished!
          (Luke 12: 49–50)

> Every one to whom much is given,
>   of him will much be required;
> and of him to whom men commit much,
>   they will demand the more.
>
>   (Luke 12: 48)

> For every one who exalts himself will be humbled,
>   and he who humbles himself will be exalted.
>
>   (Luke 18: 14)

(III) SAYINGS WHICH CAN BE CLASSIFIED AS A < B
(where the second line takes the main emphasis in the saying)

We may note here that this form of expression (*a minori ad maius*, 'from the lesser to the greater') was developed also in the Rabbinical tradition (linked with a rabbi named Hillel) in the first century CE.

> If you then, who are evil,
>   know how to give good gifts to your children,
> how much more will your Father who is in heaven
>   give good things to those who ask him!
>
>   (Matt. 7: 11 (Luke 11: 13))

> Foxes have holes,
>   and the birds of the air have nests;
> but the Son of man has nowhere to lay his head.
>
>   (Matt. 8: 20 (Luke 9: 58))

> Every one who acknowledges me before men,
>   I also will acknowledge before my Father who is in heaven;
> but whoever denies me before men,
>   I will also deny before my Father who is in heaven.
>
>   (Matt. 10: 32–3 (Luke 12: 8–9))

Not that which goes into the mouth defiles a man,
  but what comes out of the mouth, this defiles a man.

(Matt. 15: 11)

For whoever would save his life will lose it;
  and whoever loses his life for my sake, he will save it.

(Luke 9: 24 (Matt. 16: 25; Mark 8: 35))

One interesting observation here is the way that Mark and Luke in particular disrupt the parallelism with additional phrases—a practice which is particularly evident where there are Gospel parallels (e.g. Mark 8: 35; 10: 27; 14: 7; and Luke 12: 33 (cf. Matt. 6: 19–20); Luke 13: 24 (cf. Matt. 7: 13, 14). This practice seems to indicate a theological expansion (i.e. in the present literary form) of the earlier well-known and established poetic saying.

We may conclude that parallelism, as a device to make an aphorism more memorable and repeatable, is a common feature throughout Semitic thinking (whether in Ugaritic, Hebrew, or Aramaic). Furthermore, the 'one-in-three' feature (A = B; A > B; A < B) proposed earlier fits not only the Hebrew poetry of the Old Testament but also the Aramaic poetry of the New; it is thus a useful model, because it takes seriously both the distinctive features and the adaptations of parallelism in various types of Semitic poetry.

We are brought back full circle to the observation at the beginning of this chapter—that parallelism, as a poetic device, is not so much a fixed technique as a creative art. It is not so much used for its own sake, as to evoke a response beyond itself—a response encapsulated as much in the living tradition of the community, whether expressed through music or recitation, as in the written text itself.

An important implication which has arisen from this study is that Semitic poetry was composed as much to be taught (in recitation) or sung (in cantillation) as it was to be read and studied. Thus, although a literary appraisal is vital in attending to the formal issues, such as genre, style, structure, and syntax, there are nevertheless other aspects of poetic appreciation for which literary analysis alone is an inadequate tool. A more intuitive and imaginative approach is required if we are to take seriously the performative quality of biblical poetry in its various social and cultural life-settings. This issue of a living tradition behind the literary form will be the focus of attention in the following three chapters of Part II, which will assess the various influences within all types of biblical poetry other than the psalms.

PART II

Poetry outside the Psalter

5

Law Poetry, Wisdom Poetry, and Popular Poetry

If, as we have seen, Semitic poetry belongs as much to a 'setting-in-life' as it does to a 'setting-in-literature', we need first to be convinced that oral 'performative' poetry does lie behind the present literary form.

One convincing defence of this issue has been offered by Hermann Gunkel, in a seminal article on Israelite literature, written in German in 1906. He argues that, in the very first stages of cultural growth, poetry was a powerful mode of communication within the folk-religion of Israel. Poetry, linked to the music and dance of popular religion and folk-culture, was easier to memorize, and hence easier to impart to later generations, than prose. Much of the prophets' teachings some centuries later was expressed in a poetic form precisely because of this feature. Gunkel's observations in fact fit well with our own considerations concerning the poetic aphorisms found within the Gospels: the brief, binary form of Semitic verse has a distinct performative quality, and in many cases predates the prose literature into which it was later incorporated.

It is clear that only a handful of ancient poetic fragments have actually found their way into the biblical accounts. But it is equally clear that any later adaptation of an ancient poem into a literary framework gives it a very different emphasis from its earlier use in a particular life-setting. This point is important, because it shows that, in reading, we do often have to intuit the difference between oral and literary poetry. 'Poetry-in-life', on the one hand, is repeatable and has a certain typicality, because it is open to being used and reused in a variety of religious and social settings. 'Poetry-in-literature', when integrated into a prose narrative, loses this timeless quality; it becomes particularized, as it is adapted by the specific theological interests of the editor to fit into the overall sense of its literary setting.

Of the three chapters in Part II, assessing biblical poetry outside the Psalter, this chapter and Chapter 7 are mainly concerned with poetry which has been set within a narrative form, some of which suggests a 'performance-in-life' before it has been compiled as literature. The issue throughout will be that of trying to ascertain how this duality affects our understanding and appreciation. Such poetry may be contrasted with the poetry of the Psalter; the psalms stand independent of any such narrative framework and hence may be assessed as much for their setting-in-life as for their setting-in-literature. To state this contrast in a different way, it will be seen that poetry outside the Psalter is effective on account of its literary context, which gives it a more specific orientation; poetry within the Psalter is effective on account of its open-endedness, which gives it a performative quality. The issue of biblical poetry set within a prose framework is our first concern.

A. Fragments of Poetry Found within the Law

In *Wisdom and Law in the Old Testament* (also in the Oxford Bible Series), Joseph Blenkinsopp notes the difficulties in ascertaining any precise origin for Israel's legal traditions. Nevertheless, some of the briefer sayings may be traced back to the teaching of the elders of the clans and tribes in early settlement times, hence illustrating poetry-in-life which has later been adapted to become poetry-in-literature. An interesting example of adaptation is found in Genesis 4: 23–4. The verses concern the ancient law of blood revenge:

1. Adah and Zillah, hear my voice:
2.   you wives of Lamech, hearken to what I say:
3. I have slain a man for wounding me,
4.   a young man for striking me.

> 5. If Cain is avenged sevenfold,
> 6.   truly Lamech seventy-sevenfold.

The Hebrew presents this in the line-forms associated with what we might now term 'poetry'. The parallelism is evident in lines 1, 2 and 3, 4 [A = B] and in lines 5 and 6 [A > B]. The rhythm is also clear: it has a 3:3 stress. This unit takes up a legal saying couched in poetic form: its earliest purpose would have been to assert the importance of vengeance to protect certain family and clan groups. Yet its earlier use has been changed through its literary adaptation. The verse has been appropriated by the writer (following on from the story of Cain's murder of Abel in Genesis 4) to demonstrate the spread of violence throughout humankind. The song now illustrates the extent of human deprivation, and is one explanation for the inevitability of judgement by Noah's flood in Genesis 6. Hence, instead of being an ancient poetic saying used as a positive defence of tribal rights, it now serves a negative purpose as a critique of the abuse of those rights.

Another example is found in Genesis 9: 6:

> Whoever sheds the blood of man,
> by man shall his blood be shed.

This is another poetic legal saying expounding the ancient law of blood revenge (a reference to which is found in Exod. 21: 12–17). However, in its present literary context of Genesis 9: 1–19, it is used to justify God's command to Noah to exercise dominion over the earth but not to become defiled by eating animal flesh with its blood. Like Genesis 4, the literary adaptation effects an entirely different orientation.

Several ancient legal sayings are set out in the (poetic) binary form as a means of being easily memorable (for example, those in the law-code of Exod. 22: 18–23: 19). More often than not, they are found in independent legal collections, rather than being integrated with any narrative, as seen with the above examples from Genesis; and hence their later literary adaptation is of a different kind. For a more general overview of such poetry, the reader should look at Blenkinsopp's study. For the purposes of our own discussion, an assessment of poetry within the wisdom literature offers more significant insights.

B. Poetry Found within the Wisdom Tradition

Brief aphorisms in the wisdom literature have much in common with the popular morality teaching of other Near Eastern cultures, such as Babylon and Egypt. Thus they almost certainly go back to an oral tradition, and many biblical examples must have had an earlier history before their adaptation into the wisdom literature.

The most common form is the proverb. Not every proverbial saying (called *masal*, a term with a wide range of meanings) was poetic in form. Often the proverb was a simple one-line sentence. Biblical (one-line) examples include 'As the man is, so his strength' (Judg. 8: 21); 'Out of the wicked comes forth wickedness' (1 Sam. 24: 13); 'The days grow long, and every vision comes to nought' (Ezek. 12: 22); and 'Like mother, like daughter' (Ezek. 16: 44).

By adding a further line to an aphorism (either emphasizing by repetition, or expanding through explanation), the feature of parallelism occurs (where A = B; A < B; or A > B.) Most of the *mwsalîm* are in fact binary in form, and thus 'poetic', showing not only parallelism in balanced couplets but also a regular balance of rhythm. Most of these have been incorporated into the book of Proverbs.

(I) THE PROVERB AND THE BOOK OF PROVERBS

The themes of many of these proverbial sayings (particularly those found in an early collection in Prov. 10–22) point back to an older (oral) tradition of teaching on everyday morality. The context may be domestic, or may reflect a work situation, and not surprisingly the subject-matter usually concerns attitudes to issues such as wealth, temperance, honest speech, and hospitality. In many cases, the relationship between oral and literary poetry is difficult to ascertain; many of the proverbial sayings could be scribal compositions, imitating and refining more ancient oral forms. These two-line poems, set within the scribal 'instructional' tradition in Israel, fit well the term 'poetry of wit' (to borrow a phrase from Robert Alter), whereby skill is required in determining how to cap the first line with a sufficiently memorable and fitting second line.

Many of these proverbs are clearly of the A = B parallelism, although the frequent use of the word 'but' (the Hebrew *wāw*) in the second line makes the parallelism one of contrast rather than echo:

> A wise son hears his father's instruction
> but (*wāw*) a scoffer does not listen to rebuke.

(Prov. 13: 1)

> He who guards his mouth preserves his life;
> (*wāw*) he who opens wide his lips comes to ruin.

(Prov. 13: 3)

Occasionally the form is straightforward repetition:

> Even in laughter the heart is sad,
> and the end of joy is grief.

(Prov. 14: 3)

Several proverbs start with the comparative form 'like . . .' or 'better . . .'. These fall into the category of A > B parallelism:

> Like a gold ring in a swine's snout
> is a beautiful woman without discretion.

(Prov. 11: 22)

> Better is a dry morsel with quiet
> than a house full of feasting with strife.

(Prov. 17: 1)

Occasionally the saying is cast as a poetic comment on a legal saying, for example:

> Do not rob the poor because he is poor,
> or crush the afflicted at the gate.

(Prov. 22: 22: see Exod. 23: 6)

It is impossible to be sure which, if any, of the above examples actually were composed and used for a life-setting rather than a literary one. This is because it is often the theological concerns of a narrative which suggest the earlier oral nature of a proverbial saying (as seen in our two examples of legal poetry in Gen. 4 and 9), and in the book of Proverbs this is of course absent. However, a good example of such an adaptation of a proverb may be found in the book of Ezekiel:

What do you mean by repeating this proverb concerning the land of Israel,

> 'The fathers have eaten sour grapes,
>   and the children's teeth are set on edge'?

(Ezek. 18: 2)

Here the prophet is emphasizing that every individual is account-able before God; no one can blame the previous generation for their own predicament. Interestingly, the same proverb is taken up in Jeremiah, where it has again been adapted theologically, but in a different way. In Jeremiah, it serves a more positive purpose— declaring that any who open themselves to God's goodness will eventually be restored by him:

> In those days they shall no longer say:
> 'The fathers have eaten sour grapes,
>   and the children's teeth are set on edge.'

(Jer. 31: 29)

By contrast, most of the sayings which have been collected within the book of Proverbs are probably scribal reproductions of an earlier form (see Blenkinsopp, *Wisdom and Law*, ch. 2, 'Education for Life'). This is not to deny a primitive tradition: as with the legal sayings, proverbial sayings would have been used by clan and tribal elders from as early as settlement times (*c.* 1250–1000 BCE). But the period during which these would have been copied, ampli-fied, rewritten, and edited into small collections could not have been earlier than that of the royal court, possibly that of King Solomon (950 BCE), whose association with such sayings was legendary (cf. 1 Kgs. 5: 31–4). It is just possible that the earliest literary collections in Proverbs could date from shortly after Solomon's time.

A clear editorial process is evident in the book of Proverbs as a whole. There are at least seven collections of varying lengths, divided by the various superscriptions (1: 1; 10: 1; 22: 17; 24: 23; 25: 1; 30: 1; 31: 1). If some of these are as early as the time of Solomon (i.e. mid-tenth century BCE), the time of their compilation would be the latter part of the Persian period (mid-fourth century BCE). Evidence of one early collection is found in the 'Thirty Sayings' in Prov. 22: 17–24: 22. This has at least ten convincing correspondences with the thirty sayings in the Egyptian 'Instruction of Amen-em-ope' (from about 1000 BCE). It is probable that this compilation, and the other smaller collections in Prov. 10–22, were originally due to the intellectual activity of scribes in the court of the king.

The Hebrew text presents the whole of Proverbs in poetic line-forms, using the peculiar system of pointing found elsewhere only in Job and the book of Psalms. Not all the book, however, comprises brief proverbial sayings. Proverbs 1–9 is more disparate, and includes several poems extolling the virtues of wisdom. In these, wisdom is personified either as a prophetess, calling her audience to learn from her (1: 20–33; 8: 1–21, 32–6); or as a gracious hostess inviting her guests to come to her feast (9: 1–6); or as God's co-regent in creation (3: 19–20; 8: 22–31). All of these poems are probably independent compositions which have been brought together by the scribes at a later period. This is also the case with the poems at the end of the book; one is a wisdom poem in the additional collection in 30: 2–4, and another is the famous acrostic poem on the ideal (wise) wife (31: 10–31). These poems have a more sustained power of communication, in contrast to the pithy sayings of the proverbs:

> Does not wisdom call,
>   does not understanding raise her voice?
> On the heights beside the way,
>   in the paths she takes her stand;
> beside the gates in front of the town,
>   at the entrance of the portals she cries aloud:
>
> Take my instruction instead of silver,
>   and knowledge rather than choice gold;
> for wisdom is better than jewels,
>   and all that you may desire cannot compare with her.
>
> Wisdom has built her house,
>   she has set up her seven pillars.

> 'Come, eat of my bread
>   and drink of the wine I have mixed.
> Leave simpleness, and live,
>   and walk in the way of insight.'

(Prov. 8: 1–3, 10–11; 9: 1, 5–6)

(II) THE RIDDLE

As well as the straightforward *mašal*, and the developed wisdom poem, the riddle was another wisdom device set in poetic form. Judges 14: 12–18 is a good illustration of the interest in the recitation of riddles in early Israel, and the context implies that riddles were used in an early clan setting:

> And they said to him, 'Put your riddle, that we may hear it.'
> And he said to them,
>   'Out of the eater came something to eat.
>   Out of the strong came something sweet.'

(Judg. 14: 13–14)

Yet again, coming as it does within the story of the demise of Samson, the riddle in its literary context serves a different purpose from that which it would have done if it had had an earlier life-setting.

(III) RHETORICAL QUESTIONS

Poetic fragments from the wisdom tradition were not confined to clan/tribal settings, or to those at the royal court, or to scribal activity in the Persian period. The prophets also used such poems to bring impact into their message. They often used the form of rhetorical questions, and we may note the A = B type of parallelism in the following examples:

> Do horses run upon rocks?
>   Does one plow the sea with oxen?
> But you have turned justice into poison
>   and the fruit of righteousness into wormwood.

(Amos 6: 12)

Shall the axe vaunt itself over him who hews with it,
or the saw magnify itself against him who wields it?

(Isa. 10: 5)

Thus far we have emphasized the oral aspect of wisdom poetry, and observed how it has been absorbed into a literary context. But we need also to look at examples of wisdom poetry which were exclusively a literary activity. Here we may refer to the books of Job and Ecclesiastes in particular, as well as the apocryphal books of Ecclesiasticus (Sirach) and the Wisdom of Solomon.

(IV) THE BOOK OF JOB

We have already noted that the book of Job (apart from its prose prologue and epilogue) is one of three books presented throughout in poetic line-forms in the Hebrew, with its distinctive accentual system.

The poetry of Job is evident not only in its presentation, but also in rhythmic stress, which is often clear and consistent. This is mainly 3:3, although sometimes 4:4, and on occasions, for dramatic effect, the lament pattern 3:2 and the staccato rhythm 2:2 are also used. Furthermore, parallelism is everywhere apparent. This often occurs with complex adaptations, spread over a number of line-forms to create effects such as A/C; B/D, or A/D; B/C within a four-line stanza (the longer the stanza, the more complex the parallelism). Job may be dated close to the latest stages of the editing of the book of Proverbs; it is not surprising that it too contains many lengthier wisdom poems. The best example is Job 28, which is more like a hymn with two refrains (vv. 12 and 20) upholding wisdom as the exclusive possession of God. This poetry is similar to the wisdom poems in Prov. 1–10 and 30–1.

Although much of Job 3: 1–42: 6 consists of lengthy poems serving as an ongoing dialogue between Job and his friends, on many occasions within these poems we find the use of the *mᵉšālîm* common to the earlier wisdom tradition. It is as if, by reverting to older well-known poetic traditions, the point of view as expressed by the speaker is authenticated. One interesting example is in Bildad's speech in 8: 8ff., where his source of authority is stated explicitly as the proverbial sayings of old:

> For inquire, I pray you, of bygone ages,
>   and consider what the fathers have found;
>
> Can papyrus grow where there is no marsh?
>   Can reeds flourish where there is no water?
>
> Behold, God will not reject a blameless man,
>   nor take the hand of evildoers.
>
> Those who hate you will be clothed with shame,
>   and the tent of the wicked will be no more.
>
>   (Job 8: 8, 11, 20, 22)

Other proverbs used to authenticate the points of view of the speakers are found in 5: 2, 6, 7; 11: 12, 14; and 12: 12, 13.

As well as using the more established wisdom poetic form of proverbial sayings, the writer of Job is also skilled in using equally well-known liturgical poetry, often imitating the psalms: this is another means of giving the poetic speeches a familiar and conventional form. A more detailed discussion of liturgical poetry will be offered in Chapter 7, but two examples in Job are pertinent at this stage. These are the use of the *lament* and the *hymn*. The laments are placed in the mouth of Job, whereas the hymns (often used as parody) are usually attributed to Job's friends.

Job's laments are well crafted. In psalmody, laments would be offered within a more positive context, with some motif of confidence, or the hint of an oracle of assurance, suggesting a positive belief in the promise of restoration. In the case of Job, however, the laments (e.g. Job 3: 2–26; 6: 1–12; 7: 1–10; 9: 4–12; 10: 8–12; 12: 14–25; 14: 1–15 and 16: 1–17: 16) are used without any such assurance of hope. They are dark and full of despair, and the friends' false assurances following them serve only to increase the lack of resolution in Job's plight. They are part of the dramatic unity of the book, for they prepare the way for the inevitability of assurance which only God can give.

In contrast to the pessimism of Job's despair, created not only by what he says but by the literary form in which he says it, the hymns in praise of God as Creator achieve a double meaning. In the mouth of Job's friends (e.g. Eliphaz: 5: 9–16; Zophar: 11: 7–11; Bildad: 26: 6–14; Elihu: 36: 24–33; 37: 1–24) they illustrate the glib traditionalism of much of the friends' thinking, for they are seen to utter praise with a wisdom which they do not understand. When Job uses the hymnic forms (e.g. 9: 5–13; 10: 8–12; 12: 14–25), these serve to give further emphasis to his insistent belief that his suffering is black and undeserved. In contrast to the hymns of the friends, who affirm (blandly) the creative power of the God who upholds the earth and the heavens (e.g. 5: 9ff.; 26: 6ff.), the hymns used by Job speak of the negative, destructive power of God, who seals up the stars, darkens the sun, and overturns the mountains (9: 5ff.), and who creates life in order to destroy it (Job 10: 8–10). Thus, through a clever use of contrast and paradox, the integrity of Job at prayer is highlighted and the superficial hypocrisy of the friends is exposed.

In this way we may note that the writer of Job has woven into the book several established poetic forms—the proverbial saying, the lament, the hymn—in order to allow the poetry a particular power of communication. This is literary poetry at its best, evoking a response, not only through its ideas, but also through its form of expression.

Robert Alter observes that in Job the poetry 'works' by echoing at a later stage nuances found earlier in the book, giving it a dramatic unity. One good example of this, cited by Alter, is the first lament of Job (Job 3) and the first speech of Yahweh (Job 38–9).

The essence of the lament in chapter 3 is that Job is hedged in: he is confined to a dark chaotic world from which the only way out is death:

> Let the day perish wherein I was born,
>   and the night which said, 'A man-child is conceived.'
>
> Let the stars of its dawn be dark;
>   let it hope for light, but have none,
>   nor see the eyelids of the morning;
> because it did not shut the doors of my mother's womb,
>   nor hide trouble from my eyes.
>
> Why is light given to a man whose way is hid,
>   whom God has hedged in?
> For my sighing comes as my bread,
>   and my groanings are poured out like water.
>
>   (Job 3: 3, 9–10, 23–4)

The divine speech in Job 38–9 could not be more of a contrast. Here the reader is taken to a vast cosmos, teeming with life and full of light, bounded by God's ordering power. The imagery resembles other hymns of creation such as Gen. 1; Pss. 24: 1–2; 104; 136: 5–9; Prov. 8: 27–9 and Isa. 40: 12, 21–2. The birth of the cosmos plays (seemingly intentionally) on Job's curse on his own birth; instead of the stars being extinguished, instead of the womb as a symbol of death, and instead of the tears of death, there is light, life, and life-giving rains. The poetic imagery has a feminine quality, with God depicted as a midwife, supporting the earth, and wrapping up its seas as if in a blanket:

> Where were you when I laid the foundation of the earth?
> Tell me, if you have understanding
>
> .   .   .   .
>
> On what were its bases sunk,
>   or who laid its cornerstone,
> when the morning stars sang together,
>   and all the sons of God shouted for joy?
> Or who shut in the sea with doors,
>   when it burst forth from the womb,
> when I made clouds its garment,
>   and thick darkness its swaddling band
> and prescribed bounds for it,
>   and set bars and doors,
> and said, 'Thus far shall you come, and no farther,
>   and here shall your proud waves be stayed'?
>
> (Job 38: 4, 6–11)

We may conclude that within the diversity of the poetry of the book of Job we may perceive a unity of purpose. It comes as close as possible to poetry-as-story, or the epic poetry of other ancient Near Eastern cultures. Because Job's poetry has a strong narrative content, it does not display the typical and repeatable qualities of the poetry of the psalms; nevertheless, it possesses an intrinsic performative quality of its own. The analogy of the performance of music, where earlier themes are developed in new and creative ways, achieving a sense of unity within diversity, is particularly apposite in the book of Job.

(V) THE BOOK OF ECCLESIASTES

The poetry of Ecclesiastes is closer to the composite collection of Proverbs than to the dramatic unity of Job. But it is different in so far as it appears to come from the Greek period (from about the third century BCE), and its earlier poetic forms probably do not reach as far back into the early wisdom traditions as do the collections found in Proverbs.

The writer of Ecclesiastes utilizes the popular wisdom device of proverbial sayings; these are found in the longer sections, such as 2: 12–17; 5: 8–6: 9; 7: 1–22; 9: 17–10: 20. There are occasional quotations of one-line traditional aphorisms, unknown elsewhere in Scripture, to which a second line is added, creating a poetic form:

> But he who is joined with all the living has hope,
>   for a living dog is better than a dead lion.

(Eccles. 9: 4)

Most significant are those poems which deal at length with the hiddenness of God and the inaccessibility of divine wisdom—a theological contrast to the wisdom hymns of Job 28 and 38–9. A well-known poem is in Eccles. 3: 2–8, concerning the fatalism which predetermines the pattern of life:

> For everything there is a season,
>   and a time for every matter under heaven;
> a time to be born, and a time to die;
> a time to plant, and a time to pluck up what is planted;
> a time to kill, and a time to heal;
> a time to break down, and a time to build up,
> a time to weep, and a time to laugh;
> a time to mourn, and a time to dance;

(Eccles. 3: 1–4)

A similar poem is found in 1: 2–11, on the emptiness of all human effort to change the course of things, or to achieve wisdom, or to possess happiness. The book is a composite work: its poetry consists of collections of poetic proverbs (of between two and twenty lines) and two longer poems, with the rest being straightforward narrative sections (e.g. 4: 13–16; 5: 13–17; 9: 13–16) and prose (e.g. 1: 12–14; 2: 7–9, 18–23; 3: 18–21; 5: 17–19; 6: 1–3). In addition, soliloquies, parables, and dialogues are used in order to gain the attention of the supposed audience. (The audience is called a *qahal*, or assembly; hence the Hebrew name for the book is *Qoheleth*, for one who addresses an assembly; the Greek word 'Ecclesiastes' is a translation of it.) The Greek influence both in theology and in form is everywhere apparent: but, unlike Job, the worth of the book is more in the radical ideas about wisdom and knowledge of God than in its poetic expression of them.

(VI) THE BOOKS OF ECCLESIASTICUS AND WISDOM OF SOLOMON

The case is somewhat different as regards two other apocryphal wisdom books, also from the Greek period, dating from between the second and first centuries BCE. Ecclesiasticus (Sirach) comprises fifty-one chapters of reflections on wisdom in various poetic forms. The interesting feature here is that although the work has survived in a Greek translation of the Hebrew (soon after 132 BCE, by the grandson of Ben Sira, who identified himself in the Prologue), the original Hebrew has been lost and copies survive only in fragments—some of which, quite different from the Greek, have been found near Qumran. On account of this, Sirach is relevant for our purposes only in so far as it gives us an important comparison with earlier Hebrew poetry. It takes up a good deal of traditional wisdom, and develops it in an extensive, more abstract, and reflective way. The most significant chapters are 1, 14–15, 39, and 51: 13–30. We note the familiar themes in wisdom poetry. The following extracts from Ecclesiasticus 1 reveal the author's use of wisdom poems such as Proverbs 3 and Job 28, although there is a greater stress on the value of pious devotion. We may note too that there is less sense of rhythmic stress or of clear parallelism, a lack evident even in the English translation of the Greek:

> All wisdom is from the Lord
> and is with him for ever.

> .   .   .   .

To fear the Lord is the beginning of wisdom;
    she is created with the faithful in the womb.
She made among men an eternal foundation,
    and among their descendants she will be trusted.
To fear the Lord is wisdom's full measure;
    she satisfies men with her fruits.

(Ecclus. 1: 1, 14–16)

The Wisdom of Solomon marks one stage further in the development of wisdom poetry, in that it was actually composed in Greek, although there is evidence that the first few chapters may have had a Hebrew original. The book seems to have been written in Alexandria, probably by a Hellenistic Jew, in the latter part of the first century BCE. Again, its value in a discussion about Hebrew poetry is that it enables us to compare these more extended, often pedestrian reflections on wisdom with the earlier, more vibrant examples of Hebrew poetry which have influenced it. Of the nineteen chapters in praise of wisdom, set in poetic line-forms throughout, many are an imitation of the older wisdom forms, such as the personification of wisdom (6: 12–16) and instructions to live in the way of wisdom (6: 21–5).

In this way we see a vast development in wisdom poetry—from the brief binary proverbial saying, to the expanded wisdom poem, to various composite collections (Prov. and Eccles.) to long poetic wisdom tractates (Job, Ecclus., Wisdom).

Within these last few sections, the issue of the literary adaptation of previously oral poetry has not been as relevant, simply because much wisdom poetry pertains to a more pervasive literary tradition. This is not the case with the following section, where the dissonance between the earlier oral poetry and the later literary adaptation is far more apparent.

C. Popular Poetry

As with the earliest legal and wisdom poems, popular sayings would most probably have originated among various tribal groups before the monarchy, and suggest ancient origins. Not surprisingly, popular poetry is found in several different forms. The first we might term *aetiological sayings*, concerning the meaning of place-names, often serving to defend disputed territorial claims, sometimes set in poetic line-forms. The second is the *song*—typical songs which one would expect from any ancient Near Eastern culture: working songs, harvest songs, love songs, and funeral dirges lamenting the death of relatives and friends, often accompanied by music. A third category is that of *tribal blessings and curses*; and a fourth is that of *war poetry*—victory songs celebrating some military success undertaken in the name of Yahweh. Many of these examples of popular poetry are in brief, fragmentary form. Their main significance is that they offer good examples of the dissonance between the use of 'poetry-in-life' and its adaptation as 'poetry-in-literature'.

(I) FRAGMENTS OF POETRY IN AETIOLOGICAL SAYINGS

Many of these pertain to disputes over wells and watering rights, and in content suggest an early origin amongst clans and tribes as they defended their possession of new terrain. Several are found in the early stories of Genesis. Four such sayings are found in Genesis 26: 20, 21, 22, and 32. The best example is in v. 22:

> So he called its name Reho'both [= ? wide places] saying,
> For now the LORD has made room for us,
> and we shall be fruitful in the land.

The earlier life-setting of the poetic saying is concerned with the quarrels of herdsmen over the right of access to water. This has been readapted by the editor of Gen. 26 to make a different point concerning the superiority of the people of Israel (represented by Isaac) over the Philistines (represented by Abimelech). This is a clear illustration of the dissonance between an ancient 'well-saying', set in a binary poetic form, and its later theological use in literature.

Similar accounts of territorial disputes, ratified by the appeal to a place-name indicating the presence and protection of God in the land, are found, for example, in Genesis 16: 13–14; 21: 31; 31: 46–9;

32: 2–3; Exodus 17: 7; and Numbers 11: 3, 34. In each case the aetio-logical saying, explaining the significance of the place-name, is adapted for a different purpose in its later literary setting. Another good example is Exodus 17: 15–16, which in its earliest form could relate to the period of enmity with the Amalekites (see Num. 24: 20 and Deut. 25: 17–19):

15 And Moses built an altar and called the name of it,
     The LORD is my banner, saying,
16 'A hand upon the banner of the LORD!
     The LORD will have war with Amalek from generation to genera-
     tion.'

The earliest poetic fragment is probably the 'Banner Song' in v. 16 ('A hand upon the banner of the Lord'). The editor has taken this fragment of early war poetry and combined it with an aetiological saying about the antiquity of a cultic site from the time of Moses (v. 15). The composite poetic unit has been further developed to fit into the larger narrative about the murmurings in the wilderness (Exod. 17: 1–16), to illustrate God's faithfulness in contrast to the people's complaints. This narrative framework has again changed and developed the more crude and war-like character of the earlier poetic unit.

(II) POEMS OF WORK AND LEISURE, BIRTH AND DEATH, LOVE AND MARRIAGE

Alongside the poetic saying, another category of popular poetry is that of the song.

1. One example of a *working song* is found in Num. 21: 17–18:

     Then Israel sang this song:
A   'Spring up, O well!—Sing to it!
B   the well which the princes dug,
C   which the nobles of the people delved,
D   with the sceptre and their staves.'

This song begins with an acclamation at the 'springing-up' of the water in a freshly dug well. There is good reason to suggest this is ancient poetry, and the occurrence of other poetic fragments in this chapter in Numbers (see vv. 14–15, 27) would further confirm this observation. The parallelism (A = B) is evident in lines two and three, whilst the final lines (C + D) fit with the images of 'princes/nobles' and 'dug/delved' in the preceding lines. Again, the literary context has changed the impact of this poem; a general working song has been given a specific orientation by the editor, to ratify the divine provision of water as the people journeyed through the wilderness.

2. *Songs of leisure*, such as drinking songs, are referred to only obliquely. Isaiah 22: 13 quotes from one ('let us eat and drink, for tomorrow we die'), and uses it in parody against the people. Wisdom 2: 6–9, written (in Greek) probably as late as the first century BCE, takes up a much later song, although the sentiments of enjoying life before death ends are akin to Isa. 22: 13.

3. *Songs and sayings on the birth of a child* are more in evidence. Just as places were named with a deliberate play on their meaning, so too children's names had certain symbolic significance, often of a theophoric kind. The following examples have again been taken from Genesis:

> Behold, you are with child,
>   and you shall bear a son;
> you shall call his name Ishmael [God hears],
>   because the LORD has given heed to your affliction.
>
>   (Gen. 16: 11)

> And Sarah said,
>   'God has made laughter [Isaac] for me;
>   every one who hears will laugh over me.'
>
>   (Gen. 21: 6)

Another aetiology concerned with the meaning of names, given a new framework of reference by its narrative context, is found in Gen. 2: 23. This is clearly poetic in form; as such it is also ambiguous, being linked in some way with the poetry in 3: 14–19:

> This at last is bone of my bones
>   and flesh of my flesh;

> she shall be called Woman [Hebrew: *iššâ*.],
>   because she was taken out of Man [Hebrew: *îš*].

The prophets also appear to have used the same poetic form for explaining the naming of their children, where again it has been adapted to fit a particular theological message. Although the poetic form is not as clearly evident, Hosea 1: 4–5, 6–7, 8–9 and 2: 1 and Isaiah 7: 3–5 and 8: 1–4 are examples of this.

4. *Songs offered on the death of a loved one* are evident in two longer poems. Both of these are funeral dirges for great heroes fallen in battle. These are found in 2 Sam. 1: 19–27 (David's lament over Jonathan) and 2 Sam. 3: 33–4 (David's lament over Abner). The reference to 'The Book of Jashar [the upright]' as a source-book for such laments in 1 Sam. 1: 18 (also in Josh. 10: 13) indicates that these songs, sung over the fallen, were preserved in particular collections of war poetry. The interesting feature about both of these poems concerns their lack of any religious reference. In 2 Sam. 1, we may note the typical features of parallelism and (despite a corrupted text) a discernible 4:4 rhythmic stress. The following verses offer an illustration of the parallelism:

> From the blood of the slain,
>   from the fat of the mighty,
> the bow of Jonathan turned not back,
>   and the sword of Saul returned not empty.
> Saul and Jonathan, beloved and lovely!
>   In life and death they were not divided;
> they were swifter than eagles,
>   they were stronger than lions.
>
> How are the mighty fallen,
>   and the weapons of war perished!

> (vv. 22, 23, 27)

An interesting development of this poetic form is again found in the message of the prophets, who used the same funeral-dirge form, but instead applied it to the enemy nations and so sang proleptically of their downfall and death. A detailed discussion of this feature will be reserved until Chapter 7, but an interesting example is found in the so-called prophetic oracles of Balaam in Num. 21:

27–30, which uses in parody a dirge concerning the Moabites and Chemosh their god:

> Therefore the ballad singers say
>
> . . . .
> 'Woe to you, O Moab!
> You are undone, O people of Chemosh!'
>
> (Num. 21: 27, 29)

Other examples found in the prophets include Isa. 14: 4–21 (over Babylon), 23: 15–16 (over Tyre), Ezek. 27: 2–10, 25–36; 28: 12–19 (over Tyre) and 32: 2–16 (over Egypt). One striking illustration of this is found in Amos 5: 2 (already quoted on account of its 3:2 *qinâ* rhythm) where Israel's downfall and death are lamented as if they had already occurred:

> Fallen, no more to rise,
> is the virgin Israel;
> forsaken on her land,
> with none to raise her up.

Not only the parallelism, but also the 3:2 beat characterize this poetry as a typical form of lament, used over individual war-heroes (2 Sam.) and over enemy nations (as in Num. 21 and in the prophets) and even over Israel herself (as in Amos).

5. *Songs of love and marriage* are found in several different traditions of the biblical literature. Although there are no explicit examples in the early narratives, Ps. 45 is an example in the Psalter of a secular wedding song composed for a royal marriage. The prophets use the form and imagery of such secular songs to create a dramatic effect in their message, depicting God as the lover of his people. One example is Hos. 2: 14–15:

> Therefore, behold, I will allure her,
> and bring her into the wilderness,
> and speak tenderly to her.
> And there I will give her her vineyards.

Other examples include Hos. 6: 1–3; 11: 3–4, 8; Isa. 5: 1–7; Jer. 3: 1–5, and Isa. 49: 14–18; 51: 3; 54: 4–8. Of all the prophets, second Isaiah adapts the secular love song in a poignant and creative way:

For a brief moment I forsook you,
 but with great compassion I will gather you.
In overflowing wrath for a moment I hid my face from you,
 but with everlasting compassion I will have compassion on you,
 says the LORD, your Redeemer.

(Isa. 54: 7–8)

Without a doubt, the songs which are most renowned as love songs are found in the Song of Solomon. This book comprises about twenty-five lyric poems, collected together around the third century BCE. Some are clearly literary creations, and these have been interwoven to create poems serving as a dialogue between two lovers, which in turn are interspersed with a commentary by a chorus. Some smaller fragments could well have had an earlier setting-in-life: the descriptive wedding procession song in 3: 6–11 has some correspondences with the marriage song of Ps. 45, for example, and the antiphonal sections in some of the poetry (e.g. in 1: 12–17 and 2: 1–4) may suggest a wedding liturgy between bride and groom. Just as we have noted the passion for vengeance expressed in the early poetry of Israel, so we cannot exclude the possibility that in Song there are poetic fragments expressing a similar passion for love.

Song is a composite work. However, like the book of Job, its final form is a dramatic unity, being performative poetry of a literary nature. The erotic imagery offers sensuous and suggestive allusions to a couple enacting ancient myths of the love between a god and goddess, whose consummated passion creates the fertility throughout all nature.

The interchange of voices between the female and male lover also allows the whole poetic unit to be stylized like a drama. In a way which is impossible to depict in the English translation, the Hebrew often indicates when the man or woman is being addressed; the voice of the woman both opens and closes the dialogues at the beginning and end of the book. The Hebrew depicts three parts, or three voices. First, the female lover, as found in 1: 2–4*ab*, 5–6, 7; 2: 1, 3–4, 5–7, 8–10*a*, 16–17; 3: 1–5; 4: 16; 5: 2–8, 10–16; 6: 2–3, 11–12; 7: 10–13; 8: 1–4, 5*bcd*, 6–7, 8–12, 14; then the male lover, as in 1: 9–11, 2: 2, 10*b*–15, 4: 1–7, 8–15, 5: 1, 6: 4–10, 7:

1–9*c*; and also the chorus, whose role is to incite the couple in the consummation of their love, as found in 1: 4*cde*, 8; 2: 7, 15; 3: 5; 4: 1*ef*; 5: 9; 6: 1, 10, 13; 8: 5*a*, 13.

The following extracts illustrate the unashamed eroticism of these songs. Whatever their origin, their desire and longing are both suggestive and evocative. The interplay of imagery, whether of landscape or of bodyscape, offers an immediacy which is both literal and figurative: the human body evokes pictures of the fertility of the land, and the land speaks of the sensuality of the human body. Although the usual characteristics of metre and parallelism are everywhere in evidence, the substance of the poetry is as much in its imagery as in the sound and form.

He: Behold, you are beautiful, my love;
            behold, you are beautiful;
            your eyes are doves.
         Behold, you are beautiful, my beloved,
            truly lovely.
         Our couch is green;
            the beams of our house are cedar,
            our rafters are pine.

She: I am a rose of Sharon,
            a lily of the valleys.

He: As a lily among brambles,
            so is my love among maidens.

She: He brought me to the banqueting house,
            and his banner over me was love.
         Sustain me with raisins,
            refresh me with apples,
            for I am sick with love.

                     (S. of S. 1: 15–2: 2; 2: 4, 5)

Chorus: Awake, O north wind,
            and come, O south wind!

She: Blow upon my garden,
            let its fragrance be wafted abroad.
         Let my beloved come to his garden,
            and eat its choicest fruits.

HE: I come to my garden, my sister, my bride,
                  I gather myrrh with my spice,
                I eat my honeycomb with my honey,
                  I drink my wine with my milk.

CHORUS: Eat, O friends, and drink:
                  drink deeply, O lovers!

                                (S. of S. 4: 16–5: 1)

It is in Song, more than anywhere else in the Hebrew Scriptures, that we hear the distinctive voice of female love—a theme often scorned elsewhere, not least in other wisdom writings—and its capacity for endurance:

SHE: I am my beloved's, and his desire is for me.
                Come, my beloved,
                  let us go forth into the fields,
                  and lodge in the villages;
                let us go out early to the vineyards,
                  and see whether the vines have budded,
                whether the grape blossoms have opened
                  and the pomegranates are in bloom.
                There I will give you my love.

                                (S. of S. 7: 10–12)

SHE: Set me as a seal upon your heart,
                  as a seal upon your arm;
                for love is strong as death,
                  jealousy is cruel as the grave.
                Its flashes are flashes of fire,
                  a most vehement flame.
                Many waters cannot quench love,
                  neither can floods drown it.
                If a man offered for love
                  all the wealth of his house,
                  it would utterly be scorned.

                                (S. of S. 8: 6–7)

It is not surprising that the rabbis were uncertain about the value of Song. Their assent to its worth was to interpret it as a theological analogy of the love between God and Israel. Interestingly, their very affirmation of this typological approach informs us that this is far from how Song was used and understood by the people, as seen in the following quotation from Rabbi Akiba: 'He who trills his voice in the chanting of the Song and treats it as a secular song, has no share in the world to come' (Tosefta).

By the Middle Ages, Song was part of the literature used in the Jewish mystical tradition (called the *kaballâ*) which contemplated the divine glory (called the *šekinâ*). The *šekinâ* represented the female elements of the Deity; a procreative fusion with the male elements of the godhead released divine power and life. Song was seen as ideal in rehearsing this drama within the godhead, whereby the male/female voices were no longer those of human lovers, but those of God. In this way, Song was received not so much as love poetry about God and Israel, as about the inner nature of God Himself.

The earlier Rabbinic attitude to Song is also mirrored in the commentaries of the early Christian Fathers. Like their Jewish contemporaries (from whom they may indeed have discussed interpretations) they searched for the hidden meaning of a text in contradistinction to its obvious sense. In this way, Song was understood as an expression of the mystical bond between Christ and his Church. The sensual meaning of the poetry was superseded by its spiritual meaning. Thus Origen could plot a spiritual pilgrimage through the struggle against human passions (following the teaching of Proverbs) into a perception of the world's transience (as found in Ecclesiastes) which ended with the soul's rapturous contemplation of God (using Song). Gregory of Nyssa also adhered to this view: Song for him represented the final stage of the soul's ascent to and unification with the love of God. This type of exegesis was most fully explored in the writings of Bernard of Clairvaux.

What is evident from such interpretations, whether from the Jewish or the Christian tradition, is the way in which the original, more passionate vibrancy of the poetry was reappraised and eventually obscured beneath layers of theological or spiritual adaptation. Whatever value one gives to the subsequent levels of meaning (and because we are again dealing with poetry without a narrative context, it can be used in an infinite number of ways), modern reading of such poetry with its different framework of reference at the very least should start by appreciating it first and foremost within its 'setting-in-life'.

(III) TRIBAL BLESSINGS AND CURSES

This type of poetry illustrates in a negative sense the ardour of Semitic poetry. Given that we are often dealing with fragments of oral poetry placed within a literary context, the issue of dissonance between early traditions and their later literary adaptation is again apparent.

    1. The first set of examples concerns *the blessings*. One illustration of this is Gen. 14: 19–20, a blessing for Abram spoken by a non-Israelite priest-king, Melchizedek:

> Blessed be Abram by God Most High,
>   maker of heaven and earth;
> and blessed be God Most High,
>   who has delivered your enemies into your hand!

The poetic nature of this blessing is clear, both in the repetition of 'blessed' (lines 1 and 3), and in the parallelism A > B (lines 1 and 2 with lines 3 and 4). That this has liturgical connotations is evident in the references to 'God Most High', which was a title for God used in the psalms sung at the Jerusalem Temple (cf. Pss. 46: 4; 47: 2). It is probably quite ancient, and may have once been a liturgical blessing from the pre-Israelite Jebusite cultus in Jerusalem (on which account it postdates Abraham by some five hundred years). Whatever its origins, it has been adapted into the narrative of Genesis 14 to justify the ancient claims of the people of Israel to the land, placed in the mouth of a non-Israelite priest-king in order to create a more universal sense of authority. In this way, the early use of the poem has again been transformed by its literary context.

    Another poetic blessing is found in Gen. 27: 27–9 and 39–40. As an early tribal blessing, it would have pertained to the conflicts between the Edomites (who traced their ancestry back to Esau) and the Israelites (who were the 'house of Jacob': cf. Gen. 25: 23, 30). But in its present context, the writer has used it to emphasize above all

Israel's unique claim to God's blessing. Within the story about
Esau tricking Jacob of his father's blessing, the writer inverts the
former blessing on Esau/Edom (vv. 27–9), so that it now falls on
Jacob/Israel (vv. 39–40). For example:

> Be lord over your brothers,
>> and may your mother's sons bow down to you.
>
>> (v. 29*b*: to Esau)

> By your sword you shall live,
>> and you shall serve your brother;
> but when you break loose
>> you shall break his yoke from your neck.
>
>> (v. 40: to Jacob)

Two other long poems of blessing, which in their composite
form are literary creations, make a similar point concerning the
superiority of the people of Israel within the land. The best
example is Gen. 49: 2–28. This is a collection of tribal blessings,
dating from several different stages in Israel's history, compiled at a
time after the prominence of the tribe of Judah in the south (vv.
8–12) and of Joseph in the north (vv. 24–6). The writer has brought
these together as a deathbed speech by Jacob to the twelve sons, in
order to emphasize the early unity of the disparate tribes. Again we
may note how early tribal blessings have been given a different
theological purpose in their literary context.

The second example is Deut. 33: 1–29, which is also a collection of
tribal blessings, probably brought together at a later stage than Gen.
49, in that there is clear evidence of the divided kingdom (vv. 7 and
17—Judah and Joseph); furthermore Dan has moved to the north (v.
22) and Simeon has disappeared. Again the blessing is used dramati-
cally as a deathbed speech, this time by Moses to the twelve tribes,
and again we may note the same dissonance between the earlier
independent tribal sayings and the later literary adaptation.

2. From poems of blessing we move to *poems of cursing*. One
interesting example is in Genesis 9:

> 25 Cursed be Canaan;
>> a slave of slaves shall he be to his brothers.

·   ·   ·   ·   ·   ·   ·

> 26 Blessed be the LORD, the God of Shem,
>   and let Canaan be his slave.
> 27 God enlarge Japheth,
>   and let him dwell in the tents of Shem;
>   and let Canaan be his slave.
>
> (Gen. 9: 25–7)

Verse 25 is probably the earliest part of this saying, and suggests a form of curse on the disobedient son (cf. Exod. 21: 15, 17). By adding vv. 26–7, the Yahwistic writer demonstrates the uneasy relations between Israel and Canaan during his own time. The context here is a story about Canaan's sexual depravity, which implies the writer's animosity to the Canaanites' fertility practices. The later literary adaptation, concerning the increase of hostilities during the growth of civilizations, has again changed the impact of the earlier saying of the simple curses against Canaan.

The Oracles of Balaam in Num. 23: 7–10, 18–24; 24: 3–9, 15–24 (within the larger literary unit of Num. 22–4) offer another example of ancient poems used to curse other peoples. These probably date from before the time of the monarchy. The view of prophecy here, and its link with military concerns, suggest an early period. One fragment is undoubtedly ancient in that it concerns the enmity between the Israelites and Amalekites, and has links with the hatred of the Amalekites in the 'Banner Song' in Exod. 17: 16, referred to earlier:

> By Jacob shall dominion be exercised,
>   and the survivors of cities be destroyed!
>
>   .   .   .   .   .   .
>
> Amalek was the first of the nations,
>   but in the end he shall come to destruction.
>
> (Num. 24: 20)

The literary adaptation has heightened the effectiveness of these ancient curses by adding to them the power of the prophetic word. The editor has also woven into the story the irony of Balaam who is supposed to speak on behalf of the Moabites against Israel, but instead blesses Israel and (by implication) curses Moab: the motifs found in Gen. 27 and the Jacob/Esau blessing are again apparent.

(IV) WAR POETRY

Just as the blessings and curses recall ancient land disputes, ethnic
conflicts, and national idealism, so too the songs of military victory
indicate the same territorial and nationalistic concerns. Many of
these are lengthy and composite literary poems, like the blessings
of Gen. 49 and Deut. 33, but there are a number of briefer, earlier
fragments of war poetry which again have been reused by the
literary editors.

One example, quoted as from 'the Book of Jashar' (see 2 Sam. 1:
18), is found in Josh. 10: 12–13, which takes up two ancient ideas—
Israel's God is not only a 'holy warrior', but also he controls the
forces of nature:

> 'Sun, stand thou still at Gibeon,
> and thou Moon in the valley of Aijalon.'
> And the sun stood still, and the moon stayed,
> until the nation took vengeance on their enemies.

Another example is from Exod. 15: 21, a brief fragment
celebrating the victory at the Red Sea, being placed after a longer
literary poem composed to celebrate the same event (15:2–18). The
poem is attributed to Miriam but is very similar to v. 1, which is
attributed to Moses. Here we may note the rhythm (2:2; 2:2) used
in the call to praise God:

> And Miriam sang to them:
> 'Síng to-the-LÓRD, for-he-has-tríumphed glóriously;
> [the] hórse and-his-ríder he-has-thrówn into-the-seá.'

The cultic background to this song is apparent not only in the
larger literary unit (chs. 12–15, which recount the events connected
with the festival of Passover) but also in the smaller unit (15: 2ff.),
which speaks of the celebration in music and dance after military
victory (v. 20). The antiquity of the poem is evident not only on
account of its brevity, but also because of its various correspondences with Ugaritic poetry, including the allusions to the deity
fighting the chaotic forces of the sea. An interesting correspond-

ence is the epic poem describing the fight between Ba'al and Yam. (The tricola 'now, thine enemies, O Ba'al' which was used in Chapter 2, p. 41 belongs to this same epic poem). The 2:2 staccato stress is similarly evident:

Sea (Yam) fell,	He sank to earth,
His joints trembled,	His frame collapsed.
Ba'al destroyed,	Drank Sea!
He finished off	Judge River.

(CTA 2. iv. 25 ff.)

yamma la-mitû	Sea is indeed dead
ba' lû-mi yamlû(ku)	Ba'al indeed rules!

(CTA 2. iv. 32)

The motif of the deity's fight against the power of the sea is common throughout the ancient Near East. Several examples also occur in the biblical accounts (cf. Pss. 74: 15 ff.; 77: 17–20; 89: 10 ff.; 93: 1–4; Isa. 27: 1; 51: 9–11; Hab. 3: 8–9). The evidence points towards a repeated adaptation of a popular motif.

Another example of a victory poem, probably composed close to the event, is found in Judg. 5: 2–31 (also referred to on pp. 35–6 and pp. 81–2). This is hardly a brief poetic fragment, but rather one lengthy song—an ancient text which is so corrupt that in places it is difficult to ascertain its meaning. Verses 12–30 (and perhaps vv. 6–8 also) form the core of the song, celebrating tribal victory. The introduction (vv. 1–11) and the conclusion (v. 31) are more hymnic in style, attributing the victory not to tribal prowess but to the God of Israel. The earlier verses demonstrate again the use of ancient Near Eastern mythology, in their depiction of God coming from the desert region, probably of Kadesh, in the Sinai peninsula. God marches to defend his people; his coming is described in the anthropomorphic terms of a warrior-god:

> LORD, when thou didst go forth from Seir,
> when thou didst march from the region of Edom,
> > the earth trembled,
> > and the heavens dropped,
> > yea, the clouds dropped water.

> The mountains quaked before the LORD,
>   yon Sinai before the LORD, the God of Israel.

> (Judg. 5: 4–5)

The rhythmic stress is less regular, although a pattern 3:3 (common to hymns of praise) is in evidence. The parallelism is A = B (lines 1 and 2), with staircase parallelism in the tricola (lines 3–5) and A > B in the bicola (lines 6–7). Like Exod. 15, Ugaritic motifs are evident: examples include the heavens and clouds dropping water (*CTA* 6. iii. 6–7, 12–13), and the mountain-god appearing on earth in a violent thunderstorm (*CTA* 6. v. 70–1). The correspondences of this poem with other biblical poems reflecting Canaanite influence (e.g. Ps. 29: 6/Judg. 5: 3; Ps. 68: 7–8, Deut. 33: 2; Hab. 3: 4–5/Judg. 5: 4–5) suggest further the possibility of some 'borrowing'. Like Exod. 15: 21, it is more than likely that such songs would have been composed for a celebration of victory within the liturgy of the cult.

Another example celebrates the military might of King David. This brief song occurs three times (1 Sam. 18: 7; 21: 11; 29: 3) in the accounts of the early monarchy. The literary context changes the meaning of the poem in each case:

> Saul has slain his thousands,
>   and David his ten thousands.

Another example of a similar fragment occurring twice and adapted differently each time is in 2 Sam. 20: 1 and 1 Kgs. 12: 16:

> We have no portion in David,
>   and we have no inheritance in the son of Jesse;
>   every man to his tents, O Israel!

Other examples of different types of war poetry being adapted into a literary context include the song of the watchman in Isa. 21: 11–12 and the 'last words of David' in 2 Sam. 23: 1–7. The latter is probably a literary copy of earlier war songs, compiled to highlight David's military exploits as recounted in 2 Sam. 23: 8–39.

Even as late as the second century BCE we find a victory poem in 1 Macc. 14: 4–15, which, like 2 Sam. 23, is another literary copy of war poetry used centuries earlier:

The land had rest all the days of Simon.
He sought the good of his nation;
his rule was pleasing to them,
as was the honour shown him, all his days.   (v. 4)

At the beginning of this chapter it was proposed that Semitic poetry often has a 'setting-in-life' prior to its 'setting-in-literature'. This observation has been confirmed, even though the process of the separation of one from the other is usually difficult to prove.

Two other types of poetry outside the Psalter still require some attention. The first is the poetry of the prophets (and the prophets' use of other traditional poetry has been seen frequently in this chapter); and the second pertains to the poetic forms used in cultic worship. These two types of poetry, each interwoven in various ways within a prose framework, will be the focus of our study in the following two chapters.

6

Prophetic Poetry

Throughout the previous chapter we noted the various ways in which the prophets used the poetry from their culture in order to communicate effectively. In itself this is little different from any adept contemporary preacher using a variety of illustrations in order to capture the imagination of a congregation. Prophets such as Amos and Isaiah borrowed from the proverbial poetry and rhetorical sayings of wisdom; they used secular songs (Isa. 22: 13); they appropriated funeral laments—over nations, if not over individuals (Amos 5; Isa. 14, 23; Ezek. 27, 28, 32); they used love songs to depict the depth of Yahweh's love for Israel (Hos. 2, 6; Isa. 5; Jer. 3; Isa. 49, 51, 54); they took up oracles of blessing and cursing (Num. 22–4); and they utilized war poetry in order to dramatize the coming judgement on Israel before the other nations (Amos 3, 6, 9; Isa. 5, 10, 28; Jer. 4, 5, 6). In addition, the prophets used a good deal of liturgical poetry from the cult, sometimes in short poetic fragments, and at other times in longer, sustained verse.

Rather than focusing on the possible dissonance between the life-setting and the literary setting in prophetic poetry (a theme to be developed in the following chapter) this chapter will attend instead to the more fundamental question of whether the prophetic literature might be properly termed 'poetic'. The critical issue in discussing prophetic poetry has already been discussed in part in our earlier chapter on poetry and prose.

A. Prose and Poetry in the Prophetic Writings

We have already noted with reference to Hermann Gunkel's observations that it is likely that the prophets articulated some of their message in poetic form, so that it could easily be recalled and repeated by those who heard it. Nevertheless, this is not as straightforward as it may first appear. In spite of Lowth's claims that, being inspired, the prophetic literature must be poetic, the Hebrew gives us conflicting evidence in this respect. Firstly, it fails to present much of the so-called poetry in the line-forms used to indicate clear poetic units; and secondly, it gives no indication from the accentual system that the Prophets should be read in a similar way to the poetry of the Psalms, Job, and Proverbs. The English translations interestingly reflect this confusion: some present the prophetic material almost entirely as prose, whilst others set much of it out in terms of line-forms and stanzaic structures.

This problem is peculiar to the prophetic literature. In the Pentateuch (Genesis to Deuteronomy), as also in the Deuteronomistic and Chronicler's material (Joshua to 2 Kings; Chronicles, Ezra and Nehemiah), the material is essentially narrative in form, with small portions within it being 'poetic': the greatest proportion of material is in prose. In the wisdom literature, by contrast, particularly in Proverbs, Job, and the Psalms, the literature is more clearly set out in the typical line-forms associated with poetry, with little explanation by way of prose narrative: almost all of the material is in verse. Between these two extremes of biblical literature being predominantly prose or predominantly poetry, the prophetic literature falls somewhere between the two.

In different ways, the three major prophetic books of Isaiah, Jeremiah, and Ezekiel, as also the twelve minor prophets, offer an amalgam of prose and poetic material. The *story* in the prophetic literature is of course in prose, following the form of the material in Joshua–Kings (called in Hebrew the 'Former Prophets'). By contrast, the *oracles* of the prophets are found both in prose and in poetry. It is as if the purported historical context, into which each prophetic message fitted, required a prose form, whereas the material which was less rooted in one historical context, and which made little appeal to any specific life-setting, could be expressed in the poetic mode. The details of particular circumstances within the prophetic literature normally create a prose form, with a narrative-story appeal, whilst the prophetic oracles which suggest a more general, timeless quality are often more appropriate for the genre of poetry.

This uncertainty in determining poetry and prose in the prophets is best illustrated by reference to selections from the prophetic literature in various different English translations. It will be seen that there are vast differences with respect to the perceptions of poetry and prose.

(I) JEREMIAH

The most controversial book by far with respect to the issue of prose and poetry is that of Jeremiah. Most scholars would agree that there are probably three distinctive literary sources within this book: poetic oracles (mainly of judgement on Judah and Jerusalem), prose narratives (in the third person, mainly describing the sufferings of the prophet on account of the message of judgement on the eve of the exile), and prose sermons (resembling in style and language the sermons in Joshua, Samuel, and Kings, and believed to be the work of the Deuteronomists). The main problems lie in determining what is a poetic 'oracle', and what is a prose 'sermon'. It is interesting to see that many scholars gauge what might be 'authentic' Jeremianic material by this criterion; they assume that the material from the prophet himself is that which is couched in poetic style (poetry being the most obvious memorable form of oral communication, following Gunkel's hypothesis). Such scholars would argue that an oracle which suggests an utterance by the prophet must, by definition, be poetic.

Most of the disputable poetic material is found in Jeremiah 1–25; any sample chapter from this collection would illustrate the widely varying views of scholars on this issue. An interesting example is found in Jer. 21: 12 and 22: 3. Although the Hebrew presents both of these examples in prose (as it does for the greatest proportion of the book), the RSV chooses to present the first in poetic line-forms, and the second as prose:

O house of David! Thus says the LORD:
Execute justice in the morning,
and deliver from the hand of the oppressor
him who has been robbed ...

(Jer. 21: 12)

Thus says the LORD: Do justice and righteousness, and deliver from the hand of the oppressor him who has been robbed ... (Jer. 22: 3.)

We may surmise that the reasons behind this are that Jer. 21: 12 is believed to be closer to the words of the prophet, and thus suggests a memorable poetic medium, whilst Jer. 22: 3, within its whole narrative 'story' context, is from a later hand, and so suggests a prose style.

Even apart from the differences between an English translation and the Hebrew text, what is more surprising is that there are occasionally the same inconsistencies in different editions of the Masoretic text of the Hebrew Bible. For example, Jer. 11: 21 contains a quotation of Jeremiah's contemporaries in Anathoth: 'Do not prophesy in the name of the LORD, or you will die by our hand.' An earlier edition of the Hebrew (called *Biblia Hebraica*, or *BH*, printed at the beginning of the twentieth century) presents this as prose; a later edition (called *Biblia Hebraica Stuttgartensia*, or *BHS*, first printed in Stuttgart in 1968) presents this as poetry, probably on account of the parallelism of prophesy/die; name of the LORD/our hand.

The argument can be presented on a much larger scale than a comparison of two or three verses. If we take the first chapter of Jeremiah as an overall model, the comparisons in Table 1 emerge (the abbreviations for biblical translations are given on pp. xii–xiii).

What is clear is that, in translation, the decision between poetry and prose has been made on grounds other than those of metre and parallelism; it has been made partly on an assessment of what may be 'authentic' Jeremiah (and hence, poetry), and partly on an assessment of what counts as narrative (story) within the text, and thus deserves a prose form.

TABLE 1. Prose and poetry in translations of Jeremiah 1.

RSV

vv. 1–3	Prose	Historical introduction
v. 4	Prose	
v. 5	Poetry	
vv. 6, 7a	Prose	Call of prophet
vv. 7b–8	Poetry	
v. 9a	Prose	
vv. 9b–10	Poetry	
vv. 11–12	Prose	Visions
vv. 13–19	Prose	

NEB

vv. 1–3	Prose	Historical introduction
vv. 4–10	Prose	Call of prophet
vv. 11–14a	Prose	Visions
vv. 14b–19	Poetry	

NJB

vv. 1–3	Prose	Historical introduction
v. 4	Prose	
v. 5	Poetry	
v. 6	Prose	
vv. 7–8	Poetry	Call of prophet
v. 9a	Prose	
vv. 9b–10	Poetry	
vv. 11–12	Prose	
vv. 13–14a	Prose	Visions
vv. 14b–19	Poetry	

NIV

vv. 1–3	Prose	Historical introduction
v. 4	Prose	
v. 5	Poetry	Call of prophet
vv. 6–10	Prose	
vv. 11–12	Prose	
vv. 13–15a	Prose	Visions
vv. 15b–16	Poetry	
vv. 17–19	Prose	

Note: In this case the NRSV follows the RSV; and the REB follows the NEB.

(II) ISAIAH 1–39

The same observation on the issue of prose and poetry holds true in first Isaiah. Apart from the obvious narrative prose of the biographical stories of the prophet before the king (Isa. 6–8; 36–9) the remaining chapters move (uncertainly, it seems at times) between didactic prose passages and poetic oracles. Even within the narratives themselves, the English translators have attempted to present poetic fragments, apparently to add a certain focus and immediacy (as if the prophet is speaking) to the backcloth of the prose story. This is in contrast to the Hebrew manuscripts, where almost the entire book is presented in continuous prose. The AV (King James Version, or the Authorized Version, dating from 1611) follows the Hebrew in writing in continuous prose, subdividing verse by verse, as it does with all the prophets; this is not the case with established English translations from the twentieth century, which mix together poetry with prose, and so depart from the Hebrew original.

Even in a narrative passage such as Isaiah 7–8 the translations reflect a great number of variations, particularly with respect to the depiction of the prophet's 'own words' in poetry or prose. For example, the oracle concerning the sign of Immanuel (Isa. 7: 10–25) is in prose in the RSV and the NRSV, as also in the NEB, REB, and NIV; but it is in poetry in the NJB. Or again, Isaiah's teaching in 8: 16–22 is in prose in the RSV and in the NRSV; it is in prose and poetry in the NEB, REB, and NIV; but it is all in poetry in the NJB. These variations are illustrated in Table 2. (See p. 128.)

(III) EZEKIEL

The variations in the book of Ezekiel are also noticeable, with most translations recognizing much longer prose sections, and presenting various smaller sections in poetry. Taking Ezek. 1–23 as a unit, there is a good deal of disagreement: for example, the RSV presents only parts of chapters 19, 21, 23, and 24 as poetry, whereas the NRSV also includes parts of chapters 7 and 17, and additional parts of chapters 21 and 24. The NEB presents as poetry 15: 6–8 as well as

TABLE 2. Prose and poetry in translations of Isaiah 7–8.

RSV

Isa. 7: 1–6, 7*a*	Prose	Isaiah and Ahaz
7*b*–8*a*	Poetry	
8*b*	Prose	Judgement on Judah
9	Poetry	
10–25	Prose	Sign of Immanuel
Isa. 8: 1–4, 5	Prose	Assurance to Ahaz
6–8	Prose	
9–10	Poetry	God will deliver
11–15	Prose	
16–22	Prose	Isaiah's teaching

NRSV
Follows RSV exactly as above

NEB

Isa. 7: 1–6, 7*a*	Prose	Isaiah and Ahaz
7*b*–9	Poetry	Judgement on Judah
10–25	Prose	Sign of Immanuel
Isa. 8: 1–4, 5	Prose	Assurance to Ahaz
6–8	Poetry	
9–10	Poetry	God will deliver
11–15	Prose	
16–22	Poetry	Isaiah's teaching

REB
Follows NEB as above

NJB

Isa. 7: 1–6, 7*a*	Prose	Isaiah and Ahaz
7*b*–9	Poetry	Judgement on Judah
10	Prose	
11	Poetry	
12	Prose	Sign of Immanuel
13–25	Poetry	
Isa. 8: 1–8	Prose	Assurance to Ahaz
9–22(23)	Poetry	God will deliver; Isaiah's teaching

NIV

Isa. 7: 1–6, 7*a*	Prose	Isaiah and Ahaz
7*b*–9	Poetry	Judgement on Judah
10–25	Prose	Sign of Immanuel
Isa. 8: 1–4, 5	Prose	Assurance to Ahaz
6–8	Poetry	
9–10	Poetry	God will deliver
11	Prose	
12–17	Poetry	
18–22	Prose	Isaiah's teaching

15: 2–5, and 18: 2*b* (not poetry in the RSV or NRSV). The REB replaces 15: 6–8 as prose, although apart from this follows the NEB; the NJB overall also follows the NEB; whereas the NIV preserves chapters 15 and 17 as prose, whilst presenting 18: 5–9, 11*b*–13*a*, 15–17 also in poetry. This is illustrated in Table 3.

TABLE 3. Poetic passages in Ezekiel 1–23.

RSV

19: 2–14	Lament on Israel
21: 9*b*–10*a*	Sword of the Lord
23: 32*b*–34	Allegory of Samaria
24: 3*b*–5	Announcement of siege
NRSV	
7: 2*b*–4, 5–9, 10–12, 14–19, 21–7	End of Israel
15: 2–5	Parable of the vine
17: 3*b*–10, 22*b*–24	Allegory of the eagle
19: 2–14	Lament on Israel
21: 9*b*–12, 14–17, 25–7, 28*b*–32	Sword of the Lord
23: 32*b*–34	Allegory of Samaria
24: 3*b*–5, 6–8, 9*b*–13	Announcement of siege
NEB	
15: 2–5, 6*b*–8	Parable of the vine
17: 3–10, 22*b*–24	Allegory of the eagle

TABLE 3 *(cont.)*

18: 2*b*	Proverb of the grapes
19: 1–14	Lament on Israel
21: 9*b*–11, 14–16, 28*b*–32	Sword of the Lord
23: 32–4	Allegory of Samaria
24: 3*b*–6*a*, 6*b*–8, 9*a*–13	Announcement of siege
REB	
15: 2–5	Parable of the vine
17: 3*b*–10, 22*b*–24	Allegory of the eagle
18: 2*b*	Proverb of the grapes
19: 2–14	Lament on Israel
21: 9*b*–11, 14–16, 28*b*–32	Sword of the Lord
23: 32*b*–34	Allegory of Samaria
24: 3*b*–5, 6*b*–8, 9*b*–13	Announcement of siege
N*J*B	
15: 1–5, 6*b*–8	Parable of the vine
17: 3–10, 22*b*–24	Allegory of the eagle
18: 2*b*	Proverb of the grapes
19: 1–14	Lament on Israel
21: 14–22	Sword of the Lord
23: 32*b*–34	Allegory of Samaria
24: 3*b*–5, 6*b*–8, 9–11	Announcement of siege
NIV	
18: 2*b*	Proverb of grapes
18: 5–9, 11*b*–13*a*, 15–17	Explanation of proverb
19: 1–14	Lament on Israel
21: 9, 11–12, 14–17, 28*b*–32	Sword of Yahweh
23: 32–4	Allegory of Samaria
24: 3*b*–5, 6*b*–8, 9*b*–12	Announcement of siege

(IV) AMOS AND HOSEA

The same issue is evident in the minor prophets. This is best illustrated by referring to two typical eighth-century (pre-exilic)
prophets, Amos and Hosea. Taking Amos first, the variations occur

with regard to the prose; most translations present the book primarily in poetry. Amongst the most variable passages, the RSV and NRSV depict 1: 1; 3: 12; 5: 1, 25–7; 6: 9–10; 7: 1–2*a*, 4, 7–8*a*, 10–11*a*, 12–15; and 8: 1–2*a* as prose; the NEB presents 1: 1; 3: 1; 7: 1–17 and 8: 1–7 entirely as prose, whilst the REB adds to this 3: 11*b*; 5: 1; and 6: 9–10. The NJB is more sparing with prose, presenting only 1: 1; 3: 1 and 7: 10–16 as such. The NIV has a more complicated alternating schema, with 1: 1; 3: 1, 13; 5: 1; 6: 9–10; 7: 1–2, 4–5, 7–8*a*, 8*c*, 10–11*a*, 12–15; and 8: 1–4, 7 as prose.

Similar variations are found in Hosea. These and those of Amos are again more clearly shown in a chart (Table 4).

TABLE 4. Prose passages within the poetic sections of Amos and Hosea. (The passages in italics are the most variable passages of prose.)

AMOS	
RSV	1: 1
	3: 1, *12*
	5: 1, *25–7*
	6: 9–10
	7: *1–2a*, 4, 7, *8a*, 10–11*a*, 12–15
	8: *1–2a*
NRSV	
Follows the RSV above	
NEB	1: 1
	3: 1
	7: 1–17
	8: 1–7
REB	1: 1
	3: 1, *11b*
	5: 1
	6: 9–10
	7: 1–17
	8: 1–7
NJB	1: 1
	3: 1
	7: 10–16

TABLE 4 *(cont.)*

NIV	1: 1
	3: 1, *13*
	5: 1
	6: *9–10*
	7: *1–2, 4–5, 7–8a, 8c, 10–11a, 12–15*
	8: *1–4, 7*
HOSEA	
RSV	1: 1–11
	2: 1, *16–20*
	3: 1–5
NRSV	
Follows the RSV above	
NEB	*1: 1, 2–4a, 8*
	2: 1, *18–23*
	3: 2
	14: 9
REB	*1: 1, 2–6a, 8*
	2: *18–23*
	3: 2
	4: 1
	14: 9
NJB	1: 1, 2–9
	2: 1
	3: 1–5
NIV	1: 1–11
	2: 1
	3: 1–5

(V) HAGGAI AND ZECHARIAH

The later prophetic books are interesting, in that (like Ezekiel) the balance of poetry to prose is reversed. In Haggai, not only the Hebrew but also every one of the six translations presents the entire book in continuous prose. In Zechariah 1–8, the prose again predominates: the RSV, NRSV, NEB, REB, and NIV assign only the later chapters (9–14) as poetry. Only the NJB presents Zech. 2: 10–17 and 8: 2–8 (celebrations of the restoration of Zion) as poetry. The prophetic oracles are presented as part of a particular narrative (story) account, and so retain the prose form.

(VI) ISAIAH 40–55

Another interesting example of the mix between poetry and prose is found in the oracles of second Isaiah. Although in the Hebrew these chapters (Isa. 40–55) are in prose (and the AV also follows this model) all the modern translations present most of second Isaiah in poetic line-forms, with the exception of Isa. 44. It is hard to read these oracles as anything other than sustained poetry, and the lack of any historical contextualization within second Isaiah (there being no biographical details about the prophet) increases the sense of timelessness in the substance of the oracles, and so suggests the more natural medium of poetry. To illustrate this, the following extract is taken from the RSV as set in line-forms and hence read as poetry; this same extract is then transposed into prose, in order that readers may judge the artistic effect for themselves. The extract is from Isa. 46: 1–4, a satirical passage which contrasts God's support for Israel with the impotence of the Babylonian deities and idols:

> Bel bows down, Nebo stoops,
>   their idols are on beasts and cattle;
> these things you carry are loaded
>   as burdens on weary beasts.
> They stoop, they bow down together,
>   they cannot save the burden,
>   but themselves go into captivity.
>
> Hearken to me, O house of Jacob,
>   all the remnant of the house of Israel,
> who have been borne by me from your birth,
>   carried from the womb;
> even to your old age I am He,
>   and to grey hairs I will carry you.
> I have made, and I will bear;
>   I will carry and will save.

Bel bows down, Nebo stoops, their idols are on beasts and cattle; these things you carry are loaded as burdens on weary beasts. They stoop, they bow down together, they cannot save the burden, but themselves go into captivity. Hearken to me, O house of Jacob, all the remnant of the house of Israel, who have been borne by me from your birth, carried from the womb; even to your old age I am He, and to grey hairs I will carry you. I have made, and I will bear; I will carry and will save.

B. Criteria for Determining the Poetry of the Prophets

What, then, are we to conclude from these various surveys? First, that with few exceptions, the printed editions of the Hebrew text are extremely cautious about the use of poetry in the prophetic writings, following more an aesthetic and theological effect. Second, that the older English translations, not least the AV (1611), follow with precision the prose of the earlier Hebrew editions. Third, and most significantly, that the more recent translations are apt to be more bold in their presentation of poetry. This may be due to a presumption that rhythm and parallelism can be found in the line-forms. But it may also be on account of a Lowthian-type of assessment of what is a 'genuine' saying of the prophet (thus requiring poetry) and of what is an explanation or interpretation from a later hand (and therefore more likely to be written in prose as a type of explanation of the text). Another reason for choosing either more poetry or more prose is a practical one: it achieves greater continuity within an entire text (very much a feature of the NEB and NJB), so that the material flows in one form or another, creating either a sense of a historical narrative, or a sense of timeless expressions of thought.

What emerges from this overview is that, within the prophetic literature, neither metre nor parallelism is a sufficiently convincing feature in distinguishing poetry from prose; other literary and theological criteria come into play as well. It is clear that intuition plays a very large part; and in this sense, the comparison of poetry and music, and of poetry and art, is still a useful one, in that the 'performances' of earlier 'scores' (the analogy here being to the English translations of earlier Hebrew versions) are multivariant, being dependent as much on intuitive interpretation as on slavish adherence to tradition and convention.

Given that we have affirmed that the nature of poetry is as much to conceal as to reveal, then a good deal of the work of translators is in part inspired intuition: an analogy might be the use of the same insight when interpreting nuances within the score in producing a great opera or symphony. Just as there is an infinite variety of performances of the same score, so there can be a similar variety of presentations of poetry from the same prophetic material.

This does not mean that intuition is the only way of assessing the poetry of the prophets. As we noted at the beginning of this chapter, a large number of unmistakable fragments have been incorporated into this literature—wisdom poetry, popular poetry, cultic poetry not least. Of these three, we have already assessed wisdom and popular poetry; but the poetry of the cult, as yet unexplored, would appear to have been by far the most formative influence in the prophetic books. The following chapter will attend to the issue of cultic poetry in some detail.

7

Cultic Poetry

In early Israelite culture, the cult and its sacral associations were bound up with the whole of life. It is thus not surprising that cultic poetry is evidenced throughout wisdom, popular, and prophetic traditions, at all stages of Israel's history.

An illustration of this pervasive influence of cultic poetry has been noted with respect to the close relationship between the cult and warfare. We have already observed this in the discussion of the victory songs implying cultic celebrations in Exod. 15 and Judg. 5 (see Ch. 6, sect. C). A further illustration is found in the sayings concerning the ark, the chest which symbolized the presence of God on the battlefield; for example:

> And whenever the ark set out, Moses said,
>> 'Arise, O LORD, and let thy enemies be scattered;
>> and let them that hate thee flee before thee.'
> And when it rested, he said,
>> 'Return, O LORD, to the ten thousand thousands of Israel'
>>> (Num. 10: 35–6)

This saying would be spoken by cultic officials (priests or prophets) before and after battle, as in the stories in 1 Kgs. 22 and 2 Kgs. 6; it probably dates from the early monarchy, if not before. That it is early is suggested by the depiction of God as a 'warrior', defeating Israel's enemies (Exod. 15: 3; Judg. 5: 4–5). Its cultic associations are further illustrated by its occurrences in some psalms, for example Pss. 68: 1–2 and 132: 8.

In this chapter the extensive influence of cultic poetry will be assessed under two headings: first, the *fragments of cultic poetry* which have been incorporated into a narrative framework; and second, the *more developed cultic poems*, some of which might also have had a life-setting before being used in a literary framework, and others of which are entirely literary compositions using cultic forms.

A. Fragments of Cultic Poetry

This category may be subdivided further: first, cultic poems used by the priests; second, those used by the people; and third, those mediated as if by God (probably through a priestly or prophetic voice). This sort of liturgical poetry pertains as much to a setting-in-life as it does to a setting-in-literature. Thus, when we read such poetry now integrated within a narrative framework, the familiar problem of dissonance will be evident—whereby the specific theological purposes of the editor have transformed the earlier performative qualities of the verse from its use within some liturgical setting. This may be seen for each of the three categories referred to above.

(I) CULTIC SAYINGS USED BY THE PRIESTS

A well-known priestly saying, most probably from the Temple liturgy, is the so-called 'Aaronic Blessing' in its tricola form:

> The LORD bless you and keep you:
> The LORD make his face to shine upon you,
>   and be gracious to you:
> The LORD lift up his countenance upon you,
>   and give you peace.
>
>   (Num. 6: 24–6)

In spite of the absence of any regular rhythmic pattern, the parallelism of A > B > C, set out in three pairs of jussive clauses, is very clear. Again we may note the ways in which the phrases of the blessing have been taken up into the psalms (e.g. 'make his face to shine': see Pss. 31: 16; 80: 3, 7, 19), thus illustrating further the cultic associations. When or where this was used by the priest and community is unclear; but that it eventually became incorporated into the liturgy of the Temple is almost certain. In its present literary context, the blessing is set amongst various ancient ritual laws concerning the holiness of the cultic community (Num. 6) and of the appropriate dedication offerings for the altar (Num. 7). The priestly writer has transformed the liturgical setting for the blessing so that it now serves a different purpose: that of emphasizing the rewards due for such ritual propriety.

(II) CULTIC SAYINGS USED BY THE PEOPLE

Cultic poetry was not the preserve of the priesthood. It would have been learnt and recited by the people as well. Deuteronomy 26: 5–6 is an interesting example. It is possible that this was once an early credal saying, which has now been placed (rather like Num. 6: 24–6) into a composite literary work. The cultic context suggested by this saying would have been the harvest service of first-fruits, performed at the central sanctuary:

	And you shall make your response before the LORD your God,
A	'A wandering Aramean was my father;
B	and he went down into Egypt
C	and sojourned there, few in number;
B	and there he became a nation,
C	great, mighty and populous.'

(Deut. 26: 5–6)

This saying compresses together several diffuse traditions from the people's history, from Abraham to Moses, and thus cannot be very ancient; its summary form suggests some editing by the Deuteronomists. But it could, nevertheless, point to an earlier saying in poetic form. For example, we may note the parallelism, which after the first line A is: B > C, B > C. It may well have developed into a poetic creed, recited by the people at harvest thanksgiving but developed for different theological reasons into a Deuteronomistic literary context, as a fitting preamble to Moses' speech before the people in Deut. 28 ff.

Another credal saying which may pertain similarly to cultic usage is found in Deut. 6: 4–9. This is the *Shema*—so called because the first word is *šᵉma*, which in Hebrew means 'hear'—and it begins as follows:

A Hear, O Israel:
B   The LORD our God is one LORD;
C and you shall love the LORD your God
D   with all your heart,
E   and with all your soul,
F   and with all your might.

(Deut. 6: 4–5)

Its poetic form (for example, the tricola pattern in lines D, E, and F) would facilitate it being learnt and recited. It may well have had an independent life-setting before being incorporated in Deut. 6; if so, then it also has a double orientation. Its purpose here is to explain the meaning of the first of the Ten Commandments set out in Deut. 5.

(III) CULTIC SAYINGS SPOKEN ON BEHALF OF GOD

As well as cultic sayings sung or spoken by priests to the people, or by the people to the priests, there are other such sayings whereby the priest or prophet mediates in oracular form to the people on behalf of God. One example is found in Exod. 33: 19:

I will be gracious to whom I will be gracious,
    and will show mercy on whom I will show mercy.

This phrase concerning the 'merciful and gracious God' occurs several times in prose prayers and narratives throughout the Old Testament (e.g. Exod. 34: 6; Deut. 4: 31; Neh. 9: 17; Jonah 4: 2). It is probably a prayer developed by the Deuteronomists. Its occurrence in many of the psalms testifies further to its having become a cultic saying (e.g. Pss. 86: 15; 103: 8; 111: 4; 112: 4; 116: 5; 145: 8), as does its use in texts with cultic associations as far apart as Joel 2: 13; Nahum 1: 3; and 2 Chr. 30: 9. It is interesting to note in this case that the *same* cultic prayer can be used within a variety of literary settings. In each case, the general, liturgical nature of the verse is particularized in different ways according to its context.

These examples demonstrate that the relationship between oral and literary poetry is highly complex. Sometimes an early cultic saying has been adapted for a particular literary purpose (as in Num. 6; Deut. 6, 26); at other times a poetic saying appears to have been developed mainly for literary purposes (as in Exod. 33). Although poetry in a literary context serves a particular theological purpose, rather than having the more general and open-ended features of liturgical poetry, it is impossible to ascertain that there was always an earlier setting-in-life before the setting-in-literature. The poetic fragments are too brief to confirm this.

B. Developed Cultic Poetry

Having assessed examples of short cultic verses, we now turn to the longer liturgical poems. These can be categorized into four groups: first, the *hymns*; second, the *laments*; third, the *thanksgivings*; and fourth, *miscellaneous cultic poetry*—a mixed group including poems about the king, hymns extolling Zion, and songs celebrating the eternal rule of God. Each of these forms reveals that cultic poetry occurs extensively in all of Israel's traditions. The prophets not least borrowed and adapted these four cultic forms with great frequency, for this gave their message both familiar continuity and creative originality.

(I) HYMNS

These are poems which focus on the goodness of God not only in creation, but also throughout history. A large proportion of psalms (a fifth of the Psalter) fit this category; non-psalmic hymns are found in some of the prophets, in some narrative passages, and in the later wisdom material.

Amos

Two prophetic books which incorporate a substantial amount of hymnic material from Temple liturgy are Amos and Isaiah. The book of Amos incorporates at least three such hymns (often called 'doxologies', because each ends by praising the name of God) in 4: 13; 5: 8–9 and 9: 5–6. These doxologies are unusual, because they praise God as the one who brings darkness as well as light. They speak not only of the preserving and re-creating activity of God, but also of a more negative relationship between the Creator and the created order, where God uses nature to destroy evil and chaotic forces. These hymns fit with the dominant message of judgement in the book of Amos; it is as if every established tradition implying the well-being of the people—even their hymnody—is used to speak not of well-being but of judgement, in order to shake the audience out of their complacency:

A He who made the Pleiades and Orion,
B   and turns deep darkness into morning,
C   and darkens the day into night,
D who calls for the waters of the sea,
E   and pours them out upon the surface of the earth,
F the LORD is his name.

(Amos. 5: 8)

Other examples of hymnic fragments in Amos, used similarly to evoke a sense of impending doom and judgement, are found in 1: 2 and 8: 8.

Isaiah

Isaiah 40–55 also incorporates several hymns of creation; in contrast to the hymns in Amos they serve the message of comfort and restoration (the judgement of the exile in 587 BCE having occurred). Instead of being a means of indictment, they offer solace and renewed hope. One hymn compares interestingly with Amos: the two aspects of God's nature are again recalled, but this time to reinforce a creative rather than a destructive message:

I form light and create darkness,
    I make weal and create woe,
I am the LORD, who do all these things.

(Isa. 45: 7)

When these hymns occur in second Isaiah, they always serve to emphasize (in contrast to Amos) that a new creative act of God is about to take place. It is again difficult to know whether these have been borrowed from previous Temple liturgy, or whether they illustrate the prophet's own literary skill. The best examples are found in 40: 9–11; 42: 10–13; 43: 14–21; 44: 23; 52: 7–10; 54: 1–3, 4–8, 9–10; 55: 12–13.

In addition to creation hymns, which in Isaiah imply not only God's sovereign rule over the natural order of the cosmos but also his rule over all the nations within it, another theme is that of God's special care for 'Zion' (whether this means the city or the people is often unclear):

> Break forth together in singing,
>   you waste places of Jerusalem;
> for the LORD has comforted his people,
>   he has redeemed Jerusalem.
>
> (Isa. 52: 9)

This has clear correspondences with the hymns of Zion in the book of Psalms:

> Thy right hand is filled with victory;
>   let Mount Zion be glad!
> Let the daughters of Judah rejoice
>   because of thy judgements!
>
> (Ps. 48: 10c–11)

This use of the hymnic motifs concerning Jerusalem is interesting, because it links the hymns of second Isaiah (chs. 40–55) with the hymnic fragments of first Isaiah (chs. 1–39), where the hymns are used not so much to praise God for his creative activity everywhere, as to affirm his kingly rule in Zion in particular. The hymn incorporated into the call of Isaiah in the Temple at Jerusalem is one example:

> Holy, holy, holy is the LORD of hosts;
>   the whole earth is full of his glory.
>
> (Isa. 6: 3)

A similar hymnic fragment concerning Zion, from the eve of the exile, is found in Zephaniah:

> Sing aloud, O daughter of Zion;
>   shout, O Israel!

Rejoice and exult with all your heart,
O daughter of Jerusalem!
The LORD has taken away the judgements against you,
he has cast out your enemies.
The King of Israel, the LORD, is in your midst;
you shall fear evil no more.

(Zeph. 3: 14–15)

Other hymns in the prophetic literature which also emphasize God's good purposes for his people are found in Isa. 2: 1–4, 12: 5–6, Mic. 4: 1–3, and Zeph. 3: 14–15. The final chapters of Isaiah (56–66) include several hymns of rejoicing (Isa. 61: 10–11; 66: 22–3) as does the later collection of oracles in Isa. 24–7, for example, Isa. 25: 9 and 26: 1–6. In every case, the inclusion of hymnic material reinforces to the people, in traditional liturgical language and in established cultic forms, that the God whose praises they still sing will soon turn again to act in their favour. The earlier hymnic fragments, sung in liturgy, take on a different orientation when taken up into a larger literary work.

Four other hymns deserve particular mention, in so far as they are lengthier poems, each combining ancient cultic material and interweaving it into a composite literary whole. These are Exod. 15: 1–18; Deut. 32: 1–43; Judg. 5: 2–31; and Hab. 3: 2–19. The complexity of these forms suggests that ancient poems have evolved into literary artefacts over a period of time.

Exodus 15

Exodus 15 is a hymn which has been placed within the particular literary context of the Passover Festival and the Feast of Unleavened Bread (cf. Exod. 12–13). The chapter serves to celebrate in hymnic form the main motif of this combined festival—namely, that an enslaved people is now free. Passover was celebrated in spring, at the time of the creation of a new order, and the hymn uses mythological motifs to create a sense of renewed hope for the future. Some scholars have likened Exod. 15 to various psalms that were used for the same purpose: although their link with any spring festival is less clear, the most obvious psalms which similarly celebrate the crossing of the Red Sea are Pss. 77 (vv. 17ff.); 89 (vv.

10 ff.); and 93 (vv. 1 ff.) Psalm 114 is another interesting example: it combines the victory over the sea (as here in Exod. 15) with the crossing of the river Jordan into the promised land (as told in Josh. 5). It also takes up the ancient mythological motifs from Ugarit regarding Ba'al's victory over 'Judge River and Prince Sea' ('The sea looked and fled, Jordan turned back'), thus interweaving mythology with traditions about Israel's own history.

Several other psalms on the same theme as Exod. 15 were used in the Temple liturgy. Two examples are Pss. 78 and 105. This then raises the question: why has Exod. 15 not been included in the Psalter, particularly given its close associations with the Passover Festival? The opening verses could be those of any psalm, and indeed are found in Ps. 118: 14, taken up similarly in Isa. 12: 2:

> The LORD is my strength and song,
>   and he has become my salvation;
> this is my God, and I will praise him,
>   my father's God, and I will exalt him.
> The LORD is a man of war;
>   the LORD is his name.

> (Exod. 15: 2–3)

Then follows a description of the drowning of Pharaoh's host (vv. 4–6, full of Holy War imagery); this leads into a description, using mythological language, of a divine battle with the sea (vv. 7–10), which concludes, in the language of Pss. 86: 8 and 89: 7–8:

> Who is like thee, O LORD, among the gods?
> Who is like thee, majestic in holiness,
>   terrible in glorious deeds, doing wonders?

> (Exod. 15: 11)

The psalmic influence is further demonstrated in the closing verses, which suggest a much later tradition about God's kingly rule in Zion—hardly a theme relevant to the Exodus, before Zion (Jerusalem) was even known about:

> Thou wilt bring them in, and plant them on thy own mountain,

the place, O LORD, which thou hast made for thy abode,
the sanctuary, O LORD, which thy hands have established.
The LORD will reign for ever and ever.

(Exod. 15: 17–18)

Exodus 15 offers a good example of an ancient brief hymn (v. 21 — the Song of Miriam) expanded later on account of some cultic use (parts of vv. 1–16), and adapted for Temple liturgy (vv. 17–18). Nevertheless, it was *not* included in the Psalter: instead it became associated more particularly with a specific narrative framework. In this way, the cultic associations of the hymn have again been overshadowed by the literary concerns of the editor, who, by giving it a different theological emphasis in a narrative setting, has limited its performative value to this context alone.

Deuteronomy 32

Deuteronomy 32, like Exodus 15, is one of the few poems in which the Hebrew is presented in distinct line-forms; this is probably more because of the link with Moses than because of the nature of the poetry. It is a lengthy didactic hymn, probably once associated with the cult, although in its literary framework it serves as a prophetic sermon which forms part of the conclusion of the book of Deuteronomy.

Judges 5 and Habakkuk 3

Judges 5 and Habakkuk 3 are also similar in this respect. They too were once brief fragments of war poetry, but have grown into composite works serving more literary than liturgical purposes. Both cultic poetry and war poetry may be seen in each of them. Judges 5 has already been referred to in Ch. 2, sect. D; the following example is from Habakkuk:

> The mountains saw thee, and writhed;
> the raging waters swept on;
> the deep gave forth its voice,
> it lifted its hands on high.
> Thou didst bestride the earth in fury,
> thou didst trample the nations in anger.

Thou didst trample the sea with thy horses,
the surging of mighty waters.

(Hab. 3: 10, 12, 15)

That this poem once had cultic associations is also clear from the introduction (3: 1—'A prayer of Habakkuk the prophet, according to the Shigionoth'), the middle section (3: 9—'Selah'), and the conclusion (3: 19*d*). However, like Exod. 15, Deut. 32, and Judg. 5, it is now placed within a literary framework: Hab. 3 serves as a collection of prophecies uttered on the eve of the exile, compiled under the theme that God will march for his people and will overthrow the might of Babylon. In this sense, the poem is no longer open-ended for general use, but has rather a particular theological emphasis.

The Chronicler

The relationship between the liturgical and the literary use of hymns is also apparent in the books of Chronicles. The Chronicler's adaptation of various psalms from the Psalter does not only tell us a good deal about the use of psalmody in the restoration period when the Chronicler was writing (about the fourth century BCE), but also shows how hymns of praise could again be adapted for a dual purpose—liturgical and literary.

1 Chronicles 16 records a feast of dedication which purports to be set in Davidic times (1000 BCE) but which includes psalms, and combinations of psalms, from a later period, more relevant to the worship of the Chronicler's own time, some seven hundred years later. In 1 Chr. 16: 8–22 we find parts of Ps. 105: 1–15; in vv. 23–33, Ps. 96: 1–13; and in vv. 34–6, Ps. 106: 1, 47–8. 2 Chronicles 5: 13 similarly picks up a common psalmic refrain, which occurs, for example, throughout Ps. 136:

For he is good,
for his steadfast love endures for ever.

The Chronicler's purpose in including such psalms is to demonstrate that the worship of the post-exilic community in Judah drew its authority from hymns associated with 'the house of David' in the first Jerusalem Temple, some seven hundred years earlier. Such traditional use of earlier psalms legitimized the community in the face of threats to its identity from within (the northern Israelites) and from without (the imposition of Persian rule). Thus in post-exilic times, as in pre-exilic times, a hymn which had previous liturgical use was incorporated into a narrative framework so that it also served a theological purpose within the literature into which it had been grafted. This is another clear case of the shift of emphasis between genuine liturgical poetry, performed in the cult, and literary poetry, given a different theological purpose through the work of the editor.

Daniel

Another illustration of the use of hymns in this way comes from the book of Daniel, finally written in the second century BCE. The first six chapters, set in a narrative form, are taken up in part with the same concerns about the identity of the Jewish community that pre-occupied the Chronicler: Daniel, by his example of piety and prayer, displays to the pagan rulers of Babylon (and Persia) just what it means to be a Jew in a foreign land. Setting aside Dan. 7 (to which we shall turn later) there are four hymns in Dan. 1–6, three times spoken by Gentile kings, using the style and language of psalms which would have been used in the cult, but which in the Daniel narrative context, as in the Chronicler's narrative, serve a different theological purpose. These four hymns are found in Dan. 2: 20–3, which has several themes from Ps. 103, and also Pss. 41: 14 and 139: 12—all quite late psalms; Dan. 4: 3, linked to Pss. 77: 19 and 145: 3; Dan. 4: 34–7, linked to Pss. 102: 24 and 145: 13; Dan. 6: 26–7, linked to Ps. 145: 12–13. The last example, spoken by 'Darius the Mede', is as follows:

> for he is the living God,
>   enduring for ever;
> his kingdom shall never be destroyed,
>   and his dominion shall be to the end.
> He delivers and rescues,
>   he works signs and wonders
>   in heaven and on earth
> he who has saved Daniel
>   from the mouth of the lions.
>
> (Dan. 6: 26–7)

> . . . to make known to the sons of men thy mighty deeds
> and the glorious splendour of thy kingdom.
> Thy kingdom is an everlasting kingdom,
> and thy dominion endures throughout all generations.
> The LORD is faithful in all his words,
> and gracious in all his deeds.
>
> (Ps. 145: 12–13)

We may note here the familiar theme of God's world-rule and kingly power—a theme popular in the exile, as seen in the hymns of second Isaiah, and a theme which, not surprisingly, fits well the story of Daniel, which is set within the exilic period. The use of a familiar psalm in Daniel makes the theological point that, within the chaos of earthly powers of the exilic period, the heavenly rule of Israel's God continues, and, exhibited through the deliverance of Daniel from the lions, is duly confessed by the pagan earthly powers. The use of the hymn is intended to reinforce the flagging hopes of the restoration community in the second century BCE—the God of Israel had the powers of foreign nations such as Persia in his sovereign control. (Interestingly, other hymnic additions to the text of Daniel are found only in the Septuagint. These are Dan. 3: 25–45, the Prayer of Azariah, and 3: 46–90, the Song of the Three Young Men; they both draw extensively from Pss. 136 and 148, and make the same point about God's kingly rule and the frailty of human powers.) Yet again we may note that cultic hymns serve a more specific purpose when set in narrative form; examples are found as early as pre-settlement times (? twelfth century BCE, as seen in Exod. 15) and as late as the time of the book of Daniel (in the second century BCE, as seen in the above hymns).

Hymns in Wisdom Literature

Finally, reference must be made to the earlier discussion on the use of cultic hymns in wisdom literature. Overall, these hymns are later literary compositions rather than developments of earlier liturgical fragments. The hymns which are found in Prov. 8 and 30 and Job 28 (referred to in Ch. 5, sect. B), which testify to the value of wisdom as offering true knowledge of God, are good examples of this: they are not really 'cultic' hymns at all, for their praise concerns not so much the community before God, as the individual and the pursuit of wisdom. The two much later wisdom 'hymns' in Ecclus. 39: 14–35 and 42: 15–43: 33 also illustrate this point. These examples are not so much later literary adaptations of earlier cultic hymns, but rather copies of cultic poetry set within the wisdom tradition.

In this way we have moved successively from ancient fragments of cultic hymnody, possibly from as early as settlement times, to early hymns connected with the rise of the monarchy (around the ninth century BCE), to the later literary development of such material during the period of the later monarchy and the exilic period (eighth and seventh centuries BCE), to the restoration period (fourth century BCE), down to the time of the Maccabees (second century BCE). We have seen the influence of liturgical hymnody serving particular purposes in the case of several different writers—the prophets, the Deuteronomistic editors, the priestly writers, the Chronicler, and the editor of Daniel. Cultic hymnody—the traditional language of the praise of God—whether performed in liturgy, or developed in literature, exhibited a profound influence on the theological world-view of the biblical writers.

(II) LAMENTS

The lament form of poetry comprises two interrelated types: the communal laments and individual laments.

Communal Laments

The lament would have been used in cultic worship as a means of invoking the presence of God within a situation of distress. Its form is recognizable in two ways. First, in the Hebrew, it normally has a 2:3 (or 3:2) rhythm (as seen in Chapter 3: the *qinâ*, on account of its 'limping' rhythm, is a phonetic illustration of suffering). Second, the contents (usually set in the two-line form of parallelism A = B) depict a context of distress, suffering, and complaint before God.

Laments Used in Parody. One of the most interesting literary uses of this form is again found in the prophetic literature, where it takes on a type of parody, used as a mourning or complaint song depicting the downfall of a nation. We have already noted its use in Amos 5: 2, where it portrays the downfall of Israel herself:

> Fallen, no more to rise,
>   is the virgin Israel;
> forsaken on her land,
>   with none to raise her up.
>
> (Amos 5: 2)

The prophet Micah, preaching in Jerusalem only a few years after Amos' message to the people of Israel in the northern kingdom, similarly uses the lament form to depict the people's sufferings. Although the 3:2 rhythm is discernible, the parallelism and imagery in this particular example are more unusual and memorable, as the personification of the people's distress is depicted:

> Woe is me! For I have become
>   as when the summer fruit has been gathered,
>   as when the vintage has been gleaned:
> there is no cluster to eat,
> no first-ripe fig which my soul desires.
>
> (Mic. 7: 1)

Similar uses of the lament form as a funeral dirge upon the people are found in several other prophets. Habakkuk 1: 2–4, 12–17; Ezek. 19: 1–9, 10–14; Joel 1: 15–18; and Isa. 59: 9–15 all provide good examples, from different stages in the people's history, thus showing the pervasiveness of this form throughout the prophetic literature.

The lament form occurs in parody against Israel only infrequently, as a warning to Israel of her coming destruction; its more frequent use was to act as a judgement oracle, or threat, against other nations. In Nahum 3: 1–10 we see it used against Assyria; in 2 Kgs. 19: 21–8 (repeated in Isa. 37: 22–9) it is also used against Assyria; in Isa. 14: 4–21 it is used against Babylon; in Ezek. 27: 3–9, 25–36 it is used against Tyre; and in Ezek. 32: 1–8 it is used against Egypt. In both of these different parodies of the lament form, whether used against Israel or against the other nations, we may see again the way in which the later use of a cultic lament gives it an entirely different orientation.

Laments Used as Personal Expressions of Distress. This is not to say that there is not good evidence of the communal lament form being used by the prophets to indicate a genuine situation of distress. Isaiah 64: 1–12 is a good example from the later period after the exile:

> O that thou wouldst rend the heavens and come down,
>> that the mountains might quake at thy presence—
> as when fire kindles brushwood
>> and the fire causes water to boil—
> to make thy name known to thy adversaries,
>> and that the nations might tremble at thy presence!

The most poignant illustrations of a prophet lamenting on behalf of the people are found in the book of Jeremiah. These laments, full of the typical cultic language of lament found in the Psalms, are all found in the first part of the book (4: 19–21; 8: 18–9: 1; 10: 19–21; 14: 17–22; 23: 9–12), with the same theme of pain and horror in the face of coming devastation and destruction. The imagery of weeping and grief is deeply personal, and the prophet identifies his suffering with that of the people and of the land:

> O that my head were waters,
>> and my eyes a fountain of tears,
> that I might weep day and night
>> for the slain of the daughter of my people!   (9: 1)

> Woe is me because of my hurt!
>> My wound is grievous.
> But I said, 'Truly this is an affliction,
>> and I must bear it.'   (10: 19)

> Let my eyes run down with tears night and day,
>> and let them not cease,
> for the virgin daughter of my people
>> is smitten with a great wound,
>> with a very grievous blow.   (14: 17)

One other unusual lament form used in Jeremiah, consonant with the theme of bearing suffering and pain, is found in chapter 12, following immediately the complaint 'Righteous art thou' noted in Ch. 1, sect. C. Here the speaker is apparently God, whom the prophet depicts as being drawn into the people's predicament rather than being aloof from it:

> My heritage has become to me
>   like a lion in the forest,
> she has lifted up her head against me;
>   therefore I hate her.
> Many shepherds have destroyed my vineyard,
>   they have trampled down my portion,
> They have made my pleasant portion
>   a desolate wilderness.　　　　　(12: 8, 10)

We may note in the above examples the intensity of suffering evoked within the imagery, and alongside this, the use of parallelism, as well as some evidence in the Hebrew of 3:2 metre. By content and general rhythmic pattern, the lament form is clear.

Another book most appropriate for a discussion of the communal lament form, and not surprisingly associated in tradition with the prophet Jeremiah, is Lamentations. Although the distinctive style and content make Jeremianic authorship unlikely, it is possible that all five laments could have been written for use as public laments of fasting and mourning in memory of the devastation of the Temple by the Babylonians in 587 BCE. They are important because they are genuine cultic songs, without any narrative framework. The 3:2 rhythm is particularly clear, even in translation. In addition, the artistic form has been honed further by using an acrostic device: the first four chapters have one stanza for each of the twenty-two letters of the Hebrew alphabet, and the fifth chapter similarly conforms to twenty-two verses—thus revealing the close relationship between literary devices and public recitation. Just as in Amos, the subject-matter (especially in chapters 1, 2, and 4) resembles a funeral dirge over the fallen city; the difference in this case is that this lament is used as a catharsis for genuine grief, rather than in parody as indictment and judgement:

> How lonely sits the city
>   that was full of people!
> How like a widow has she become,
>   she that was great among the nations!

> She that was a princess among the cities,
>   has become a vassal.

(Lam. 1: 1)

Occasionally the personification of suffering is intensified by the use of the 'I' form, as in Jeremiah:

> Is it nothing to you, all you who pass by?
>   Look and see
> if there is any sorrow like my sorrow
>   which was brought upon me,
> which the LORD inflicted
>   on the day of his fierce anger.

(Lam. 1: 12)

That the lament form continued long in Israel's history is evidenced by the use of it at the time of suffering and persecution in the second century BCE; we may note here 1 Macc. 2: 7–13 and 3: 45, 50–3.

Individual Laments

We have already noted how an individual poet (whether Jeremiah or another) could embody the suffering of the community. In addition, there are at least two instances in biblical poetry (outside the psalms) where the 'I' used in the lament form is distinctively individual and personal. Several examples of these so-called 'individual laments' are found again in the book of Jeremiah; others are found in the book of Job.

Scholars have questioned whether, before the time of the devastation of the land and the exile to Babylon in 587 BCE, it was possible for an individual to compose personal prayers of distress. The debate has been focused on six prayers in Jer. 11–20, set within a narrative which depicts the sufferings of the prophet—one isolated from his people on account of the message of judgement he is compelled to offer to them. Jeremiah 11: 18–23; 12: 1–6; 15: 10–12, 15–21; 17: 12–18; 18: 18–23; 20: 7–18 have been called 'Confessions' in so far as the bold protests at the conflict of faith and experience appear to give us insights into the inner turmoil of the prophet himself. We read of cries of personal dereliction and isolation (15: 17;

20: 8–10); protests of innocence (15: 11; 18: 20); and threats of vengeance upon those close at hand (17: 18; 18: 23). All of these clearly separate the condition of the prophet from the fate of the community, and thus are more personal and individual than communal in orientation. These 'Confessions' are notable for their radical rebuke and reproach of God in prayer. The traditional lament form and language are creatively applied for a particular personal use, as can be seen in the following example from Jer. 15:

> I did not sit in the company of merrymakers,
>   nor did I rejoice;
> I sat alone, because thy hand was upon me,
>   for thou hadst filled me with indignation.
> Why is my pain unceasing,
>   my wound incurable,
>   refusing to be healed?
> Wilt thou be to me a deceitful brook,
>   like waters that fail?
>
> (Jer. 15: 16, 17)

The sixfold collection of 'Confessions' has been dispersed throughout Jeremiah 11–20 to create a particular literary impression: the movement is towards greater depths of despair, and God appears to become increasingly silent. The lament in 20: 7ff. is full of bold accusations of God's faithlessness, for he has not brought about the words of judgement spoken by the prophet; Jeremiah, forbidden to marry (Jer. 16), couches his rebuke in strong sexual imagery:

> O LORD, thou hast deceived me,
>   and I was deceived;
> thou art stronger than I,
>   and thou hast prevailed.
> I have become a laughing stock all the day;
>   every one mocks me.
>
> (Jer. 20: 7)

It is no surprise to find that the author of the book of Job chooses the lament form to depict repeatedly Job's cries of despair in his own (seemingly undeserved) suffering; Job 3, in which Job laments the day of his birth, has many similarities with Jer. 20, particularly in vv. 14–20, where we read:

> Cursed be the day
>> on which I was born!
> The day my mother bore me,
>> let it not be blessed!
> Cursed be the man
>> who brought the news to my father,
> A son is born to you,
>> making him glad.

.   (Jer. 20: 14, 15)

The correspondences in Job are clear:

> Let the day perish wherein I was born,
>> and the night which said,
>> 'A man-child is conceived.'
> Let that day be darkness!
>> May God above not seek it,
>> nor light shine upon it.

(Job. 3: 3–4)

In Job, the irony of the mockery of life is all too apparent:

> Why is light given to a man whose way is hid,
>> whom God has hedged in?
> For my sighing comes as my bread,
>> and my groanings are poured out like water.
> For the thing that I fear comes upon me,
>> and what I dread befalls me.
> I am not at ease, nor am I quiet;
>> I have no rest; but trouble comes.

(Job 3: 23–6)

This same individual lament form, discernible not only by sense (the imagery of complaint and distress) but also by sound (the *qinâ* rhythm), is found in Job 6: 1–12; 7: 1–10; 9: 4–12; 10: 8–12; 12: 14–25; 14: 1–15; and 16: 1–17: 16. As we have seen earlier, these examples illustrate that the author has used this lament form as skilfully as he has the hymn—with freedom as well as with adherence to convention. The lament, being well established in liturgical tradition, and having been popularized by the prophets, is used in Job to depict the tension between piety and experience of life. As we noted earlier with respect to the use of hymnic forms in Job, this lament form also serves to create a stark contrast between Job's fearless honesty before God, and the bland superficiality of the friends.

We may conclude that the scope of the lament form is vast: it is found not only in the psalms where the use is more straightforwardly liturgical, but also in the various adaptations and modifications of the prophets and wisdom writers, where the lament is used for different purposes. The tension between the setting-in-life and the setting-in-literature is again apparent.

(III) THANKSGIVINGS

Thanksgiving songs, whether in the Psalter or outside it, are not as much in evidence as are the hymns and laments. It is possible to see the thanksgiving as another form of the hymn, in that it praises God for a *particular* act of restoration, rather than being more general in its orientation. In view of this, some scholars (for example, Claus Westermann) have termed thanksgiving songs 'declarative praise'—declaring before the congregation specific answers to a prayer; this is in contrast to the broader category, 'descriptive praise'—a type of hymn describing in more universal terms God's goodness throughout creation.

Whether related to the category of hymn or not, in purpose and in use the thanksgiving stands at the opposite pole to the lament. In the thanksgiving, the individual or community celebrate in the cult their well-being in an ordered world. This is in stark contrast to the lament; there the liturgy is used as a focus for the experience of order which is otherwise absent in a chaotic world.

Communal Thanksgivings

A large number of communal thanksgivings have been incorporated into Isaiah 40–55. These chapters date from the time of exile, and hence from the experience of chaos rather than order. The prophet uses thanksgivings (as he also used hymns) to celebrate

proleptically the good promises of God who brings light out of
darkness and hope out of despair. These songs thus look forward to
the time of restoration—to use them is to look ahead to the light at
the end of the tunnel of the exile. The best example is found in Isa.
52: 7–10:

> How beautiful upon the mountains
>   are the feet of him who brings good tidings,
> who publishes peace,
>   who brings good tidings of good,
>   who says to Zion, 'Your God reigns.'
>
> Break forth together into singing,
>   you waste places of Jerusalem;
> for the LORD has comforted his people,
>   he has redeemed Jerusalem.   (vv. 7, 9)

Unlike the lament form, the communal thanksgiving form,
noticeable even in translation, has no clear, regular rhythm; nor is
the parallelism always clearly evident. Yet this is still poetry, and
much of the imagery and phraseology comes from the psalms. It has
been used with a specific theological aim in mind, and in this way,
in its overall literary setting, it evokes a more particular response
than would be the case if it were used as a psalm on its own.

Individual Thanksgivings

These occur less frequently than the individual laments. In each
case, they are set within a particular narrative context, which
results in the readaptation of the poem to suit the particular
theological designs of the editor. This is akin to the use of the
hymns (e.g. Exod. 15; Deut. 32; Judg. 5; Hab. 3) discussed earlier.
Setting aside a very late example of this form in 1 Macc. 14: 4–15,
there are four clear biblical examples.

Hannah's Song. Hannah's Song of thanksgiving is related to the
dedication of Samuel in the temple at Shiloh, found in 1 Sam. 2.
One of the peculiarities of this individual thanksgiving is that very
little of the substance of the poem is apt for Hannah's own situation
(i.e. her state of barrenness and the gift of her child, Samuel, as
described in 1 Sam. 1). The thanksgiving is more nationalistic in its

connotations, for it concerns military victory and the success of the king (v. 10). Nevertheless, the brief phrase in v. 5:

> The barren has borne seven,
>   but she who has many children is forlorn

is most probably the reason for its inclusion within this particular narrative. This phrase, alongside the theme of the reversal of fortunes of the downtrodden and oppressed (compare here Luke's Magnificat, in Luke 2, almost certainly influenced by this song), would suggest its appropriateness in spite of the irrelevant allusions in other verses. This individual thanksgiving thus illustrates the point that a cultic poem (used in an entirely different context), when appropriated into a particular piece of literature, actually loses something of its more repeatable and more typical performative nature.

David's Song. Another example is 2 Sam. 22, which is a song of thanksgiving by David after his many military victories, not least those against the house of Saul. It is used to make a particular theological point—that David's successes were not due to human might but rather to the sovereign power of God. The first verses of the song make this very clear:

> The LORD is my rock, and my fortress, and my deliverer,
>   my God, my rock, in whom I take refuge,
> my shield and the horn of my salvation,
>   my stronghold and my refuge,
>   my saviour; thou savest me from violence.
> I call upon the LORD, who is worthy to be praised,
>   and I am saved from my enemies.

> (2 Sam. 22: 2–4)

There is good evidence that this was a particular thanksgiving song which was used in cultic worship: it is found in an almost identical form in the Psalter, as Psalm 18. Were we to read this same song as Psalm 18, with no reference to any narrative framework, our interpretation of the poem would be quite different, for we would not be constrained by particular theological concerns brought into the poem by an editor: we would read and use the poem as liturgy, in an open-ended way.

Hezekiah's Song. Another similar example is in Isa. 38. This is a prayer of thanksgiving attributed to Hezekiah after his recovery from illness through the mediation of the prophet Isaiah. The editors have included this thanksgiving to validate the authority and effectiveness of Isaiah's ministry. Isaiah 38 reflects the same peculiarities that we noted for 1 Sam. 2: the lament form in vv. 10–16 (contrasting the past distress with present recovery) is very general in its description of despair, and very little of it relates at all to Hezekiah's particular situation.

If this were a lament/thanksgiving used only for cultic worship, the language would be deemed sufficiently typical for anyone to use it, without drawing too many necessary correspondences; but because we read it here as a poem adapted into a specific literary setting, our use of it is quite different. Again, the adaptation from a setting-in-life to a setting-in-literature has changed the orientation of the poem.

Jonah's Song. Perhaps the best example of the literary adaptation of cultic poetry is found in the book of Jonah. The story concerns a prophet who refused to obey God's call to preach repentance to the Gentiles, who was cast into the sea and swallowed by a 'great fish' because of his resistance to God's purposes. The thanksgiving song has been included at this, the lowest point in the story (ch. 2), and is put into the mouth of Jonah in the belly of the fish. It serves not so much to express Jonah's distress, as to anticipate his deliverance. A reading of this thanksgiving, in Jonah 2: 2–9, reveals again that the thanksgiving song has little to do with Jonah's own story. The end of the song (vv. 7–9) certainly reads rather anachronistically, as it concerns praying and making vows in the 'holy temple'. The references in the lament form in vv. 2–6 are the only really appropriate motifs, referring to 'the belly of Sheol' in v. 2, and to being 'cast into the deep', 'into the heart of the seas', and into 'the flood' in v. 3; similarly, v. 5, perhaps originally intended to be understood metaphorically, corresponds literally with Jonah's plight:

> The waters closed in over me,
>   the deep was round about me;
> weeds were wrapped about my head
>   at the roots of the mountains.
> I went down to the land
>   whose bars closed upon me for ever;
> yet thou didst bring up my life from the Pit,
>   O LORD my God.

Frequently in the psalms the poet speaks of his distress in terms of 'drowning' and being 'overwhelmed' by the waters of despair (cf. Pss. 42: 7; 69: 1–2). By taking metaphorical imagery and giving it a literal meaning, the poem 'fits' its narrative context. Rather like the thanksgiving songs in 1 Sam. 2 and 2 Sam. 22 and Isa. 38, this poem again demonstrates how cultic poetry can serve a different theological purpose in a literary setting. Instead of being used typically and repeatedly by anyone in danger or threat of death, where the metaphorical imagery has a typical and timeless appeal, the thanksgiving now makes a more specific, time-bound point: the God who can rescue his prophet from the chaotic waters of the deep to effect repentance, has also the power to rescue other nations (i.e. Nineveh) from their idolatrous unbelief to effect repentance. This theological meaning could hardly emerge from reading Jonah 2: 2–9 on its own, as an independent poem; it is only evident in its narrative setting.

The thanksgiving poems together make the now familiar point— that the literary use of a poem changes its earlier performative impact in liturgical worship.

(IV) MISCELLANEOUS CULTIC POETRY

This category includes songs connected originally with the *king and the royal court*, which speak of a coming deliverer, and songs which celebrate the *rule of God*, mainly over the city of Zion but also within the entire cosmos.

Poems Originally Associated with the Royal Cult

The earliest such poems are connected with the royal court from the tenth to the seventh centuries BCE. Because the king assumed a sacral as well as a political role, they would have been used in Temple liturgy. Within the Psalter, such poems are called 'royal psalms'. After the demise of the monarchy at the end of the sixth century BCE, they were given a future orientation, where the 'deliverer' was not so much a present or past Davidic figure as a future one (Pss. 2 and 110 are particularly pertinent in this respect, as we shall see in a later chapter). Much of the cultic 'royal' poetry—not only in the Psalter, but elsewhere in the Old Testament—was used long after there was a king, and such poems which had been preserved from the past were appropriated because they could be used to look ahead to the future. One could argue that they are in fact good examples of poetry which conceals as much as it reveals. On this account they have often been used in later Jewish and Christian literature as poems which speak of a Messianic figure—a deliverer sent by God to bring in the kingdom of the new age.

Isaiah 9. Outside the psalms, there are several examples of such poetry. A good example is found in Isaiah 9: 2–7, the kernel of which may well be an oracle offered by the prophet at the time of the birth of an heir to the throne (possibly Ahaz's son, Hezekiah). Although the poem has probably been modified to fit a later situation when there was no king (e.g. v. 9, which in idealized language speaks of the everlasting 'throne of David'), the military imagery in vv. 3–5 and some of the royal titles in v. 6 could well suggest a royal poem celebrating God's promises to perpetuate the Davidic dynasty from one generation to another:

> For to us a child is born,
>   to us a son is given;
> and the government will be upon his shoulder,
>   and his name will be called
> 'Wonderful Counsellor, Mighty God,
>   Everlasting Father, Prince of Peace.'

The exaggerated imagery concerning the king as the divine representative among the people was not unusual in this sort of royal verse. It is found in royal psalms such as Pss. 2: 7 (where the king is God's adopted son), 45: 6 (where the king's throne is 'divine'), and 89: 26–7 (where the king addresses God as 'Father'). Certainly, in Isaiah, the religious and political responsibilities of the reigning king play a large part in his message, so it is more than possible that this was an adaptation of some 'royal psalm' which was then given a prophetic orientation. However the poem arose, the significant point is that no Davidic king fulfilled the hopes expressed within it, and so its use after the end of the monarchy was to perpetuate a 'prophetic' orientation, so that it always referred to the future and to a coming deliverer.

Isaiah 11. Less clear is another song about a coming royal figure, in Isa. 11: 1–9. Like Isa. 9, this has been adapted to a later situation of exile when there was no king. Verse 1, concerning the 'stump of Jesse [David]', suggests its use (if not its origin) in a period when the monarchy was all but finished. Verses 2–5, which concern a wise and understanding figure, on whom God's spirit rests, correspond in some measure with the concerns of Isaiah for Jerusalem (for example, the hoped-for reign of peace), but, like vv. 6–9, they may well have been added in the exilic period instead, so that the figure pertains to a future and idealized hope:

> And the Spirit of the LORD shall rest upon him,
>   the spirit of wisdom and understanding,
>   the spirit of counsel and might,
>   the spirit of knowledge and the fear of the LORD
>
>   .   .   .   .
>
> with righteousness he shall judge the poor,
>   and decide with equity for the meek of the earth.
>
> (Isa. 11: 2, 4)

Micah 5. Two other poems in the pre-exilic prophetic material are also relevant in this respect. One is found in the book of Micah, a contemporary of Isaiah:

> But you, O Bethlehem Ephrathah,
>   who are little to be among the clans of Judah,
> from you shall come forth for me
>   one who is to be ruler in Israel,

> whose origin is from of old,
> from ancient days.
>
> (Mic. 5: 2)

Whether this is at all the work of the prophet is unclear. But the oracle, found in a book which is orientated to eighth-century Judah and the issues of king, court, and people, is certainly part of the belief that the Davidic dynasty must continue, even when the monarchy in Judah is ended. This is still 'royal poetry', although it is more linked to the future than to the present.

Jeremiah 23. Similarly, we may refer to an example set within the book of Jeremiah. This has other interesting ramifications, because many translations (including the RSV) offer it as prose, not poetry. The REB, however, is as follows:

> The days are coming, says the LORD
> when I will make a righteous Branch
> spring from David's line,
> a king who will rule wisely,
> maintaining justice and right in the land.
> In his days Judah will be kept safe,
> and Israel will live undisturbed.
> This will be the name given to him;
> The LORD our Righteousness.
>
> (Jer. 23: 5–6)

Although the imagery is less rich and idealized than that in Isa. 11, the substance is the same. This could be a song composed on the eve of the exile, to celebrate the coming rule of another Davidic heir: he will right all the wrongs of the monarch of the prophet's time, and he will therefore become the coming deliverer.

Second Isaiah: The Servant Songs. A number of songs in a similar vein have been incorporated into the book of second Isaiah (40–55). In this case, the royal connotations are more concealed. The figure who is to come has other features which make his identity ambiguous—he is in part king, in part prophet; in part an embodiment of the community, and in part an unknown, mysterious figure, who appears to suffer and die for his people. These songs have been called the 'Servant Songs', and are found in Isa. 42: 1–4; 49: 1–6; 50: 4–7; and 52: 13–53: 12. The work of this coming figure, particularly in 42: 1–4, is to bring in justice and righteousness, upheld by the Spirit of God: one cannot help but associate this with the song in Isa. 11: 2–5.

Whether these songs form a separate collection of poems is most unclear; each poem fits so well into its context that it is difficult to know where the actual ending is (for example, 42: 5–7, 49: 7, and 50: 8–9 could also be part of these poems). In spite of the ambiguity about identity—the concealing as well as the revealing features of poetry—the figure of the 'servant' in each poem has a distinctive and separate role from that in the song before it, although at the same time there is also some continuity; this changing figure always acts on behalf of God, and accomplishes his purposes in obedient fidelity—a role not evident when the servant is referred to (usually as Israel) elsewhere in the book.

These songs, echoing some of the earlier songs concerning a coming royal figure, but by no means bound by that tradition, look forward to the future: the last song (Isa. 52–3) in particular has been used many times to refer to a coming deliverer, not only in the later Jewish tradition, but also in the Christian tradition with regard to the person and work of Christ:

> Surely he has borne our griefs
>   and carried our sorrows;
> yet we esteemed him stricken,
>   smitten by God, and afflicted.
> But he was wounded for our transgressions,
>   he was bruised for our iniquities;
> upon him was the chastisement that made us whole,
>   and with his stripes we are healed.
> All we like sheep have gone astray;
>   we have turned every one to his own way;
> and the LORD has laid on him the iniquity of us all.
>
>   (Isa. 53: 4–6)

Here we may refer to but one of the many New Testament allusions to this song:

For to this you have been called, because Christ also suffered for you,
leaving you an example, that you should follow in his steps. He com-
mitted no sin; no guile was found on his lips. When he was reviled, he
did not revile in return; when he suffered, he did not threaten; . . . By
his wounds you have been healed. For you were straying like sheep,
but have now returned to the Shepherd and Guardian of your souls.
(1 Pet. 2: 21–3, 25.)

Similarly, Isa. 61: 1–11, set within a larger collection of oracles in
60: 1–62: 12, refers to a coming deliverer who will comfort and heal
both the city and the people. Unlike Isa. 52–3, there is less about
the purpose of his death, and more about the purpose of his life.
Like Isa. 52–3, the passage has been appropriated in the New
Testament to refer to Jesus Christ:

> The Spirit of the Lord GOD is upon me,
>   because the LORD has anointed me
> to bring good tidings to the afflicted;
>   he has sent me to bind up the brokenhearted,
> to proclaim liberty to the captives,
>   and the opening of the prison to those who are bound.

(Isa. 61: 1: cf. Luke 4: 18–19)

What is most interesting is the variety of interpretations which
may be given to each of these songs. They possess an 'open-
endedness' which, in each case, is due to the lack of any narrative
context which constrains the meaning of the poem to that of the
intentions of the editor. (We may note by contrast here the more
'closed' interpretation required from the hymns and individual
thanksgiving poems which *were* set in narrative contexts.)

Thus far, all the songs about a coming deliverer have been found
in the prophets: it is as if the prophetic concerns with hope for the
future (and their setting within oracular material rather than in
narrative) provided the most suitable setting for their expression.
With one or two exceptions (namely a couple of much later songs in
the apocryphal Psalms of Solomon, chapters 17 and 18, and a short
passage in 1 Macc. 3: 3–9) the only other context where such songs
are found is in the apocalyptic literature, which has its own distinctive future orientation. Some of the songs in the book of Enoch look

towards a future deliverer, but not being in the canon of Scripture, they lie beyond our concern. The relevant examples from biblical apocalyptic are found in the books of Zechariah and Daniel.

Zechariah 9. Zechariah 9: 9–10 is an interesting example. The whole chapter concerns the hoped-for reign of God, but vv. 9–10 focus on a particular figure—the 'Prince of Peace'. Probably dating from the third century BCE, when the monarchy had long since ceased, this is a poem which is similar in content and function to Isa. 11:

> Rejoice greatly, O daughter of Zion!
>   Shout aloud, O daughter of Jerusalem!
> Lo, your king comes to you;
>   triumphant and victorious is he,
> humble and riding on an ass,
>   on a colt the foal of an ass.
>
>   (Zech. 9: 9)

Daniel. In the Zechariah poem, as with the preceding examples, the reference is to an earthly, royal figure who will bring in the reign of God. Only the Book of Daniel is different in this respect. In this case, the coming figure is in part supernatural. Daniel 7: 9 ff., dating from the time of the Maccabees in the second century BCE, and clearly rich in liturgical and courtly imagery, is the one obvious example. Here the picture is not so much of an earthly court and royal throne as of a divine council and a divine seat of judgement; the picture is set within the 'night visions' where the reader looks into heavenly realities, and here we find a song, again concealing as much as it reveals, about a coming deliverer:

> I saw in the night visions,
> and behold, with the clouds of heaven
>   there came one like a son of man
> and he came to the Ancient of Days
>   and was presented before him.
> And to him was given dominion and glory and kingdom,
>   that all peoples, nations and languages should serve him;
> his dominion is an everlasting dominion,
>   which shall not pass away,

> and his kingdom one
> that shall not be destroyed.
>
> (Dan. 7: 13–14)

Chapters 2–7 of Daniel were originally written in Aramaic: this, then, offers the one clear Old Testament example of Aramaic poetry. Although this poem is in contrast to the picture of the marred appearance of the suffering servant in Isa. 52–3, in so far as we perceive in Daniel only a victorious figure, the force of both poems is nevertheless similar. The identity of Daniel's figure is equally ambiguous and mysterious, and the poetic medium serves to increase this impression. But, like the poetry concerning the servant in Isaiah, the concealing nature of this song would serve to keep alive the hopes of the beleaguered community of Jews in their time of intense persecution under the Seleucid Antiochus Epiphanes. Their assurance would be that some day soon a deliverer would arise and restore order out of chaos, justice and righteousness out of persecution and oppression.

It is interesting to surmise that a line of continuity might be drawn from poetry which once served the purposes of the royal court and human rule (for example, the royal psalms, and Isaiah 9), to poetry, some six hundred years later, which offers insights into the affairs of the divine court and divine rule. The precise identity of the coming deliverer constantly changes, but the voice within the poetry is overall unchanged: when vulnerable and powerless amongst the affairs of foreign nations, Israel must await her deliverer promised by God.

Poems Celebrating the Rule of God

Two other types of cultic poetry, both prevalent in the psalms, but used for different theological purposes outside them, are also used mainly in the prophetic material. One of these is poetry which celebrates (or looks ahead to) peace and security in Jerusalem, Zion, where a redeemed and purified community is described, offering worship which befits its God. These may be called *Zion hymns*. Another category consists of those poems which celebrate the kingly rule of God, whose sovereign power is affirmed and unthreatened, in spite of human appearances to the contrary.

These are the *kingship hymns*. Very often, the kingly rule is seen to take effect in the royal city, so that the two types become interlinked.

Both these types occur mainly in the books of Isaiah and Micah. For example, of the so-called 'Zion hymns', we may note Isa. 2: 2–4, paralleled in Mic. 4: 1–4; Isa. 33: 20–2; 35: 8–10; 40: 9–11; 52: 1–2, 7–10; 60: 1–3. Of the so-called 'kingship hymns', we may note Isa. 40: 21–3; 44: 6–8; 49: 22–6; 51: 4–6. As was seen with the poetry concerning the royal cult, these songs are ambiguous in their allusions to a future hope: Isa. 2 is a good example of this, because it intertwines the themes of Zion's re-establishment with God's kingly rule:

> It shall come to pass in the latter days
> that the mountain of the house of the LORD
> shall be established as the highest of the mountains,
> and shall be raised above the hills;
> .　.　.　.　.　.　.　.
> He shall judge between the nations,
> and shall decide for many peoples;
> and they shall beat their swords into plough shares,
> and their spears into pruning hooks;
> nation shall not lift up sword against nation,
> neither shall they learn war any more.
>
> (Isa. 2: 2, 4; see also Mic. 4: 1, 3)

These themes occur frequently in the hymns and thanksgivings of the Psalter, thus confirming the liturgical influence within the poetry of the prophets:

> Great is the LORD and greatly to be praised
> in the city of our God!
> His holy mountain, beautiful in elevation,
> is the joy of all the earth
> .　.　.　.　.　.　.
> For lo, the kings assembled,
> they came on together.
> As soon as they saw it, they were astounded,
> they were in panic, they took to flight . . .
>
> (Ps. 48: 1–2, 4–5)

In conclusion, it is clear that when the biblical writers, not least the prophets, use cultic poetry to suit their own theological concerns, the poetry (on account of its literary context) offers a limited range of meaning. This more specific and particular adaptation contrasts with the liturgical poetry proper in the Psalter, where there is an open-ended orientation because of the re-usable nature of the psalms for all types of cultic occasions.

Ironically, this issue of the 'open-endedness' of the poetry in psalmody has resulted in a plethora of views regarding the origins and meaning of the psalms; this will be the focus of our attention in the following chapters.

PART III

The Poetry of the Psalms

8

The Psalmists as Poets

The issue of a 'setting-in-life' and a 'setting-in-literature' is quite different with respect to the poetry of the psalms. The absence of a narrative context means that each psalm is a self-sufficient unit, and as its meaning is not controlled by an editor's narrative commentary, a 'setting-in-life' has to some extent still been preserved. Clearly there is some interpretative framework—for example, the superscriptions which identify particular psalms with events in the life of King David, and the interrelationship between one psalm and its neighbour within the collection—but this has not the same effect as the lengthy narrative framework which surrounds non-psalmic poetry; it most certainly does not predetermine the overall meaning of a psalm.

Although the absence of a narrative context makes it easier to read Hebrew poetry, from the point of view of its performance 'in life', it is nevertheless difficult to establish the precise life-setting for which a psalm was composed. The specific origins of the psalms are unknown; their later use is usually unclear. Inevitably, hypotheses abound: studies of the Psalter proliferate in various theories regarding not only the purpose of the psalms but also the identity of the psalmists.

Since the early part of the nineteenth century, five emphases have emerged in psalmic studies, each one mirroring the changing concerns of biblical scholarship. This chapter will assess each of these emphases in turn. Presenting an overview of scholarship will illustrate the sheer diversity of opinion in identifying the psalmists: again this will demonstrate the futility of attempts to overclarify and overcategorize as complex a genre as Hebrew poetry.

A. The Psalmists as Individual Poets

This stage marks a growing interest in what has been called 'historical criticism' (also known as 'biblical criticism' or 'literary criticism', although the last term has a different meaning today). The main concern of historical criticism is to ascertain where possible the date, place, and author of the biblical material. When applied to the psalms, its first result was an emphasis on the life of the individual poet, so that a type of personal autobiography was assumed from the allusions within a psalm.

This sort of approach to the psalmists is found in early German commentaries on the Psalter, dating from the 1820s onwards, especially in scholars who were influenced by the Romantic movement in Germany in the nineteenth century. The ideas of theologians such as Friedrich Schleiermacher and Johannes Herder were applied to readings of religious poetry, including the Psalter. German commentators thus placed great emphasis on individual religious experience, and the ways in which this experience finds expression in the outpourings of the heart. Examples of such German commentators include W. M. L. de Wette (1823), H. G. A. Ewald (1866), H. Graetz (1882), B. Duhm (1899), R. Kittel (1905), E. Balla (1912), and M. Lohr (1922).

This autobiographical approach was developed some time later in English commentaries on the psalms: examples include A. F. Kirkpatrick (1902), W. T. Davison and T. W. Davies (1904–6), and S. R. Driver (1915). A common assumption was that the personal experiences of the psalmists, expressed in the poetic medium, were influenced by the preaching of the prophets. (Here again we may note the influence of Lowth.) On this account the psalms were dated late, after the pre- and post-exilic prophets, from the time of the restoration period until the Maccabees. Kirkpatrick's commentary illustrates well the personal and autobiographical reading of the psalmists:

In the Psalms the soul turns inward on itself, and their great feature is that they are the expression of a large spiritual experience. They come straight from 'the heart to the heart', and the several depths of the spirit. (*The Psalms*, p. v.)

This approach provided an important continuum between scholarly study and the more devotional reading of the psalms in the Judaeo-Christian liturgical tradition. A typical example of this way of thinking is found in *The Psalms in Human Life*, by R. E. Prothero, who illustrates the ways in which individuals throughout the centuries have identified with the heights and depths of the personal experiences of the psalmists—their poems were 'from the heart to the heart'. Not only German and British scholars, but also French Catholic commentators have adopted this way of reading: examples include E. Podechard (1949), P. Drijvers (1958), and L. Jacquet (1975). It was also used by American writers on the Psalter such as M. Buttenweiser (1938), F. James (1938), and R. Pfeiffer (1941); more general and devotional works have also taken up this interpretation, such as the writings of C. S. Lewis (1961), T. Merton (1963), D. Bonhoeffer (1970), and M. Israel (1990).

In many ways, there is little difference between this personalized view of the psalmists and that expressed through the earlier centuries of the Judaeo-Christian tradition, which read the psalms primarily as 'psalms of David'. The main distinction of historical criticism is that it permits a variety of opinions about the actual identity of the poet. Some scholars would still see the Davidic king as the principal author; others, a prophet or cultic official in the court of the king; others, scribes or wisdom writers working in the post-exilic period; yet others, various individuals writing during the turbulent times of the Maccabees. But the critical historians share with earlier interpreters the belief that the psalmists were writing out of personal circumstances—in sickness, exile, defeat, persecution, near death, suffering from doubt and scepticism, or in times of recovery from illness and restoration to the community.

In this sense, the reading of the 'I' form in the psalms is literal and particular: it is some sort of individual autobiography, akin to that of the great independent prophets (not least, the Confessions of Jeremiah), even though the actual experiences were usually hidden behind the formulaic prayer language and the typical liturgical forms of the day. And even when the references within the psalm imply the concerns of the whole community (for example, defeat in battle, harvest time, or the affairs of the royal court) the assumption is still that the personal insights of the psalmist are uppermost in the composition of the psalm.

B. The Psalmists as Poets Serving the Community

It is possible to affirm the use of the historical-critical method, but to infer that the psalms were not so much personal prayers as representative expressions of the experiences of the entire community. This means that the use of the 'I' form is read in a representative, corporate light. Scholars developing this interpretation (from about the 1880s onwards) were influenced not only by the resurgence of national consciousness in response to the political and international events of the last century, but also by new developments in the study of the corporate element in comparative ancient Near Eastern religions—the folklore, myths, rituals, and customs, the language and the literature (much of it poetic in form) of so-called 'primitive peoples'. There was a renewed interest in the psyche of nations, and in the impulses within these cultures towards national survival.

It is not surprising that many scholars and commentators believed that the psalmists were also writing from the same corporate consciousness. In Germany, works on the Psalter by J. Olshausen (1853), R. Smend (1888), D. F. Baethgen (1897), and J. Wellhausen (1898) represent this view. In England, commentaries by T. K. Cheyne (1891, 1904) and C. A. and E. G. Briggs (1906–7) also demonstrate a more corporate interpretation. The psalms were attributed to the various political and national events in the life of the community—in terms of military victory and defeat, of national expansion or oppression—from as early as the monarchy (where the king was seen to play an important religio-political role) to as late as the Maccabees (when the high priest replaced the role of the king). Even where the 'I' form in a psalm was understood as personal, its inclusion into the Psalter was the result of its having been taken up into the life of the *whole* community. Hence, instead of being understood as personal auto-biographies by individual psalmists, the psalms were seen more as corporate biographies by representative poets.

The fact that the historical-critical method should yield such diverse results says as much about the nature of the method as it does about the identity of the psalmists. Biblical criticism is not an objective science; it is part of its own culture, and can often be highly subjective in its assumptions. When appropriating such time-conditioned modes of interpretation to the poetry of the psalms, which are themselves ambiguous because they are devoid of a particular context, the results are bound to be highly variable. Various scholars, writing about the psalms in the 1920s and 1930s, noted the vast areas of uncertainty which still remained:

for the most part internal evidence—the tone, language and theological outlook of the individual poems—is practically the only criterion on which critical judgements can be based, and it leaves the door wide open for subjectivity. (T. H. Robinson, *The People and the Book*, 175.)

Scholars appropriating the historical-critical method were of course aware of this problem: the discussion of the 'I' of the psalms became a major issue in psalmic studies. It was out of this context of uncertainty that a different emphasis emerged, in part continuous with the old and in part entirely different from it. This method, known as form-criticism, was popularized and applied to the psalms by a German scholar to whom reference has already been made—Hermann Gunkel. As a result of form-critical studies, a process began whereby the psalmists became more consistently associated with liturgy, in other words, with the affairs of the Temple cult and its festival worship.

C. The Psalmists as Liturgical Poets Serving the Cultic Community

Instead of seeing the individual's concerns or the nation's concerns at the heart of psalmody, this third interpretation (emerging in the 1920s) moved the focal point of attention to the worshipping community itself. It was not that previously the cult was seen to be unimportant; it was obviously a vital influence on the hymns and liturgies. It was more a question of emphasis: earlier scholars had understood the cult to be only one of the processes through which individual and corporate needs were expressed, rather than being the beginning, middle, and end of the process.

At least three factors contributed to this more pan-cultic reading of most of the psalms. As noted above, one factor was the work of Hermann Gunkel; another concerned the new appraisal of the role of the king in pre-exilic Israelite worship, in response to comparative research concerning the status of the king in other ancient Near Eastern cultures; the third factor was the influence of a Norwegian scholar, Sigmund Mowinckel.

Gunkel's form-critical studies developed in relation to a group in Germany called the History of Religions School. As far as the psalms were concerned, the more corporate interpretation was preferred: the 'I' of the psalms was seen as a figure representative of the entire community. Gunkel's own work on the psalms holds together at least four concerns: first, an interest in the spirituality of Israel as it was expressed through the life of the liturgy of the cult; second, an awareness of the influence of myths and rituals from other cultures which also gave life to the cult; third, a conviction that the prophetic movement gave the Israelite cultus a distinctive identity *vis-à-vis* other cultures, in terms of its monotheistic faith. Fourthly, in a slightly different category, Gunkel understood that the poetry of Israel grew out of oral traditions which were later transposed into literary forms through the influence of the prophets, so that by the end of the eighth century, poetic genres could be expressed within larger representative literary types.

Gunkel's first book on the psalms was published in 1904. Several articles followed, but it was not until the years 1926–32 that his seminal introduction and commentary appeared. The four concerns noted above were all interwoven into his study of the history of the poetry of the psalms—discussions on the corporate life of the cult, on the borrowings from other cultures, the influence of the prophets, and the development of poetic literature into two basic 'representative types'—prayer and praise. Gunkel recognized full well the limits of trying to overcontextualize the psalms; instead of adopting a thoroughgoing historical approach, he attempted instead to concentrate on the religious feeling within the poetry, offering a more aesthetic description of the patterns of psalmic language than any one specific historical context, whether personal or communal. But his was not an abstract process. Having classified the two representative types of prayer and praise, Gunkel then differentiated these into at least five basic poetic genres which recurred (with modifications) throughout the Psalter. These genres were hymns, laments, thanksgivings, royal psalms, and didactic psalms. As we shall see shortly, only a minor adjustment to Gunkel's work was needed in order to see that such classifications were due to the work of a particular class of skilled cultic poets, trained in poetic composition for liturgical occasions.

We noted in the previous chapter, with respect to the prophets' use of cultic poetry, that the interest in the role of the king in Israelite religion became a predominant concern in Old Testament studies (cf. Ch. 7, sect. B), which referred to the influence of royal ideology in passages such as Isa. 9 and 11; Mic. 5; Jer. 23; Zech. 9; and Dan. 7. This interest was readily applied to the psalms. Scholars who preferred a more personal interpretation understood the individual poet to be a Davidic figure; those who appropriated a more communal reading would see that the king, who embodied the well-being of the entire nation, was the speaker who represented the greater whole. In taking seriously the role of the king, there was much support for reading the psalms as cultic poetry to be used in the royal court, and hence for dating them during the period of the monarchy (1000–587 BCE). Gunkel similarly understood the role of the king to be paramount in the early history of psalmody: his categorization of a group of psalms as specifically 'royal psalms' is an example of this.

One group of scholars took their interest in a 'royal reading' of the psalms one stage further. In the 1930s the Myth and Ritual School (comprising mainly a group of scholars from Oxford) advanced the theory that Israel, like the cultures of Babylon, Egypt, and Canaan, also had a view of sacral kingship, whereby the king in Israel had a special religious status (as the son, or adopted son, of God) which was enacted in the Temple cult at particular festivals throughout the year. In spite of the critical attitude to kingship in the books of Samuel and Kings, expressions in the psalms such as 'You are my son, today I have begotten you' (Ps. 2: 7); 'Your divine throne endures for ever and ever' (Ps. 45: 6); 'Thou art my Father, my God, and the Rock of my salvation' (Ps. 89: 26); and 'You are a priest for ever after the order of Melchizedek' (Ps. 110: 4), offered support for such a view.

This theory of sacral kingship had been expressed previously by a number of Scandinavian scholars who were also interested in the role of myth and ritual in Nordic legends of somewhat later times. It is not surprising that Sigmund Mowinckel, a pupil not only of Gunkel but also of a Danish anthropologist, Grønbech, should develop the ideas of both these scholars and apply them to the psalms. One of Mowinckel's earliest studies (1916) was on the so-called 'royal psalms' as classified by Gunkel; by the time Mowinckel wrote his six-volume work on the psalms (1921–4) he was becoming increasingly convinced that well over half of the Psalter could be loosely termed 'royal psalms', written for the king to use at an annual festival.

This festival, he contended, took place at the turn of the New Year: Mowinckel believed this to be autumn time in Israel. Following the pattern of similar festivals in Babylon, the king and cultic personnel would act out God's ordering of the chaotic forces in the natural world and his protection of his people against the threatening power of foreign nations, and so gain the promise of provision and protection for the coming year. The relevant psalms were composed by gifted cultic poets in the royal court. As the significance of the annual festival increased (not least, because it upheld both the religious and the political power of the king) so too did the number of psalms composed for this same festival.

Mowinckel wrote on various aspects of psalmody for some fifty years. His most notable study, a two-volume work translated into English as *The Psalms in Israel's Worship* (1951; tr. 1962) reflects very clearly his major interest in the psalmists as 'royal cultic poets' and his minimal interest in other (more personal) types of psalmody. Mowinckel does not deny that the psalmists appropriated their own personal piety into their composition of the psalms: but the primary reason for such psalms, he believed, was to serve as ritual texts for the king and for the cultic community. For example:

The content, the formal language and the thoughts [in the psalms] are determined by purpose and custom . . . The personal contribution by the poet consisted in finding new variations of the fixed forms . . . In ancient Israel personality with the quality of originality and uniqueness was neither an ideal nor a reality. The personality became conscious of itself through the common experiences and emotions in which the Israelite entirely merged. (*Psalms in Israel's Worship*, ii. 126.)

The psalmists are no longer to be seen as individual poets, reflecting on their experiences of life at all stages in Israelite religion; nor are they even poets who wrote only on behalf of their people, in good times and bad. Instead, according to Mowinckel, the psalmists are, quite simply, professional poets, gifted in the conventions of liturgy, working for the king in the royal cult.

Mowinckel's reading of the psalms has become known as the 'cult-functional method'. His approach has influenced many different scholars. In Germany these include G. von Rad (1957, 1962), N. Muller (1961), and H. Zirker (1964). In Scandinavia, Mowinckel's pupils H. Birkeland (1933, 1955) and A. Bentzen (1941), as well as H. Ringgren (1937) and I. Engnell (1943, 1948), popularized the same views. In England, Mowinckel's views are most associated with W. O. E. Oesterley (1929) and with the many monographs by A. R. Johnson (1935, 1942, 1944, 1949, 1955, 1979) and J. Eaton (1967, 1976, 1979, 1981) and latterly by S. Croft (1987). To different degrees, but clearly following the same lines of argument, each of these scholars has viewed the royal cult as the backcloth against which not only the psalms but also the religion of the Old Testament could be properly studied.

We have already noted that, according to the more cult-centred interpretation, the professional poets wrote their psalms not only for the king but also for a particular New Year festival. Mowinckel adduced that the key theme in this festival was the celebration of the kingship of God, for whom the human king stood in a representative role. (Here we refer back to the earlier discussion of this theme in cultic poetry in Ch. 7: see pp. 163–5, with reference to passages from Isa. 40, 44, 49, and 51.) Observing that a great number of other psalms referred to the sovereign rule of God over the entire world, Mowinckel deduced that some ritual enactment of Yahweh as king (also involving royal processions with the ark of God) was the major part of this festival, in keeping with the New Year theme of the establishment of order for the following seasons. It is a moot point whether the psalmists used the liturgical expression 'The LORD reigns' (*Yahweh malak*) to signify a belief in actually 'remaking' Yahweh as king, or whether they were simply reaffirming Yahweh's continuous and everlasting kingship. The latter view is the most probable, and seems to be the most likely reading of those psalms which refer to this idea of the sovereign rule of God, for example:

> The LORD reigns; he is robed in majesty;
> the LORD is robed, he is girded with strength.
> Yea, the world is established; it shall never be moved;
> thy throne is established from of old;
> thou art from everlasting.

(Ps. 93: 1–2)

Two other scholars have also made a significant contribution in this area. They too start with the view that the psalmists wrote for the king for one particular autumnal festival, but each in different ways alters the main emphasis of the festival. For Mowinckel, the model for the enthronement festival came from the *akītu* New Year festival held in Babylon—curiously, in spring. A German scholar, H.-J. Kraus (writing in the late 1950s and publishing a commentary on the psalms in the early 1960s), upheld instead that the most important influence on the psalmists came not from Babylonian culture, but from Canaan. Kraus believed that the psalmists adapted aspects of Canaanite mythology in order to support their own belief in God's protection of his holy dwelling-place, Zion: the key purpose of the annual festival was to celebrate God's choice of Jerusalem, the founding of the Temple, and the security and protection of God's chosen people. (Here we may note how this theme of Zion was expressed in the hymns used by the prophets: see Ch. 7, sect. B, which referred to examples from Isa. 2; Mic. 4; Isa. 33, 35, 40, 52, and 60.) Several psalms clearly illustrate Kraus's views; the best examples are Pss. 46 and 48, which include the use of the Canaanite name for God (El Elyôn, the Most High God), as well as the Canaanite allusions to the dwelling-place of their deities:

> There is a river whose streams make glad the city of God
> the holy habitation of the Most High,
> God is in the midst of her, she will not be moved;
> God will help her right early.

His holy mountain, beautiful in elevation,
  is the joy of all the earth,
Mount Zion, in the far north,
  the city of the great King.

(Pss. 46: 4–5; 48: 2)

A. Weiser offered a further modification of the psalms' orientation around one autumnal festival. Weiser wrote at the same time as Kraus in the early 1950s, and similarly published a German commentary in 1959. He deduced that the psalmists were primarily influenced neither by Babylonian rituals, nor by Canaanite mythologies: the roots of psalmody grew from Israel's own soil—from a distinctive sense (mediated by the prophets) of God's activity in Israel's own history. This peculiar belief was expressed in a covenant-renewal festival which was celebrated even before the founding of the Temple. This took place in the various prominent sanctuaries, and eventually only in Jerusalem, at the time of the New Year in autumn (possibly every seven years, according to Deut. 32). Like Kraus and Mowinckel, Weiser still affirmed that the psalmists were professional poets, working in the royal cult, producing psalmody for this one predominant festival; however, their compositions drew as much from the great credos of Israelite faith as from Babylonian rituals or Canaanite mythologies. The psalmists also drew material from the special Israelite traditions of the escape from Egypt, the appearing of God on Sinai, the protection in the wilderness, and the provision of the land of Canaan. Weiser made particular reference to Pss. 50, 81, and 95 in support of his theory, of which Ps. 81 is a convincing example:

Blow the trumpet at the new moon,
  at the full moon, on our feast day.
For it is a statute for Israel,
  an ordinance of the God of Jacob.
He made it a decree in Joseph,
  when he went out over the land of Egypt.

(Ps. 81: 3–5)

Clearly Mowinckel, Kraus, and Weiser cannot all be right: the psalmists could hardly have been writing for three different autumnal festivals, each occurring at the same time. It is of course possible that there was more than one New Year in Israel, and thus more than one key annual festival: in this case, elements of Weiser's festival, associated with the Exodus and so with the Passover, may well have been celebrated instead in springtime. It is similarly possible that Mowinckel's theme of God's enthronement and Kraus's theme of God's protection of Zion were brought together in the same pre-exilic Jerusalem cultus, and that these were both celebrated in the autumn. From all this, we can conclude only that the psalmists probably wrote for several festival occasions, and that some of these were royal, corporate affairs at key points in the liturgical calendar: but as to the one autumnal festival, and the precise number of psalms—this we can never really know.

Nevertheless, according to the cult-functional view, we may conclude that the psalmists were not only gifted poets but also gifted dramatists. They were highly capable of writing poetry to be performed publicly in liturgy. This reading, in spite of its overconfident claims, takes seriously what has frequently been referred to as the 'performative' nature of early Hebrew psalmody, and rightly brings out a distinctive dramatic quality of the poetry of the psalms over and against the poetry set within the biblical narratives.

D. The Psalmists as Liturgical Poets Serving a Private Cultus

The previous understanding of the psalmists as professional liturgical poets saw them as part of the royal Jerusalem cultus. By contrast, from about the 1960s onwards, other scholars, whilst still maintaining a cult-functional reading, have redefined the meaning of the cult, so that it also refers to a more personal and independent liturgical activity. This was in part attached to the Temple, but also to outlying local sanctuaries, and catered for the needs of individuals rather than for the entire nation. Furthermore, instead of this cult presupposing a pre-exilic setting (in that it involved the court of the king), the context for such psalmody also included a post-exilic date, since it pertained not only to pre-exilic local sanctuaries but also to post-exilic synagogue-type communities. The psalmists are still seen as professional poets, composing ritual texts. However, instead of these being used only for public annual festivals, and instead of being orientated around the king, the psalmists, it is held, also composed poetry which served as prayers for individuals to use at various stages in the history of the cult.

The impetus for this view has come almost entirely from Germany, and is in part again the result of comparisons with other ancient Near Eastern cultures (not least Babylon and Egypt) where similar cultic material, serving the needs of individuals, has been discovered. Various anthropological studies on the practice of folk-religion and on the importance of the *rites de passage* in more popular and familial circles, have also been influential: German scholars such as G. Fohrer (1967), E. Gerstenberger (1971, 1974, 1980), R. Albertz (1978), H. Vorländer (1975), J. Baumgartner (1979), and E. Conrad (1980) have popularized this view within Old Testament studies, although Gerstenberger and Albertz have been responsible for applying the theories of a more popular 'folk-culture' to studies of the psalms.

Although most of the (German) scholarly work dates from the 1960s, H. Schmidt applied these ideas to the psalms as early as 1927. Schmidt saw many of the more individually orientated psalms as compositions for individuals to use when falsely accused and unjustly brought to trial. C. F. Barth (1961) and W. Beyerlin (1970) proposed that a number of psalms which are preoccupied with the fear of death were ritual texts composed for those to use who had had an experience of near-death. In addition, L. Delekat (1967) and O. Keel (1969) each assessed the many individual psalms of lament which speak of personal isolation and individual distress and persecution, and in different ways they adduced these to be compositions of gifted poets for suppliants to use when they chose to take refuge from their persecutors in the sanctuary. By contrast, K. Seybold (1973) also examined those psalms which seem to suggest personal sickness and proposed that these were ritual texts—close to incantations—to be used against illness and sorcery.

As with the various views regarding the autumnal festival, not all these theories are mutually inclusive. Nevertheless, these scholars have shown that the category of individual lament cannot be subsumed (as proposed by Mowinckel) into a more public enthronement festival, on the grounds that the 'I' is a poetic means of personifying the cultic community. It is more than likely that, on the analogy of our own hymn-books and prayer-books, we can suppose the psalmists wrote for various kinds of cultic occasions—public and private—for use at all times in the liturgical year, and at all stages in Israel's history.

We are now in a position to list (with caution) the most obvious psalms which suggest the two different types of cultic occasion.

The first category consists of *psalms composed for cultic use by the whole community*: into this we may place the royal psalms (e.g. Pss. 2, 18, 20, 21, 45, 72, 89, 110, 132, 144), several early hymns (e.g. Pss. 29, 100, 114, 135), the hymns which speak of God's kingship (e.g. Pss. 47, 93, 96, 97, 98, 99), the psalms which speak of God's protection of Zion (e.g. Pss. 46, 48, 76, 87, 122), the psalms which may be part of some covenant festival (e.g. Pss. 50, 75, 81, 95), and liturgies which suggest some procession to the Temple (e.g. Pss. 15 and 24).

The second category concerns *psalms composed for cultic use by private individuals*: this list is notoriously difficult to ascertain, on account of the difficulty of knowing exactly when these psalms were written. We may include here those psalms which seem to speak of illness and near-death (e.g. Pss. 6, 13, 22, 30, 31, 38, 41, 69, 71, 88), and of individual isolation, and physical dangers (e.g. Pss. 7, 17, 25, 27, 35, 40, 56, 57, 142).

It should be apparent that this list includes less than half of the psalms in the Psalter. This is in part because there are still many other spiritualized and individual psalms, as well as other didactic poems. The list also excludes a mixed category of liturgical poetry which is impossible to date because of its composite nature.

So is there a way of understanding the poetry of the psalms which includes all the Psalter, whilst also giving due attention to the psalmists as poets? The fifth emphasis (which can be dated from about the 1970s onwards) is an interesting response to this dilemma.

E. The Psalmists as Poets of Life

The previous four emphases were each concerned with 'historicizing' or 'particularizing' the psalms, whether in the context of specific individual and communal experiences, or of more general public and private cultic occasions. In so doing, the primary emphasis was on the psalms as ancient texts, with a relevance only to the liturgical life of ancient Israel. Some scholars have attempted to find a radically alternative solution by reading the majority of psalms as private, non-cultic prayers, set apart from the mainstream of Israelite religion (for example, G. Quell (1926); A. Szörenyi (1961)); but this view has had little following. Another way forward was required; this had to be one which avoided reducing the relevance of the poetry to only one historical or cultic context, but rather allowed for it to be appropriated within any number of life-settings, on account of its typical and evocative nature.

It is evident therefore that any alternative reading should not only avoid being over-selective in its use of relevant psalms, but should also allow for the way in which a poem resonates with meaning beyond its original one.

Scholars who have attempted to write a 'theology' of the psalms have recognized and even partly overcome this problem, for if one looks at the psalms from a theocentric point of view as much as from an anthropocentric one, the abiding relevance of their substance is all too apparent—not only in terms of their theological ideas, but also in terms of their expressions of faith. H.-J. Kraus's *Theology of the Psalms* (1979; tr. 1986) is a good example of the work of a scholar with a predominantly cult-historical bias who nevertheless wrestles with the problem of the 'life-centredness' of the poetry beyond any one specific cultic context.

Similarly C. Westermann, a German scholar who, from the 1950s, has written several books and articles on this issue, has repeatedly made the point that, although many of the psalms point towards some particular 'worship-event', they also point (more significantly) towards a more generally understood 'life-event', whereby that which is common to their human experience is also common to 'everyman'. Westermann observes that in the cult-functional reading of the psalms:

This whole tendency to explain as many as possible or even all of the Psalms either by the 'ideology' of a specific (and only just discovered) festival, by a cultic schema, ... seems to me ... to have produced meagre results for the understanding of the individual Psalms. . . . In the Old Testament there is no absolute, timeless entity called 'cult', but that worship in Israel ... developed gradually in all its various relationships, those of place, of time, of personnel, and of instrumentality ... (*Praise and Lament in the Psalms*, 21.)

According to Westermann, the psalms are not only important literary poems about the individual or the nation (as presupposed in the historical-critical approaches); nor are they simply cultic texts applicable only to a pre-exilic cult (as understood in the cult-functional interpretations); they are also examples of prayerful reflection on life, and as such, they represent the two basic experiences of prayer—praise and lament. In this way, Westermann acknowledges the value of previous studies, noting that the psalms are literary poems, and that they are cultic texts, but that they also have broader horizons. As 'reflections on life', they encompass an infinite number of settings whereby, through their medium of poetry, all may share in their 'life-centredness'.

The American scholar W. Brueggemann maintains a similar view. Taking up terms used by a French scholar, Paul Ricœur, Brueggemann classifies the psalms according to 'the flow of human life' which is evident in each of them. Instead of Westermann's two poles of human experience, Brueggemann proposes three: first, poems of disorientation (mainly the laments, where the experience is of loss and oppression); second, poems of reorientation (mainly the thanksgivings, where the experience is of restoration and recovery); third, poems of orientation (the hymns, which centre on wholeness and well-being in the presence of God). Even where the psalmists have included more than one life-experience in a single psalm, one overall theme usually predominates. In his *Message of the Psalms* (1984), Brueggemann seeks to move beyond the constraints of earlier studies which approach the psalms primarily as ancient texts, attempting instead to discover an appropriate resonance in the meaning of the poetry in a life-setting which is relevant also today. This approach is close to that which was discussed in Chapter 1, in connection with a general appreciation of all poetry: we should read poetry not only by *looking at* it as text set within its own culture, but also by *looking through* it in terms of its contemporary meaning here and now.

This life-centred approach to the psalmists may be linked with our earlier discussions in two other ways. First, it enables us to see their performative value from a broader perspective: whereas Mowinckel's work dealt clearly with the performative nature of the psalms, it was still primarily concerned with their particular performance in the cultic life of Israel. A life-centred reading allows the psalms—like a score of music—to have innumerable performances beyond one ancient cultic setting.

Secondly (and perhaps most importantly) this life-centred reading reminds us again of the enigmatic nature of Semitic poetry. Just as it has proved difficult to define the poetry in terms of predeterminable metrical formulas, or even in terms of particular techniques of parallelism, so it is equally difficult to limit the origins and purpose of the poetry to one historical or cultic method of interpretation. Like all poetry, Hebrew poetry conceals as much as it reveals, and so creates for the interpreter both possibilities and limitations: and given the absence of explicit narrative contextualization for the psalms, psalmody in particular cannot be constrained by one interpretative method alone. Moreover, Hebrew poetry is essentially more spontaneous and responsive to situations: this was illustrated in our earlier discussions concerning the biblical songs of love, death, work, leisure, blessing, cursing, and war. Such poetry is first and foremost a response to life; although using clear poetic conventions, in terms of form as well as style, the early poets—the psalmists included—were not constrained by convention, and their poetry cannot be oversystematized and controlled.

In brief, we may conclude that each of the five emphases in psalmic studies reveals an important aspect in reading the psalms; but of the five, the life-centred approach offers the present-day reader the most scope and flexibility in a fuller appreciation of Hebrew poetry in its broadest sense. The following chapter will seek to apply this approach to a more detailed study of particular psalms.

9

The Psalms as Poems (I)

We have already observed the tension in Hebrew poetry between an adherence to tradition and an expression of originality: this was especially noticeable with regard to the use of metre and parallelism. Nowhere is this tension more evident than in the psalms. In part this is because of their 'life-centredness': being responsive as much to experience of life as to liturgical formulas, the psalmists have used conventional forms with a creative freedom.

Our earlier discussion of the use of metre in psalmody made reference to this tension. Although there is no unanimity amongst scholars as to what comprises an adequate metrical system for Hebrew poetry, several psalms appear to have a discernibly regular rhythm: relevant examples include Ps. 117, with a basic 3:3 stress (Ch. 3, pp. 58–9); Ps. 46, with a 4:4 stress (Ch. 3, pp. 59–60); Ps. 29, with a 2:2 stress (ch. 3, pp. 61–2); and Ps. 5, with a 3:2 stress (Ch. 3, pp. 62–3). Nevertheless, an overall survey of the psalms revealed that although some sort of fixed metre was evident in hymns (often 3:3) and another sort in the laments (often 3:2), this was by no means uniform throughout the entire Psalter. Very few psalms appeared to conform to any one clear metrical pattern.

The same ambiguities were evident in our assessment of the parallelism in the psalms. On the one hand, much Hebrew poetry does display a clear structure of short sentences arranged in pairs, with each couplet reflecting either an A = B, A > B, or A < B relationship: examples which were used earlier included Ps. 114: 1–2 (Ch. 4, pp. 69–70); Ps. 33: 6–7 (Ch. 4, pp. 79–80); and Ps. 29: 1–2 (Ch. 4, p. 81). On the other hand, there are many instances where the relationship between the two parts is less clearly balanced; for example, Pss. 23 and 122 demonstrate a complete breakdown in parallelism throughout (Ch. 4, pp. 75–7). Our observations concerning the enigmatic nature of some aspects of biblical parallelism (see Ch. 4, sect. B) are not far from the truth.

If a psalm does not follow the conventions of poetry in terms of any consistent balance of sound (the metre) or of any continuous balance of ideas (the parallelism), then the now-familiar question may again be posed: are the psalms to be read only as poetry? In some cases, the answer might well be in the negative: we have already noted a handful of psalms where the dividing-lines between prose and poetry are somewhat blurred, so that they could be read as continuous prose. Examples include Pss. 87 and 106, 103, and 136 (see Ch. 2, sect. D).

In this and the following chapter, we shall approach the way in which the psalms can be read as poetry from two different angles. Setting aside the issues of metre and parallelism, this chapter will assess (from a more aesthetic point of view) the use of *poetic devices* in psalmody. The first section will look at devices of a more *phonetic* nature, whereby the sound of the poem is a most significant characteristic, and the second section, devices of a more *semantic* nature, whereby the meaning of the poem is enhanced by the poetic techniques applied to the structuring of the language. In the following chapter, we shall examine (from the point of view of the function of the psalms) the different *poetic forms* which have been used—referring back to the basic poetic forms which we have already established within the narrative and prophetic literature, namely the hymns, laments, thanksgivings, and liturgies (see Ch. 7, sect. B).

Poetic Devices in the Psalms

(I) PHONETIC DEVICES

Even though a consistent metrical pattern is not always discernible, the psalmists were certainly interested in their poetry affecting the ear as well as the eye. Chapter 2 established twelve specific criteria for ascertaining Hebrew poetry: at least three of these were in part phonetic in nature. For example, we noted the use of rhyming— particularly in the use of suffixes, such as the third-person feminine plural -nâ and the first-person plural -nû, and in the first-person singular ending -î (Ch. 2, sect. B, pp. 25–6, with reference to Jer. 9: 18 and 12: 7). Or again, we noted the use of repetition, whereby a similar phrase was reiterated at the beginning or ending of a sequence to create a dramatic effect (see Ch. 2, sect. B, p. 26, with reference to Jer. 15: 2). Furthermore, we noted the use of tricola, again serving to create a dramatic emphasis through a different sort of repetition (see Ch. 2, sect. B, p. 27, with reference to Ps. 27: 14 and Ps. 24: 7, 9).

We shall return to these three examples shortly. Equally important in the psalms are variations of *plays on words*. This was discussed at the end of Chapter 1, in relation to a verse outside the Psalter. In Isa. 5, the word-play was twofold—the two similar-sounding words *mišpāṭ* (justice) and *mišpāḥ* (bloodshed) were set in contrast to each other, as also the pair *ṣᵉdāqâ* (righteousness) and *sᵉʿāqâ* (cry). This sort of word-play is often used for effect by the prophets, but it is also a recurrent feature in the psalms. There are at least five particular aspects of such word-play: *assonance* (a form of vowel repetition); *alliteration* (a form of consonant repetition); *onomatopoeia* (where the sound of a word imitates its meaning); *homonymy* (where words which are identical in sound are used with different meanings); and *polysemy* (whereby the same word is used with several meanings). Two or three examples from various psalms should serve to illustrate these effects in psalmody.

One example is found in Ps. 93: 4:

> Mightier than the thunders of many waters
> miqqōlôṯ mayim rabb*îm*
>
> Mightier than the waves of the sea
> ʿaddîr*îm* mišbᵉrê y*ām*
>
> The LORD on high is mighty!
> ʿaddîr bammār*ôm* ʾᵃḏōnay

Some assonance can be seen in the repetition of the vowel sounds such as *îm*; *ām*; *ôm* (as indicated in the italic type in the example above). Alliteration is seen in the repeated use of the consonants m, r, and y. Onomatopoeia is also evident; the sounds imitate the thundering of the waves and the roaring of the waters.

The preceding verse (Ps. 93: 3) offers similar interesting features:

> The floods have lifted up, O LORD,
> nāŝᵓû nᵉhārôṯ ᵓᵃḏōnay
>
> the floods have lifted up their voice,
> nāŝᵓû nᵉhārôṯ qôlām
>
> the floods lift up their roaring
> yiŝᵓû nᵉhārôṯ doḵyām

The assonance is evident in the different combination of vowel sounds—for example, the ā-û, and the ā-ô, and the ô-ā evident in each line. The alliteration is in the repeated 'n' sound in the first two lines. Onomatopoiea is discernible in the sonorous vowel sounds imitating the waves and waters. The 's' sound in the first word of each line might suggest the crashing of the surf. There is also some use of end-rhyme in the *ām* in the second and third lines, which suggests the continuous pounding of the waves on the shore.

Another example of assonance in Ps. 102: 6, in the ā-î-î sounds of each opening line:

> I am like a vulture of the wilderness
> dāmîṯî liḵᵓaṯ miḏbār
>
> like an owl of the waste-places
> hāyîṯî kᵉḵôs hᵃrābôṯ

Psalm 48: 7a also offers another example of assonance in the repeated use of the 'a' vowel, which again creates an onomatopoeic effect of the wind and the storm:

> By the east wind thou didst shatter the ships of Tarshish
> bᵉrûaḥ kāḏîm tᵉŝabēr ᵓŏnîyôṯ tarŝîŝ

Alliteration may be found in Ps. 127: 1, where the 'b' is a repeated device in the first couplet, and the 'š' in the second, with the contrast being between the key words bānâ = build and šāmar = guard:

> Unless the LORD builds the house
> ᵓim- ᵓᵃḏōnay lōᵓ-yiḇnê ḇayiṯ
>
> those who build it labour in vain.
> šāwᵉᵓ-ᶜāmᵉlû ḇônâw ḇô

Unless the LORD watches over the city
'im-ʾᵃḏōnay lōʾ-yišmor-ʿîr
the watchman stays awake in vain.
šāwᵉʾ šāqaḏ šômēr.

Psalm 46: 9 uses the 'q' and 'ts' alliteration effectively in its description of the shattering effects of God's warfare:

He makes the wars cease to the end of the earth;
mašbîṯ milḥāmôṯ ʿaḏ-qᵉṣēh hāʾāreṣ

he breaks the bow, and shatters the spear,
qešeṯ yᵉšabēr wᵉqiṣṣeṣ hᵃnîṯ.

Psalm 137 is full of phonetic devices, its beginning imitating musically the song of Zion which is the subject of the lament; the assonance is repeated in ā- and û- and î-sounds, and the alliteration in the 'a' and the ḇ sounds and in the end-rhyming -û; for example, see vv. 1–2:

By the waters of Babylon
ʿal-nahᵃrôṯ bāḇel

there we sat down and wept,
šām yāšaḇnû gam-bākînû

when we remembered Zion.
bᵉzokrēnû ʾeṯ-ṣîyôn

On the willows there
ʿal-ʿᵃrābîm bᵉṯôḵāh

we hung up our lyres
tālînû kinnōrôṯēnû

Onomatopoeia also is used to evoke the wailing typical of laments (See Chapter 2, pp. 25–6, on Jer. 9: 18 and 12: 7). This is evident in psalms such as 74 and 79. An entirely different type of onomatopoeia might be seen in Ps. 140: 3, where the 'š' sounds are used to imitate the hissing of the serpents:

They make their tongue sharp as a serpent's
šānᵉnû lešônām kᵉmô-nāḥāš

and under their lips is the poison of vipers.
ḥᵃmaṯ ʿaḵšûḇ taḥaṯ śᵉpāṯêymô.

Examples of homonymy are also frequent. A subtle example is found in Psalm 6: 10, where the play of words is between *bôš* 'to be ashamed' and *šûb̠* 'to turn':

All my enemies shall be ashamed and sorely troubled;
yēb̠ōšû w^eyibāh^alû m^{eʾ}od̠ kol-ʾoy^ebāy

they shall turn back, and be put to shame in a moment.
yāšub̠û yēb̠ōšû rāga^ʿ.

Psalm 76 offers another subtle interchange between two similar-sounding words, môrāʾ (= 'wrath') in v. 10, and nôrāʾ (= 'to be feared') in v. 11.

Psalm 5: 9 offers several examples of homonymy, one of which is clear even in translation. There is a pun on the word *qirb̠ām* (= 'their heart', from the root q–r–b) alongside a similar-sounding word *qeb̠er* (= 'open sepulchre', from the root q–b–r):

their heart is destruction,
qirb̠ām hawwôt̠

their throat is an open sepulchre,
qeb̠er-pāt̠ôaḥ g^eronām

Several of the above examples also demonstrate some use of rhyme. This is not as common a device in Hebrew poetry as we might expect. It is usually created by the use of the suffixes at the end of the lines: although in themselves these need not be a deliberate use of rhyme, the phonetic effect is nevertheless apparent.

If the above examples illustrate the use of phonetic devices in the shorter units and the line-forms, then the *refrains* show how this can extend over into the larger unit of the psalm, moving beyond two, three, or four line-forms (which create the stanzas) into larger groupings (forming strophes). Psalm 8 is a good example of this, with the refrain in vv. 1 and 9

O LORD, our Lord,
how majestic is thy name in all the earth!

framing the entire psalm. The refrain in Ps. 118: 1 and 29

O give thanks to the LORD, for he is good;
for his steadfast love endures for ever!

works in the same way. By contrast, Ps. 136 is entirely different, whereby the refrain

for his steadfast love endures for ever

is found in every half-verse. Other examples are in Pss. 49, 57, and 99, which all have two refrains (and hence two stanzas, one at the beginning and one after the first refrain), and in Pss. 42–3 and 46, with three refrains (and hence three stanzas), and in Pss. 59 and 80, with four refrains (and hence four stanzas). Slightly different are Pss. 39, 56, and 67, each with two refrains, but with three stanzas, and hence no concluding refrain. Of these examples, the refrains in Pss. 46 and 67 are also fixed compositions (as in Pss. 8, 118, and 136); those in Pss. 39, 42–3, 49, 57, and 59 occur with minor variations, whilst those in Pss. 56, 80, and 99 have considerable variations (Ps. 99 being in tricola form). The refrains give each of these psalms a more ordered structure, not only by way of division into stanzas but also through the repetition of sound. Another important observation is that refrains suggest antiphonal responses from the congregation. Nowhere is this more in evidence than in 2 Chr. 5: 13–14, where the refrain from Ps. 136 is clearly assumed to be part of the congregational response.

Finally, an assessment of phonetic devices also requires reference to the use of acrostics, where a psalm has been composed with the first letter in each line following a sequence, usually alphabetic. Sometimes these alphabetic patterns occur between one single line-form and another (as in Pss. 111 and 112), sometimes they occur in a more extended way, between one full verse and the next (as in Pss. 25 and 37), and sometimes they are found between every three verses (e.g. Lam. 1). In Ps. 119 the pattern is in the use of the same letter at the beginning of a line, repeated eight times in succession, followed by the eightfold use of the next letter of the alphabet creating another stanza. Another example, transliterated into the English form, is from Ps. 37, with the acrostic pattern running throughout the couplets:

> Agree not to fret yourself because of the wicked,
>   be not envious of wrongdoers!
> Be confident in the LORD, and do good;
>   so you will dwell in the land, and enjoy security.

> Commit your way to the LORD;
> trust in him, and he will act.
> Do not worry about the LORD's deeds,
> but wait patiently for him.

> (Taken from J. Hempel, *Interpreter's
> Dictionary of the Bible*, 953)

We might ask whether these were phonetic devices at all: were they intended for the ear, or more for the eye? Some would argue that it requires the written page to make full sense of the alphabetic patterns, but the trained listening ear would easily also pick up the repeated use of the same letter at the beginning of each line, as in Ps. 119. The repertoire within the acrostic form is often restrictive, and such limitations make it possible to discern the patterns with the ear as much as with the eye.

Much depends on how complex the acrostic forms were; the more complicated ones were probably composed for literary rather than liturgical purposes. These might include Pss. 111 and 112, which both use the full alphabet. Psalm 145 is similar, although this has one verse out of alphabetic sequence, so that the acrostic in the middle of the psalm runs as m–l–k, rather than k–l–m: this seems to be deliberate, for the word *melek* means king, and the psalm celebrates the kingship of God. Psalm 25 is also a complete acrostic, with forty-four lines: its unity is also created by various key words occurring throughout. Similarly, Ps. 34 has a clear, recurring pattern. Psalm 119 uses the full alphabet of twenty-two letters, with each letter repeated eight times in an eight-line stanza, so that the acrostic is $8 \times 22 = 176$ verses.

There are various psalms which do not complete the acrostic device from beginning to end. One example is Pss. 9–10. Psalm 9 starts with the first letter, *alep*, and ends with the second to the last letter, *reš*; Ps. 10 starts with the tenth letter, *lamed*, but ends on the last letter, *tet*. Several letters are missing, but it does seem that there is a linking alphabetic structure between the two psalms, which have undergone several disruptions through the process of transmission.

Several implications follow from this brief selection of phonetic devices. First, the fact that the psalmists composed with a concern for the *sound* of their poems may well suggest that there may be a greater adherence to *metre* than we might suppose; our problem is that we do not have all the rules to assess metre, and in addition, where the psalm is corrupt or composite, any discernible metrical pattern has broken down. At the very least, the phonetic element in psalmody shows that the sound of a psalm *was* important.

Two other factors confirm these observations. First, these same phonetic devices were employed also by the prophets, whose message (as we have noted in the previous chapter) was in part conveyed orally. Second, many of the above devices are also to be found in other ancient Near Eastern literature, for example, that of Babylon and Canaan, whose poetry was also conveyed in an oral context. Hence we can confirm again that psalmody was associated with a setting-in-life more than with a setting-in-literature.

(II) SEMANTIC DEVICES

The poetic devices with a concern for the balance of sense within a psalm have already been discussed in Chapter 2. They include the various sorts of word-pairs (pp. 24–5) the organizing of the balance of ideas into line-forms (p. 24) and the organizing of line-forms into different sorts of chiasmus or intensification of ideas within the poem as a whole (p. 27).

The psalms have already been used to illustrate word-pairing, whereby a balance of sense within two line-forms or more is evident. Psalm 30: 5 (pp. 24–5) illustrates well the balance of opposites:

> For *his anger* is but for *a moment*
> and his *favour* is for *a lifetime*.
> *Weeping* may tarry for *the night*
> but *joy* comes with *the morning*.

Similarly, Ps. 114: 1–2 illustrates the way word-pairs build up a balance of sense, and hence reflect some form of parallelism (Ch. 4, pp. 69–70):

> When *Israel* went forth from *Egypt*
> *the house of Jacob* from *a people of strange language*
> *Judah* became his *sanctuary*
> *Israel* his *dominion*.

So too Ps. 31: 10 uses the same repetitive pairing (Ch. 4, p. 70):

> For *my life* is spent *with sorrow*
> and *my years* with *sighing*;
> *my strength fails* because of my misery
> and *my bones waste away*.

Psalm 33: 6–7 also offers the same pattern of corresponding word-pairs in a slightly different sequence (Ch. 4, pp. 79–80):

> By *the word of the LORD the heavens* were made,
>
> and *all their host* by *the breath of his mouth*.
>
> He *gathered the waters of the sea* as in a *bottle*;
>
> he *puts the deeps* in *storehouses*.

Watson (*Classical Hebrew Poetry*, 128–44) offers an interesting classification of the different types of word-pairs which occur not only in the psalms, but also in the wisdom literature and in the prophets. Much of this classification echoes our own observations concerning parallelism: Watson's concluding observations concerning the reasons why a poet composed in this way, are most important. He suggests that word-pairs gave the poet assistance in composing verse—'a certain degree of freedom betokening mastery' (p. 140); that their reiteration enabled the audience to follow the meaning better through the process of repetition or expansion; and that the word-pairs enable the poem to cohere together in some semantic relation throughout.

Hence the greater the experimentation with word-pairs, the greater unity within the poem as a whole. Alter (*The Art of Biblical Poetry*, 62–84) sees this as a purposeful process of 'intensification' used by the Hebrew poets: it is a form of thinking and imaging by way of 'binary' thinking, sometimes using elaborate and complex comparisons, in which the underlying image occurs repeatedly in different ways. The same ideas are reinforced through a type of merismus, whereby smaller parts are referred to instead of the greater whole: for example, 'earth and waters' or 'land and sea' rather than 'world' or 'creation' or 'cosmos'. Word-pairs, balanced throughout whole phrases, weave their own pattern throughout the poem. Alter refers here to Gerard Manley Hopkins's sonnets as an illustration of the same technique in English poetry: a good example of this is the sonnet 'Justus quidem tu es, Domine', quoted in Chapter 1, p. 9.

Within the Psalter, Ps. 13 is a good example of this form of intensification by way of word-pairs:

v. 1 How long o LORD? Wilt thou forget me for ever?

How long wilt thou hide thy face from me?

v. 2 How long must I bear pain in my soul,

and have sorrow in my heart all the day?

v. 3 Consider and answer me, o LORD my God;

lighten my eyes, lest I sleep the sleep of death;

v. 4 lest my enemy say, 'I have prevailed over him';

lest my foes rejoice because I am shaken.

v. 5 But I have trusted in thy steadfast love;

my heart shall rejoice in thy salvation.

v. 6 I will sing to the LORD,

because he has dealt bountifully with me.

We may also note the threefold 'how long' in vv. 1–2, the threefold repetition in the imperatives of v. 3, the twice-repeated 'lest' in v. 4, and the final resolution of trust in v. 5: 'But I . . .'. We may note also the play on the word 'rejoice', used of the enemies in v. 4, in v. 5 by the psalmist addressing God.

Other psalms which could be read with a view to the same intensification include Pss. 39 and 54, and also (partly on account of their refrains) Pss. 42–3 and Ps. 8.

A further development is the use of *chiasmus* within a psalm. Again this involves the intensification of meaning through the repetition and reinforcement of images, but it also moves one stage further. The imagery is built up into a discernible series of ideas which leads up to a climax, which then is inverted so that the ideas follow one another in a reverse way, so that the ending of the psalm matches its beginning.

Psalm 136, with its refrain after each line-form which in itself intensifies the images between one colon and another, is a good example of this climactic movement, particularly in vv. 10–15:

> to him who smote the first-born of Egypt,
>> for his steadfast love endures for ever;
> and brought Israel out from among them,
>> for his steadfast love endures for ever;
> with a strong hand and an outstretched arm,
>> for his steadfast love endures for ever;
> to him who divided the Red Sea in sunder,
>> for his steadfast love endures for ever;
> and made Israel pass through the midst of it,
>> for his steadfast love endures for ever;
> but overthrew Pharaoh and his host in the Red Sea,
>> for his steadfast love endures for ever;

Similarly, Pss. 95: 1–7 and 105: 1–11 are good examples, whereby the choice of word-pairing also helps towards the effect of the chiasmus. Pss. 7, 15, 29, 30, 51, 59, 72, 137, and 139 also provide similar examples.

Another important issue concerns the way the psalmists use a store of *formulaic language* in their adaptation of the word-pairs: this creates another familiar traditional pattern within their poems. Yet this does not mean that the psalms are bound by tradition and convention alone: formulaic expressions can be the means whereby creative freedom is allowed proper expression within a given framework and order. Alter observers that through the 'complex ordering of language', and 'within the formal limits of a poem . . . the fine intertwinings of sound and image and reported act', the poet is able 'to give coherence and authority to his perceptions of the world' (p. 136). Seybold notes that despite the 'restricted language of verse' no two psalms display the same design; the conventions become the means of expression of originality (*Intro-ducing the Psalms*, 62–3).

These stock expressions have resulted in several scholarly surveys of the language of psalmody. For Mowinckel, formulaic language is the result of the poet adhering to traditional conventions, and it suggests good evidence of the cultic background of the psalms:

> What strikes us in the biblical psalms is the uniformity and formality which characterise them ... Imagery and phraseology are often the stereotyped ones ... The set formality of the psalms can only be explained on the basis that they are not primarily meant to be personal effusions, but are, in accordance with their type and origin, ritual lyrics. (*The Psalms in Israel's Worship*, i. 30–1.)

Similarly, M. Tsevat, in *A Study of the Language of the Biblical Psalms*, offers a statistical assessment of the pervasiveness of formulaic words and phrases within the psalms, in order to demonstrate that psalmody has a distinctive tradition of language which the poets drew from; one hundred and fifty examples are given of expressions which occur three or more times in the psalms but nowhere else in the Bible. In a similar assessment entitled *Oral Formulaic Language in the Biblical Psalms*, R. B. Culley examines almost two hundred formulaic expressions, and concludes that at least twenty-six psalms are up to 40 per cent formulaic. Nevertheless, Culley still observes that in a long tradition of stock expressions, alongside this 'general stability' there is still 'considerable freedom and variety' (p. 100).

Culley's assessment is helpful in that it clarifies those psalms which best fit a formulaic category. Six of his examples are hymns: Ps. 100 (35 per cent); Ps. 111 (27 per cent); Ps. 135 (57 per cent—in part due to correspondences with Ps. 115); Ps. 96 (65 per cent—in vv. 1, 2, 3, 4, 7–9, 10, 11, 12); Ps. 97 (42 per cent in vv. 1, 2, 3, 4, 6, 8, 9, 12); and Ps. 98 (50 per cent—in vv. 1, 3, 4, 5, 7, 9). Most of the other examples are from laments, or lament forms within composite psalms: these include Ps. 79 (33 per cent—the only communal lament); and in individual laments, Pss. 6 (48 per cent—in vv. 2, 3, 5, 8, 9, 10, 11); 28 (26 per cent); 31 (40 per cent); 35 (24 per cent); 54

(53 per cent—in vv. 3, 4, 5, 8); 61 (35 per cent); 71 (36 per cent); 86 (49 per cent—in vv. 1, 2, 3, 4, 6, 11, 12, 13, 14, 15, 16); 120 (21 per cent); 142 (65 per cent—in vv. 2, 4, 5, 6, 7, 8); and 143 (60 per cent—in vv. 1, 3, 4, 5, 7, 8, 9, 10, 11, and 12); in lament forms in other psalms, examples include Ps. 27: 7–14 (40 per cent); Ps. 9: 2–15 (42 per cent); and Ps. 40: 13–18 (50 per cent, due in part to correspondences with Ps. 35).

Although this list is a very small proportion of the entire Psalter, there are of course other psalms with a lesser number of such expressions: the argument that the psalmists drew from a traditional store of expressions of faith and liturgy is a convincing one.

The formulaic language of psalmody might be seen to fall into six distinct categories. First are the *descriptions of the psalmist's enemies*: they are referred to frequently as 'workers of inquity' (*poʿălê ʾāwen* is a term which may be connected with the casting of spells, as in sorcery) as in Pss. 6: 8; 28: 3; 59: 2; and 141: 4. The enemies are also referred to as beasts: cf. Pss. 7: 2; 10: 9; 22: 13; 35: 17; 57: 4; and 58: 6; as liars, as in Pss. 10: 7; 12: 2; 27: 2; 36: 3; 41: 7; 52: 4; 55: 9; 59: 3; and 69: 4; as schemers, as in Pss. 14: 6; 52: 2; 31: 13; and 140: 4; as false witnesses, as in Pss. 27: 12; 35: 11; and 64: 5; as persecutors, as in Pss. 7: 1; 17: 10; 35: 2; 56: 6; and 143: 3; and as murderers, as in Pss. 38: 12; 40: 14; 59: 3; 69: 21; 70: 2; and 94: 21.

A second category of formulaic language is that of the *descriptions of the psalmist's plight*. Sometimes this is expressed in actual physical terms, such as weeping (Pss. 6: 6; 88: 9; 102: 9), aching (Pss. 6: 2; 22: 14–15; 31: 10; 38: 3; 63: 1; 69: 2; 109: 23–4; 116: 3; 141: 3), and groaning (Pss. 22: 1; 32: 3–4; 38: 8ff.; 102: 5). At other times it is expressed in more metaphorical imagery, such as being caught in the snares of death (Pss. 13: 3; 18: 4, 5; 28: 1; 30: 9; 40: 2; 55: 4; 88: 3; 102: 23) and drowning in deep waters (Pss. 18: 16; 32: 6; 42: 7; 69: 1ff.; 88: 7).

A third category is that of the *addresses to God in complaint or praise*: sometimes these occur in calls upon God's name (Pss. 38: 21; 52: 9; 57: 2; 66: 2; 75: 1; 143: 11), or thanksgivings for refuge and protection (Pss. 3: 3; 9: 9; 16: 5; 18: 2, 46; 27: 5; 31: 2; 32: 7; 59: 9; 61: 2–3; 62: 2; 144: 2), or pleas for God to hear (Pss. 3: 7; 7: 6; 9: 9; 10: 12; 17: 13; 44: 23; 59: 4), or praise for God's steadfast love (Pss. 17: 7; 21: 7; 25: 10; 42: 8; 62: 11; 63: 3; 69: 16; 89: 2; 138: 8).

Three further categories are also discernible, although here many of the expressions occur more frequently elsewhere. The first is *instructional advice*, which is associated also with the teaching in wisdom and law: phrases such as 'speaking the truth', 'seeking God', 'doing no evil', 'fearing the LORD', 'trusting' and 'waiting upon' God, 'considering the poor', are common. Another type is of *descriptions about God's theophany*. Much of this takes up the mythological and archetypal imagery found in hymns from Babylon and Canaan: examples include the earth reeling and shaking, God's appearing in thunder, on the clouds, in thick darkness, with lightnings, through the seas and deep, God fighting for his people, and his dwelling on his holy mountain. A final category concerns the *descriptions of Yahweh's judgement*. Many of these are also used by the prophets; for example, God sitting in the heavens, judging the peoples, seated in his holy temple, looking down from heaven, ruling over the nations, delivering Zion, maintaining the cause of the afflicted, and executing justice for the needy.

Within these categories, formulaic expressions appropriate the language of metaphor and simile. God is addressed in impersonal terms, such as rock, fortress, refuge, defence, stronghold, dwelling-place, habitation, and shield (cf. Pss. 3: 3; 7: 10; 18: 2, 30, 35; 27: 1; 31: 2, 4, 20; 32: 7; 43: 2; 52: 7; 59: 11; 61: 4; 71: 3; 84: 11; 91: 1, 2; 114: 2; 115: 9, 10, 11; 144: 2). He is also portrayed more personally as king (47: 8; 93: 1; 96: 10; 97: 1; 99: 1), shepherd (23: 1; 80: 2), farmer (80: 8, 12), craftsman (8: 4), father (68: 5; 89: 26; 103: 13), warrior (68: 1–2, 21–3; 89: 10), and mother (131: 2). The sufferings expressed in the laments are similarly rich in figurative language. For example, not only is the animal kingdom used to refer to the enemies (not least in the curses), but the psalmists often express their own sufferings in animal images—the worm (22: 6), the owl (102: 6–7), the deer (42: 1), and the grasshopper (109: 23). Perhaps most striking is the use of metaphor (often culled from mythological motifs of other cultures of the ancient Near East) to personify creation: the mountains are called upon to help and to bear witness (68: 15–16); the floods clap their hands (98: 8); the mountains skip like rams (114: 4); the sun comes out like a bridegroom (19: 6). These examples (also used with striking skill in the prophets, especially in second Isaiah) offer a sense of the 'animation' of creation responding in praise before God.

Both formulaic and figurative expressions (and often the two are the same, as may be seen above) offer the poet two important ways of using language. On the one hand, such expressions are sufficiently general and ambiguous to be used in a typical and archetypal way: they thus allow the psalm repeated use. Yet on the other hand, these expressions are an important vehicle for the psalmist's particular situation of distress or joy. Through the particular and the 'autobiographical', personal appropriation is possible. There are not many specific allusions in the psalms, but where they occur, they are usually also couched in formulaic and figurative language, for this becomes a means of structuring a situation of chaos and ordering the particular pain. Examples from the communal laments include Pss. 74: 4–8, 9; 79: 1–4; 83: 5–8, 9–12; and 137: 1–3; from the individual laments, Pss. 22: 7–8, 16–18; 31: 6, 11–13; 35: 11–16; 42: 4–6; 51: 4, 10–12; 55: 12–15, 20–1; 69: 7–8, 9–12, 21, 22; 71: 6, 9, 18; 120: 2, 5–7; and 141: 5–6; and from other individual psalms, Pss. 16: 4; 27: 7–10; 40: 6–8; and 41: 8–9.

In this way, the poet's deliberate choice of poetic devices, whether of a phonetic or a semantic kind, becomes the means of holding together the typical and the personal, the general and the specific. Even the use of a store of traditional language allows the poets to combine together the familiar and conventional with personal appropriation. This is the genius of the psalms: their poetry speaks the language of every person, because it mirrors not only the general and the typical, but also the particular and the specific.

The Psalms as Poems (II)

Poetic Forms in the Psalms

The previous chapter demonstrated how the psalms are expressions of what might be called the 'fixed' and the 'free' in their use of various poetic devices. This is also evident in the use of poetic forms.

Scholars such as Mowinckel, who saw the language of the psalms in a more fixed and formulaic way, placed great weight on the 'fixed' nature of the forms:

We have to do with the fixed style forms, where the similarities between the individual pieces within the group ... [are due] to the fixity of a traditional and conventional style ... Poetry, then exists ... with its own special rules as to content and form. (*The Psalms in Israel's Worship*, i. 25.)

According to Mowinckel, it was therefore possible to classify the forms of the psalms in the same way that one might with a study of botany—using 'objective criteria' as one would with the 'form and number of stamens, petals and sepals' (ibid. 25). Mowinckel took Gunkel's form-critical classification much further than his mentor. Gunkel frequently acknowledged exceptions to the rule: an obvious one was the royal psalms, which offered no consistent form. In their case, the family likeness was according to content, mood, and cultic setting. Similar exceptions were admitted in the case of psalms with composite elements, or with textual dislocations. Gunkel's categorization was without doubt a complex process (two major types and at least five minor ones, with other anomalous categories as well) but he always maintained that any form-critical classification required a certain amount of flexibility: the *contents* are as important as the *form*. Mowinckel's studies on the forms of the psalms hence tightened up a process which Gunkel had allowed to be much more open and free.

It is possible to reject altogether the classification of the psalms by their genre: this would involve assessing every psalm on its own merits, rather than trying to categorize it into a larger whole. For example, a Hungarian scholar, A. Szörenyi, has written a lengthy disputation in German showing that the supposed 'form' ascribed to many of the psalms suggests rather fragmentation and decay. By taking Gunkel's maxim that the contents of the psalm are also important, Szörenyi concludes that the contents are *more* important than the form, or structure: there is no such thing as a 'conventional form' in psalmody.

Assessments such as those of Szörenyi raise questions about a thoroughgoing form-critical analysis of the psalms. Not only Mowinckel's overconfidence, but also Gunkel's own assumptions, are in need of modification. For example, Gunkel supposed it was possible to trace a history of development of the forms; he assumed that shorter, more simple psalms were necessarily earlier than longer, more complex ones, and that communal psalms preceded the individual ones, and that thanksgiving forms were more primitive than the laments. Szörenyi's work shows that it seems more likely that the psalmists exercised the same freedom and creativity with forms as they did with other poetic devices. Any rigid theory of classification and history of development is bound to fail because of elements such as fragmentation, decay, expansions, and personal creativity in so many of the psalms.

It is nevertheless possible to use Gunkel's fundamental classification with some modifications. We may start with his suggestion of two basic forms, each discernible on account of a similar style, structure, content, and mood, to which all other various types are in some way related. These two forms are the hymns of praise and the prayers of lament. (Note that this suggestion has also been taken up by Westermann and Brueggemann, referred to in Ch. 8, pp. 186–9.) There is enough evidence from other literature in the ancient Near East to indicate that a theory of two major psalmic forms holds good: scholars such as F. Stummer, G. Castellino, G. Widengren, A. Falkenstein, and W. von Soden have enabled us to see that the biblical hymns correspond in form to several known Babylonian and Egyptian hymns, and similarly the biblical laments have many associations with the Babylonian laments.

The following assessment will therefore focus on the two basic psalmic types. We have already noted the predominant use of hymns and laments (as well as some of the derivations) within other parts of the biblical literature (see Ch. 6, pp. 140 ff.), and these observations will be drawn into the discussion. (For an overview of the occurrence of the various forms throughout the entire Psalter, see the Appendix at the end of this chapter.)

(I) THE HYMNS

We have already seen how fragments of hymnody may be traced back as early as settlement times (e.g. Exod. 15; Judg. 5), into the time of the monarchy (e.g. Deut. 32; Hab. 3; also the hymns of Zion in Isa. 2 and Mic. 4) as well as the time of the exile (e.g. the doxologies in Amos, and the hymns of creation in Isa. 40–55). Hymnody was also used in the late restoration period, as seen in the Chronicler (?fourth century BCE: see 1 Chr. 16) and the wisdom literature (e.g. Prov. 8, 30; and Job 28; Dan. 2: 20–3; 4: 3; and 6: 26–7). The hymnic language used to speak of God's kingship within Dan. 7 points also to the use of hymnody as late as the second century BCE. Given such a vast time-span (of some eight hundred years) for the composition and adaptation of the hymnic forms, it is clearly impossible to date with any certainty the hymns within the Psalter. Some may well belong to the early monarchy; several may well pertain to the time of the divided kingdom; and many more clearly come from the time of the exile and restoration.

The hymns within the Psalter follow, in the most general terms, a very simple threefold form. The introduction is a call to praise; the middle section gives the reasons for the praise; and the conclusion usually returns to the initial call to praise. There are some thirty examples (8, 29, 33, 100, 103, 104, 111, 113, 114, 117, 135, 136, 145, 146, 147, 148, 149, 150, 47, 93, 96, 97, 98, 99, 46, 48, 76, 87, 122, 78, 105) and all but eight are found in the latter part of the Psalter. Psalm 117, the briefest psalm in the Psalter, offers a good illustration of this structure:

> Praise the LORD, all nations!
> Extol him, all peoples!
>
> For great is his steadfast love toward us;
> and the faithfulness of the LORD endures for ever.
>
> Praise the LORD!

A further clear example is found in Ps. 113: vv. 1–3 are the call to praise; vv. 4–9 the reasons for the praise; and v. 9c the conclusion.

The Hebrew word for 'song of praise' is *tᵉhillâ*. In Hebrew, the whole Psalter is called *seper tᵉhillîm* (a masculine plural for a feminine singular noun—a title curiously reserved only for the Psalter) which means 'Book of Praises'. Yet only about one-fifth of the Psalter merits this classification, and only one psalm (145) is actually classified as such. The title of the Psalter may have been used in this way because the verb h–l–l (meaning 'praise') occurs with such frequency throughout the psalms; it may also be that, because most of the hymns of praise are found in the latter half of the Psalter, this was to signify the major note which ends the collection: a paean of praise (see especially Pss. 146–50).

We noted above that there were several ancient Near Eastern correspondences with the hymns of praise. Three examples will be given, all of which occur in the few hymns in the first part of the Psalter and all of which accordingly may well be earlier than the exile.

The first example has already been referred to on pp. 61–2 and 81 on account of its *Canaanite* correspondences: this is Ps. 29, which echoes an ancient Canaanite hymn to Baʻl-Hadad, the weathergod. This psalm celebrates God as Creator through his power and majesty expressed in the storm; the imagery of the sevenfold voice of God coming through the clouds, and the references to the cedars of Lebanon and Sirion (from which the temple of Baʻl was built) echo the same ideas as the Canaanite hymn.

The second example is Ps. 19A. In this case, two hymns have been later placed together: 19A (vv. 1–6) is an independent hymn praising God's order through nature, and 19B (vv. 7–13, 14) is a separate hymn celebrating God's order by his giving of the law.

Part of Ps. 19A (vv. 4c–6) is a hymn of praise to the sun; the imagery here (of the sun as a bridegroom emerging out of a 'tabernacle', or 'marriage tent' to circle the earth in the daylight hours) has many associations with Babylonian hymns praising the sun-god Shamesh (the Hebrew word for sun, *šemeš*, suggests further affinities), who was also known as the 'lordly hero' or the 'strong man' (cf. v. 5). The difference in the Hebrew hymn is that praise is offered to God as Creator of the sun, rather than to the sun itself.

The third example is Ps. 104, which has several correspondences (very clearly in vv. 20–30) with the Egyptian Hymn to Aton (the sun-god), which is attributed to Pharaoh Akhenaten, who in the fourteenth century BCE established a new monotheistic cult in Egypt which worshipped only the sun-disc. The difference in Ps. 104 is that God's providence extends beyond the daylight hours: Israel's God rules over the night as well.

The common theme within each of these three hymns is the praise of God in creation—a theme which doubtlessly would have many more counterparts in the ancient world. The two other hymns found in the first part of the Psalter similarly take up this theme: Ps. 8 (much more distinctly Israelite) celebrates God as Creator, but not only of the entire cosmos, but also of all human life:

> When I look at the heavens, the work of thy fingers,
>   the moon and the stars which thou hast established;
> what is man that thou art mindful of him,
>   and the son of man that thou dost care for him?

(Ps. 8: 3–4)

There are obvious links here with Gen. 1, which celebrates God's creating of the universe—the sun, moon, and stars—and ends with God's creating of humankind. In this case, the time after the exile (possibly contemporaneous with the priestly writer of Gen. 1) might be a possible date. Similarly Ps. 33 is another psalm, possibly later, apparently inspired more by wisdom-hymns such as we have seen in the book of Job. Here the praise focuses on the providence of God throughout all creation:

> For he spoke, and it came to be;
>   he commanded, and it stood forth.

The LORD brings the counsel of the nations to nought;
  he frustrates the plans of peoples.

(Ps. 33: 9–10)

Other hymns combine the theme of praise of God as Creator
with praise for his care throughout various stages in Israel's history.
Here the praise is often more specific; its style is very close to that
of narrative (indeed, two of these psalms have been referred to
earlier on account of their 'prosaic' style). It might be termed more
'declarative' praise, rather than 'descriptive' praise (so, Westermann). The best examples are Pss. 114 (God's 'parting of the sea'),
and 135 and 136: the last has an antiphonal refrain throughout ('for
his mercy endures for ever'), as one act of deliverance after another
is recalled. Such hymns may well reflect a situation before the
restoration, when Israel became increasingly conscious of her own
particular history.

Two other examples, often categorized separately as 'historical
psalms', may be added here, in that they also reflect the same
hymnic structure. Psalm 78 is a long recitation of God's goodness to
Israel from the Exodus until the founding of Zion: it suggests a pre-
exilic date when the Solomonic Temple was still standing (v. 69)
and when the concern with the fate of the northern kingdom was
still an issue (v. 67). Psalm 105 has a more expansive view of history,
recounting God's providence from the time of Abraham, Isaac, and
Jacob, through the sojourn in Egypt under Joseph, the time of
slavery in Egypt, the plagues, the escape, the wilderness wander-
ings, and the settlement in Canaan: it suggests a knowledge of the
priestly account in Genesis–Exodus, and may thus be much later
than Ps. 78.

Several other permutations of the hymnic form are evident: Ps.
145 is a hymn reflecting on the greatness of God, set out in an
acrostic form; Ps. 100 serves as a liturgy, possibly used as a sixfold
processional hymn, sung alternately by choir and congregation:
'the Lord is God; / he is Creator; / Israel is his people; / the Lord is
good; / his mercy is everlasting; / his faithfulness endures to all
generations.' Finally, the hymns in Pss. 146–50 cohere as a unity
with their 'Hallelu'—'Praise the Lord'—at the beginning and end.
These hymns are all impossible to date with any certainty.

Two derivations of these general hymns of praise are also evident. The first is a collection of hymns celebrating the kingship of God, enthroned in the heavens, ruling over heaven and earth. They have been called 'kingship hymns', and include Pss. 47, 93, and 96–9. These hymns may have some connection with a possible autumnal 'enthronement' festival (as discussed in Ch. 7, pp. 167–9, with particular reference to Mowinckel). If this is the case, then they must date from the time of the monarchy. Brief reference has also been made to the use of similar 'kingship hymns' in second Isaiah (40: 21–3; 44: 6–8; 49: 22–6; 51: 4–6: see Ch. 7, p. 168), suggesting that earlier themes were developed by this prophet in the exile. The kingship hymns have a vision which extends beyond God's providence only in the cosmos, or among the nations, or throughout history, or within each human life: the focus is on a heavenly throne, rather than an earthly one, and on an eternal rule, rather than a temporal one. Such psalms could reflect the turbulent times of the monarchy, as they also could the days of the exile, when all that remained of the hope in kingship was the rule of God above:

> The LORD reigns; let the peoples tremble!
> He sits enthroned upon the cherubim; let the earth quake!
>
> (Ps. 99: 1)

> God reigns over the nations;
> God sits on his holy throne.
>
> (Ps. 47: 8)

The second derivation is a corollary of the first. In these psalms God is praised not for his eternal, all-embracing heavenly rule, but for his specific, particular rule in Zion, 'the city of God'. The hymns in this category are usually known as the 'Zion hymns', and they are scattered throughout the Psalter (Pss. 46; 48; 76; 84; 87; 122). They were probably used as pilgrimage psalms, in a similar way to the collection called the 'Songs of Ascents' (Pss. 120–34), sung by pilgrims going up to the Temple in Jerusalem. Their common theme is God's world-rule from Zion, and his presence among his people who worship there:

> Great is the LORD and greatly to be praised
> in the city of our God!

His holy mountain, beautiful in elevation,
   is the joy of all the earth.

(Ps. 48: 1–2)

The 'Zion hymns' probably were known during the time of the
monarchy: during the time of exile, these hymns were apparently
sung in the hope of some return:

By the waters of Babylon,
   there we sat down and wept,
when we remembered Zion.
On the willows there
   we hung up our lyres.
For there our captors required of us songs,
   and our tormentors, mirth, saying,
'Sing us one of the songs of Zion!'

(Ps. 137: 1–3)

As to a possible date for the hymns, we may surmise that those
with ancient Near Eastern correspondences may well be among the
earliest (e.g. Pss. 29; 19A; 104). The kingship hymns and the Zion
hymns similarly suggest the time of the monarchy. Others reflect
later times during and after the exile. The difficulty of dating any
hymns with precision means that it is impossible to move from
'form' (establishing a psalm as a hymn) to one 'cultic setting' (for
example, the autumnal festival).

We now return to the issue of the so-called 'distinctive forms' of
these hymns. The most clear examples of hymns following the
threefold structure outlined above are Pss. 8, 29, 113, 117, 136, and
147, and also Pss. 97 and 99. Of the others, Pss. 33, 103, 104, 111, 145,
146, 148, 149, and 150 are also broadly typical, although several
verses do not fit any apparent hymnic pattern, using instead expressions of confidence and pleas for help (e.g. Ps. 33: 20–2) or didactic
expressions (e.g. Ps. 111: 10; 122: 6–9; 146: 3–5), or changing the
form of address from the second to the third person (e.g. Ps. 145:
4–13a, 13b–20). Other hymns are less typical still—Pss. 100, 148,
149, and 150 are simply extended calls to praise throughout, without middle or conclusion. Psalms 93, 48, and 76, by contrast, are
more a collection of reasons for praise, without explicit calls to do

so. Psalm 114 is also unusual, as it has no obvious introduction, but does have an apparent final call to praise in vv. 7–8, followed by further reasons for doing so. A similar interplay between 'calls to praise' and 'reasons to praise' is found in Pss. 47, 96, and 98. Psalm 87 is distinctive, comprising a collection of oracular material.

It would appear again that poetic conventions were adapted freely. That a 'form' of hymn existed is clear: but few poets felt entirely bound even by a relatively simple structure. One important implication follows from this: if a clear, consistent form is not always discernible, then a clear cultic setting in which such a form would have been used cannot always be presupposed. (This fits with our observations above regarding the various dates and provenances for the hymns.) Again, we cannot move from ascertaining form to determining a particular cultic setting: the hymns have emerged from many and various stages in Israel's liturgical life, and their precise setting must remain unknown. Their theme of praise in God as Creator and sustainer may well suggest a use at one of the three major festivals in the year, but precisely which festival, and with precisely what ritual, and by precisely which Temple personnel, are not at all clear.

(II) THE LAMENTS

Our earlier discussion of the lament forms (Ch. 7, pp. 149 ff.) showed how these were used by the eighth- and seventh-century prophets both in parody and as genuine expressions of grief and complaint. The lament occurred in both a communal form (e.g. Jeremiah and Lamentations) and in an individual form (e.g. Jeremiah's 'Confessions'). It was also found in the restoration period (frequently so in the book of Job). From its prevalence in the biblical literature outside the Psalter, it is probable that the lament form was as old and pervasive as the hymn: the two genres, one concerned with complaint and the other with praise, rightly expressed the polarities of Israel's experience from the first Temple to second Temple periods.

The structure of the lament form is more complicated than that of the hymn. The introduction is usually a call on the name of God. The middle section has several variations, but can comprise some or all of the following parts: a description of need, which serves as the heart of complaint, where the subject is either 'I' or 'We', or 'They' (the enemies) or 'You' (God); a request for help, often set in the imperative form (e.g. 'Hear', 'Arise'); reasons why God should hear and answer the suppliant; and affirmation of trust in God—often recalling previous acts of deliverance. The conclusion ends with a vow to offer praise or sacrifice once the prayer is answered.

A good example from a psalm using the 'I' form is Ps. 22: v. 1*a* ('My God . . .') is the address; vv. 2–18 is the description of distress, using 'I' (vv. 2, 6, 14–15, 17*a*), 'Thou' (v. 1*b*), and 'They' (vv. 7–8, 12–13, 16, 17*b*–18); vv. 1 and 19–21 are two requests for help; vv. 3–5 and 9–10 the affirmations of trust in God; and vv. 22–31 the vow to praise God when the crisis is over.

An example of a psalm using the 'We' form is Ps. 44. Verse 1 is the address; vv. 9–14, 22, 25 are the descriptions of distress, using both 'We' (vv. 22, 25) and 'Thou' (vv. 9–14); vv. 23 and 26 form the requests for help; vv. 1–7 are the affirmations of trust in God; and the vow to praise is in 44: 8.

From these two examples it is clear that the structure exists to be changed in innumerable ways; even the (supposedly) concluding vow can occur in the middle of the psalm (44: 8). The lament is recognizable because it contains *some* of the above elements, in *any* sort of sequence. (Sometimes when the recalling of previous acts of deliverance predominates, the psalm becomes more a psalm of thanksgiving; and when the affirmation of trust predominates, it becomes more a psalm of confidence: these two derivations will be dealt with shortly.)

The corresponding Hebrew word for 'lament' is *t^epillâ*, or prayer. Interestingly, there are more 'laments' than 'praises': there are at least forty individual laments and perhaps sixteen communal ones (see the appendix at the end of the chapter for a proposed list) but nevertheless the more positive term *t^ehillîm* (praises) became that by which the Psalter was known.

As with the hymns, we may note several ancient Near Eastern counterparts, mostly from Babylonian and Akkadian material. The differences mainly concern the greater adherence of these to the structure outlined above, with the addition of hymnic elements.

Just as the hymns recalled various themes (God as Creator, sustainer of Israel's history, king of heaven and earth, protector of Zion), so too the laments suggest several different emphases and needs. Through the formulaic and figurative expressions which comprise a large part of them, a situation of distress is usually discernible. These may be more national concerns, such as failure in war (44: 9–12; 60: 1–3; 108: 10–13), or the destruction of the sanctuary, probably referring to the events of 587 BCE (74: 3, 7–8; 79: 1–4), or conspiracies by the nation's enemies (83: 5), or exile (137: 1–6). They may also suggest more individual concerns, such as illness (31: 9–10; 38: 3 ff., 10–11; 41: 3 ff., 8 ff.), or death (6: 4–5; 13: 3–4; 22: 6–8, 14 ff.; 39: 4 ff.; 69: 15; 71: 9, 18; 88: 4 ff.; 143: 3), or physical dangers of a personal nature (7: 1–2; 17: 10–12; 25: 19–20; 27: 2, 12; 35: 1 ff.; 40: 13–15; 54: 3; 55: 3 ff., 10 ff.; 56: 1 ff.; 57: 4, 6; 59: 3–4; 62: 3–4; 64: 3 ff.; 69: 4 ff., 22; 71: 4; 86: 14 ff.; 109: 2 ff.; 140: 1–5; 142: 1–4). Obviously it is not always possible to 'read through' the allusions and to determine with certainty the precise situation within a psalm. In some cases there may be several possible interpretations, whereby the reading of the 'I' form need not assume an individual, but rather the entire community (as is evident with the 'I' form in some of the communal laments, for example 44: 4–8; 60: 5–12;//108: 7–13; 94: 16–23; 106: 4–7 and 123: 1–4). The 'I' might even be the king: this is more clearly the case in royal psalms with a lament form (such as 2, 18, 89: 38 ff., 144) and with several of the individual laments (e.g. 22, 55, 61, 69, 102, 143), where the more personal allusions to 'the enemies' and dangers could describe more metaphorically the whole community's distress. Furthermore, even if the 'I' form genuinely refers to a personal need, there is no clear way of determining whether this implies the composition of a gifted cultic poet writing a liturgical prayer for 'every person', or the prayer of one individual in a particular situation of need, rather like the Confessions of Jeremiah. As we noted in Ch. 7, scholars have offered various ideas for the context of these so-called individual laments—whether these are ritual texts to be offered by those suffering from evil spells or sorcery, or by those seriously ill, or by those unjustly accused, is most unclear. (On this issue, see Ch. 8, pp. 184 ff., and the summary by J. Day, *Psalms*, 19–38.)

These laments suggest at least three basic derivations: their use by the *community*; their use by various *individuals* in need; and their use by the *king*, or by the leader of the community (this would include both communal and individual laments, and also a number of royal psalms). Three examples, one to represent each type, should illustrate clearly different concerns:

O God, why dost thou cast us off for ever?
    Why does thy anger smoke against the sheep of thy pasture?

Remember thy congregation, which thou hast gotten of old,
    which thou hast redeemed to be the tribe of thy heritage!
Remember Mount Zion, where thou hast dwelt.

Direct thy steps to the perpetual ruins;
    the enemy has destroyed everything in the sanctuary!

                      (Communal lament—Ps. 74: 1–3)

O LORD, my God, I call for help by day;
    I cry out in the night before thee.
Let my prayer come before thee,
    incline thy ear to my cry!

For my soul is full of troubles,
    and my life draws near to Sheol.
I am reckoned among those who go down to the Pit;
    I am a man who has no strength,
like one forsaken among the dead,
    like the slain that lie in the grave,
like those whom thou dost remember no more,
for they are cut off from thy hand.

                      (Individual lament—Ps. 88: 1–5)

But now thou hast cut off and rejected,
    thou art full of wrath against thy anointed.
Thou hast renounced the covenant with thy servant;
    thou hast defiled his crown in the dust.
Thou hast breached all his walls;
    thou hast laid all his strongholds in ruins.

                      (Royal lament—Ps. 89: 38–40)

We return again to the issue of the so-called 'distinctive forms' of the laments. We have already noted that their complex structure offers greater variations for the poet than does that of the hymn. The following outline illustrates well the creative freedom of the Hebrew poets.

In the communal laments, we may note the several unusual changes in mood in Pss. 77, 106, and 126—sometimes created by expressions of confidence, at others by unexpected calls to praise (106: 1, 2–3). Psalm 79 starts with the description of distress, and moves then into appeals to God for help. Psalm 82 starts with an oracle, and ends with an invocation, having no obvious description of distress.

Of the individual laments, several have unusual endings. Psalm 12 ends with a description of distress (v. 13). Psalm 36 ends with appeals for help (vv. 11–13), as does also Ps. 38 (an acrostic) in vv. 21–2. Psalm 59 ends with two descriptions of distress after two earlier expressions of confidence (vv. 7–8, 9–11, 15–16, 17–18). Psalm 86 similarly ends with invocations after expressions of confidence (vv. 15, 16–17). Psalm 120 starts and ends with descriptions of distress. Psalm 141 ends with pleas for God to help (vv. 8–10), as does also Ps. 143 (vv. 11–12).

Other individual laments, dominated by the theme of pain and suffering, intersperse the many different elements seemingly at random. Psalm 22 does this in part; so too do Pss. 42–3, 51, 55, 69, and 71, which are all unpredictable in their use of invocations, expressions of confidence, pleas for help, and vows of praise: not one psalm follows the same structure as another. Finally, two psalms have no recognizable form whatsoever: their designation as 'lament' is entirely due to their contents and mood. Psalm 39 is almost all made up of descriptions of distress (vv. 2–4, 10, 11*b*, 12) and references to prayers once offered (vv. 5–7, 8–11, 13–14); and Ps. 88, referred to above as reflecting personal concerns on the fear of death and of dying, is almost entirely made up of descriptions of distress, interspersed with expressions of despair, ending with an unusual prayer questioning the goodness of God (vv. 11–13).

We see again that poetic conventions exist to be broken. The form-critical classification exists more for the purpose of our ordering the Psalter than for understanding individual psalms. Like the hymns, we may surmise that the laments too emerged from many and various stages of Israel's liturgical life, and their precise setting is again largely unknown. The only point we can really be clear about is that within the range of the so-called lament form, innumerable psalms were written over a long period of time, to cater for the needs of the whole community (whether at the Temple or at some more familial setting is unclear), and also for the needs of particular individuals. Throughout this period, the use of the 'I' form became increasingly blurred: laments which in the first instance were composed for individuals later would have been applied to the community, and vice versa. The process is rather like the way in which our own hymn-books have been compiled, whereby private poems are brought into public use. (Contemporary examples include the hymn 'There is a Green Hill Far Away', composed by Cecil Alexander (1818–95) at the deathbed of a sick child; Charles Wesley's 'O for a Thousand Tongues to Sing', composed on the anniversary of his conversion in 1738; and the prayer for faith in depression, composed by William Cowper (1731–1800), 'Oh! For a Closer Walk with God'.)

(III) OTHER PSALMIC FORMS

Most of the remaining categories are derivations of the basic praise and lament forms. The *royal psalms* are perhaps the most variable, with unclassifiable forms. The *thanksgivings* are related more to the lament (in so far as a number of the laments often include thanksgivings as examples of prayers previously answered, e.g. 6: 9–11; 7: 18; 13: 6; 31: 21–3), and also to hymns of 'declarative' praise (in so far as each seeks to celebrate God's goodness on account of specific benefits). The *psalms of confidence* are also related to the lament (being expansions of the 'confessions of trust' found in the lament psalms, e.g. 17: 15; 28: 6; 130: 5; 140: 14). The *liturgies* and *historical psalms* are closely related to the hymns, with their main theme being praise of God. Only the didactic psalms and the prophetic exhortations have fewer correspondences with the lament or praise forms; nevertheless, the material found particularly in these psalms is also evident throughout the Psalter. Didactic passages may be found in several other psalm types (e.g. 25: 8–14; 32: 8ff.; 34: 11–22, noting also the acrostic form; 40: 4ff.; 62: 11ff.; and 102: 23–8) and prophetic oracles are similarly evident in other psalms such as 2: 7–9; 3: 4; 18: 7ff.; 20: 6–8; 21: 5; 60: 6–8; 62: 11–12; 85: 8–13; 89: 19ff.; 108: 7ff.; 122: 6–9; and 132: 11–18.

Royal Psalms

Our earlier assessment of royal poetry outside the Psalter (Ch. 7, pp. 160–7) observed that this was used not only during the time of the monarchy, but also long after its demise. Indeed, most of the examples referred to (Isa. 9; 11; Mic. 5; Jer. 23; the Servant Songs in second Isaiah; Zech. 9; and Dan. 7) are compositions concerning a future regal figure, compiled a considerable time after the end of the monarchy in 587 BCE; they focused on an idealized, coming figure, rather than a contemporary Davidic king.

The issue then arises: were the royal psalms written during the monarchy, or after it? It is more probable that most of them were in fact early, and the poems in the prophetic and apocalyptic literature are developments from them. The figure of the king in the psalms, with his semi-divine status, and also the rituals of anointing and coronation, accord well with what we know about kingship in the ancient Near East at the same time. Furthermore, the various oracles evident in many of these psalms suggest a time when prophecy still functioned in the royal court, and the close association of the king with the city of Zion corresponds best with the situation of the monarchy such as is reflected in the eighth- and seventh-century prophets and in the books of Kings.

But there is no doubt that the designation 'royal psalms' is one made on account of content (because the king is either the speaker, or the focus of attention) rather than form. Gunkel listed ten psalms in this category: 2, 18, 20, 21, 45, 72, 101, 110, 132, and 144. To this we might add the latter part of Ps. 89. Both Pss. 89 and 144 have a clear lament form (Ps. 89 was referred to above). Pss. 18 and 21 are thanksgivings. Several have oracles of peace and blessing (2: 7–9; 8ff.; 20: 6–8; 89: 19ff.; 110: 1, 4; 132: 11ff.); others contain intercessions on behalf of the king (20: 1–5; 72: 1; 132: 1ff., 10). But not one psalm corresponds with another in terms of determinable form.

A significant element in these psalms is that they reveal various aspects of the cultic life of Israel. Psalm 45, a royal wedding psalm,

offers insights into the divine status of the king and the close
relationship between palace and Temple:

> Your divine throne
> (?Your throne, O God;
> ?Your throne is a throne of God)
> endures for ever . . .   (v. 6)

Psalm 132 gives us insights into the role of the ark at some
'covenant' ceremony where the king celebrated the founding of
Jerusalem:

> Arise, O God, and go to thy resting place,
>   thou and the ark of thy might
>
> The LORD swore to David a sure oath
>   from which he will not turn back
>
>   .   .   .   .
>
> For the LORD has chosen Zion;
>   he has desired it for his habitation
>
>   (vv. 8, 11, 13)

Psalm 110 offers insights into the sacral role of the king, inheriting
the ancient privileges of the Jebusite city-king:

> The LORD has sworn and will not change his mind,
>   'You are a priest for ever after the order of Melchizedek.'   (v. 4)

Psalms 2, 72, and 101 suggest ceremonies of enthronement of the
king, where the king takes 'a decree' (Ps. 2: 7; cf. 2 Kgs. 11: 12) and
makes vows to bring about peace and justice throughout his reign
(72: 1; 101: 1 ff.). Psalms 18, 20, 89, and 144 show the way the king
played a critical part in 'holy war' (Ps. 18 has a corresponding
variant in 2 Sam. 22, referred to in Ch. 7, pp. 158–9).

Most psalms point to a different cultic occasion, suggesting a
variety of rituals and liturgies throughout the different stages of the
life of the king. It is more than likely that the influence of the royal
cult is found in many other psalms in addition to Gunkel's collection of ten, although this certainly does not include all seventy-
three psalms which have the heading 'To David' attached to them.
Other psalms where the role of the king is also evident include Pss.
61 (see vv. 6 ff.), 63 (v. 11), 80 (vv. 17 ff.), and 84 (v. 9). (As was seen in
Ch. 8, a number of Scandinavian and British scholars, including

Mowinckel, Eaton, and latterly Croft, would include at least forty more psalms, mainly laments, into the list of royal psalms. These views are open to question on account of the reading of the figurative language of the psalms: see Ch. 8, pp. 201 ff.).

How were the royal psalms understood when the people returned to their land after the exile, with no ruling king and no suggestion of the restoration of the monarchy? As with the royal songs outside the Psalter, they would either have been democratized, whereby the people identified themselves with God's promise once made to the king; or they would have become part of a future idealized hope expressed in the later prophets and in apocalyptic literature—referring to one coming, rather than to a figure of the past. The royal psalms offer us the best examples of the ways in which psalmody can be read at many different levels: it is not surprising that the royal psalms in particular have been viewed in the Judaeo-Christian tradition as prophetic texts concerning the identity of God's promised deliverer.

Thanksgiving Psalms

The thanksgiving poems which are found outside the Psalter offer two important insights for understanding the function of thanksgivings in the Psalter. The communal thanksgivings, found in second Isaiah (Ch. 7, pp. 156–7), show the close associations with hymns of declarative praise. The four individual thanksgivings (attributed to Hannah, David, Hezekiah, and Jonah) reveal how typical and reusable such poems are: outside a narrative context they would be both personal and yet representative ritual texts.

Their structure is variable. The introduction reflects their liturgical context. The presence of a congregation is often presumed in the initial thanksgiving, for example in Ps. 138: 1, 2:

> I will give thanks, O LORD, with my whole heart;
> before the gods I will sing thy praise;
>
> I bow down before thy holy temple
> and give thanks to thy name for thy steadfast love
> and thy faithfulness.

The middle section of the psalm is a testimony of how the deliverance occurred. If the crisis was due to unconfessed sin, the thanksgiving often includes some confession of sin (e.g. 32: 5; 103: 6–14). If the innocence of the supplicant was beyond question, the psalmist pleads instead for God's justice (28: 6–7; 92: 5–9). Sometimes the middle section also contains didactic elements, so that the congregation might learn from the supplicant's restoration (34: 12–15, 138: 6). Occasionally the psalm concludes with a call to praise (32: 11; 138: 8). The ritual background is often evident in references to processions (118: 19–20), and to the offering of sacrifice (66: 13–15; 116: 12–19). Indeed, the Hebrew word for the thanksgiving (*tôdâ*) is also the word used for the sacrifice itself (e.g. Lev. 7: 12–14). The root y–d–h, meaning to give thanks, to praise, to extol, shows the close association between thanksgiving and praise: the former is a more particularized form of the latter.

Yet, as well as being closely linked to the form of hymn, the thank-offering is also a component part of the lament, in so far as it states the answer to the prayer offered. In some psalms (e.g. Pss. 9–10 and 22) it is hard to know whether the thanks or the lament is the predominant feature; and in others, the thanksgiving clearly serves to highlight the effectiveness of the lament, as in 40: 1–10 (the lament is in 40: 11–17) and 41: 1–3 (the lament is quoted in 41: 4–10).

Two derivations of communal and individual thanksgivings are discernible. Psalms 67 and 124 are the most obvious communal forms (Pss. 65, 66, 68, and 118 may be included as well, although each of these psalms may also be classified as a hymn of praise or even a royal psalm). The individual psalms are 9–10, 30, 32, 34, 40, 41, 92, 107, 116, and 138. Psalms 30 and 116 clearly refer to recovery from illness; Pss. 32 and 103 are thanksgivings for forgiveness; and Pss. 28, 92, and 138 refer to release from some sort of danger (the figurative reference to the 'enemies' makes it impossible to be precise). Hence we may again note that these were personal, particular psalms, usable by anyone in a corresponding situation of need.

Regular and consistent forms are often difficult to discern. For example, Ps. 107 is most unusual: it seems to be a composite psalm, speaking of different groups saved from distress (desert wanderers: vv. 4–9; prisoners: vv. 10–16; the sick: vv. 17–22; and seafarers: vv. 23–32), each ending with a refrain:

> Then they cried to the LORD in their trouble,
> and he delivered them out of their distress
>
> (vv. 6, 13, 19, 28)

followed by the exhortation:

> Let them thank the LORD for his steadfast love,
> for his wonderful works to the sons of men!
>
> (vv. 8, 15, 21, 31)

Psalm 68 is similarly atypical in form: it starts with a lament-like invocation (vv. 1–3), followed by a call to praise (v. 4), then an expression of confidence (vv. 5–6), then a long description of deliverance, set in mythological language (vv. 7ff.), ending with more invocations (vv. 23ff.) and calls to praise (vv. 32ff.). Psalms 9–10 are also unusual: creating a unity in their acrostic form, they intersperse a complicated collection of calls to praise (9: 1–2, 7–10, 11–12, 10: 1) with various descriptions of deliverance (9: 3–6, 15–17), as well as descriptions of distress (10: 2–11), expressions of confidence (9: 18; 10: 14, 16, 17–18), and other various invocations (9: 13–14, 19–20; 10: 12, 13, 15). Similarly, neither Ps. 40 nor Ps. 41 suggests a predictable pattern.

Our conclusions are similar to those made previously: more often than not, poetic freedom allows the contents to dictate the form, and hence a move from analysis of form to a proposal of some particular cultic setting is impossible.

Psalms of Confidence

'Psalms of confidence' are only evidenced within the Psalter. They are really an integral part of the lament. If the thanksgiving is connected to the lament in that it speaks of an earlier deliverance, the psalm of confidence is an even more intrinsic part of the lament because it speaks of trust in spite of all appearances—a confidence within the present uncertainties, for those caught in the conflict between faith and experience.

We have already noted the evidence of expressions of confidence in the laments: Pss. 44: 1–7 and 80: 8–11 (communal laments) and 13: 5 and 22: 3–5, 9–10 (individual laments) use this form. These forms have no obvious structure; the so-called 'form' is discernible more on account of the personal expressions of peace, hope, and certainty in being heard. Such expressions may be the result of the moods of the speaker, or they may be in response to some oracle of blessing offered by a cultic prophet or priest.

Four communal psalms (115, 125, 129, 133) fit this classification, as do ten individual psalms (4, 11, 16, 23, 27, 62, 84, 91, 121, 131). Some psalms, in addition to expressions of trust, also have didactic elements (e.g. 115: 9–11; 131: 3), blessing formulas (115: 14–15), lament motifs (129: 1–3), expressions of integrity (16: 3–4), thanksgiving elements (84: 10, 11–12), and even unusual addresses to the 'enemy' (4: 2 and 62: 3).

Although Gunkel classifies psalms of confidence as a specific form, it is better to apportion such psalms more according to their moods. Certainly no particular cultic occasion may be determined: the psalm serves to meet the moods and various suppliants in various situations of need. This is thus a good example of a category where form-critical analysis is a limited tool, and where reference to the life-centredness of a psalm is particularly apt.

Liturgies

If the psalms of confidence might be classified more according to mood than to form, then the liturgies suggest more a category according to style: the main criterion would be their antiphonal features. This, then, includes psalms occurring in other categories. Psalms 118 and 132 have antiphonal elements, yet these are royal psalms; so too do Pss. 50, 81, and 95, but these are 'prophetic exhortations' (see below). Hence the liturgies cross various boundaries: they contain the hymnic calls to praise, the wisdom-type didactic elements, the lament-type expressions of confidence, and suggestions of oracular material. Furthermore, any psalm classified as a liturgy is likely to be a fragment of a greater whole, although again the possibility of ascertaining the complete cultic setting eludes us.

The clearest example is Ps. 15, probably a restoration psalm which served as an 'entrance liturgy' for pilgrims about to enter the Temple. Psalm 15: 1 is a question about who may enter the Temple precincts; 15: 2–5*b* is the antiphonal reply, listing various ethical requirements (ten in number, possibly imitating the Ten Commandments); 15: 5c is the response of blessing, probably by a cultic prophet or priest.

Psalm 24: 3–6 is another example, set within a greater liturgical occasion which is hinted at before and after it:

QUESTION: Who shall ascend the hill of the LORD?
And who shall stand in his holy place?
REPLY: He who has clean hands and a pure heart
who does not lift up his soul to what is false,
and does not swear deceitfully
BLESSING: He will receive blessing from the LORD,
and vindication from the God of his salvation.

The implied references to the ark entering the gates of the Temple in vv. 7–10, and the theme of the kingship of God ('the King of glory') suggest that this may belong to some processional liturgy, possibly at the turn of the New Year, in the pre-exilic Temple.

The only other liturgical fragment is from some night ritual, which comprises the whole of Ps. 134:

Come, bless the LORD, all you servants of the LORD,
who stand by night in the house of the LORD!
Lift up your hands to the holy place,
and bless the LORD!
May the LORD bless you from Zion
he who made heaven and earth!

We may therefore conclude once again that the liturgies do not comprise a clear form-critical category, nor do they enable us to assign them to one particular cultic occasion.

Prophetic Exhortations

It was noted above that the antiphonal element in the liturgies may sometimes imply the voice of the cultic prophets. This was also illustrated in Chapter 7 with respect to the extent of cultic poetry in the prophetic material. The influence of the prophets has already been seen in the oracular material in several other cultic forms—not least in the royal psalms (2, 18, 20, 21, 89, 110, 132) and also within the laments (12, 60). Scholars such as A. Johnson, J. Eaton, and W. Bellinger see the prophetic influence as far more extensive than this: their view is to expand it to include implicit allusions to oracles which gave rise to the changes of mood occurring in many of the lament psalms. The problem lies in establishing sufficiently convincing criteria to sustain such theories.

The so-called 'form' is yet again discernible not so much in terms of structure, as in terms of style and content. The criterion in this case is neither mood (as with the psalms of confidence) nor antiphonal elements (as with the liturgies) but rather prophetic oracles. Psalms 50, 81, and 95 are good examples of such oracles (cf. 50: 5 ff.; 81: 6 ff.; 95: 7 ff.). These psalms suggest liturgical occasions before assembled congregations at particular feast days (81: 1–3), amidst sacrifices (50: 7 ff.) and processions (95: 1–2). Prophetic oracles with didactic elements are also evident in Pss. 14: 2 ff.; 53: 2 ff.; and 75: 2 ff. Although the liturgical occasion is less explicit, these psalms may also be termed prophetic exhortations.

The following example is an interesting illustration of the way that the oracle is similar in poetic form and in content to that of the pre-exilic prophets, yet in a context which is clearly liturgical:

> Blow the trumpet at the new moon,
> at the full moon, our feast day
>
> . . . .
>
> I heard a voice I had not known:
> 'I relieved your shoulder of the burden;
> your hands were freed from the basket.
> In distress you called, and I delivered you;
> I answered you in the secret place of thunder;
> I tested you at the waters of Meribah.'
>
> (Ps. 81: 3, 5c–7)

The dating of these psalms is contemporaneous with the influence of the prophets in the period between the late monarchy and early restoration. But yet again, the lack of any consistent form prevents any certainty about a precise cultic setting.

Didactic Psalms

In Chapter 5, sect. B(iv), we noted the cultic influence in didactic poetry with respect to the use of the lament and hymnic forms in the book of Job (e.g. Job 3, 6, 7, 8, 10, 12, 14, 16–17—laments; 5, 11,

26, 36, 37—hymns used by Job's friends; 9, 10, 12—hymns used by Job) and also in the longer wisdom poems in Job and in Proverbs (Job 28, 38 ff.; Prov. 3, 8). It is probable that this association took place later in Israel's liturgical life, probably in restoration times. The evidence of wisdom poetry in the Psalter at this time should not surprise us. Indeed, just as with the prophetic influence, wisdom elements also pervade a number of other psalms: we may note here the didactic passages in laments such as Pss. 25: 8–14; 31: 24–5; and thanksgivings such as Pss. 40: 5–6; 92: 7–9.

Like the prophetic exhortations, wisdom poetry offers no consistent form whatsoever. Several psalms use the acrostic form (e.g. 37, 112, 119) but by no means all. Some incorporate hymnic elements (e.g. 112: 1–6; 127: 3–5). Most are actually not so much prayer-forms, set as addresses to God, but are rather more like poetic homilies, addressing the congregation. They are discernible on account of their style—their use of comparison, admonition, and proverbial sayings ('blessed . . .'; 'better . . .': see 1: 1; 32: 1; 34: 8), and also because of their content—their concern with ordinary affairs such as piety at work (127: 1; 128: 1, 2) and family life (127, 128), and the prosperity of the wicked alongside retributive justice (37, 49, 73, 112), and the transience of life (73) as well as God's knowledge of every detail of it (139). On occasions their mood is orthodox (e.g. 127, 128, 139) and on others more radical and questioning (37, 49, 73). Their orientation is more towards the problems of life itself, rather than the issues of liturgy.

Many scholars believe the wisdom psalms were not even used in the cult, but rather served as reflective and didactic poetry (alongside Proverbs and Job) in wisdom schools. However, in the light of our initial observations regarding the associations between the cult and wisdom, some sort of later cultic setting seems probable. Psalm 49 is a good example of this, and the attendant audience could just as easily be the congregation assembled for worship (we are reminded here of the prophetic call to listen and obey) as a private school of wisdom:

> Hear this, all peoples!
> Give ear, all inhabitants of the world,
>> both high and low,
>> rich and poor together!

My mouth shall speak wisdom;
   the meditation of my heart shall be understanding.
Man cannot abide in his pomp,
   he is like the beasts that perish.

                    (Ps. 49: 1–3, 12)

The cultic orientation of wisdom is apparent in three other psalms which each focus on the meditation of the *law* as a means to blessing and wholeness of life: these are Pss. 1, 19B, and 119, known as 'Torah psalms'. Psalm 1 starts with the classic wisdom motif 'Blessed . . .' and introduces into the Psalter the theme of reflective and personal piety. Psalm 19B is a 'Torah psalm' added to the creation psalm in praise of the sun: these together reflect on two sorts of order and harmony—creation and the law—in the world. Psalm 119, an acrostic psalm, is almost certainly a literary rather than liturgical composition. Every verse of the psalm contains at least one of ten terms used for the law (for example, commandment; statute; word; judgement; testimony; precept; way) and the psalm as a whole is a complex construction. Like Ps. 1, this is another example of private contemplative piety—a point to which we shall return at the beginning of the following chapter.

What are we to conclude from this survey of the forms of the psalms? One critical point is that an analysis of form does not necessarily imply the same fixed setting, as some scholars have contended. The content dictates the form, not the reverse, and content most certainly does not always suggest the same life-setting. The psalms cover a huge spectrum of Israel's history, and within this, the poets combine in differing degrees an adherence to convention with their own expressions of creativity. The external structure of a psalm (whether by way of its parallelism, its metre, or its other semantic and phonetic devices) is the means by which the contents are given coherence, order, and shape; but these elements are the means to a more important end—that of communicating the substance of the psalm.

The sheer variety of forms is more than evident. Because of this, the precise liturgical settings behind the psalms are thus largely unknown. All we can surmise is *that* many psalms mirror the great liturgical occasions from the time of the monarchy into the late restoration period; but *how* they were used within the constantly changing and developing liturgy still largely eludes us. The fact that the psalms conceal as much as they reveal has of course been the reason for their survival in the Judaeo-Christian tradition, for, detached from the constraints of a specific cultic occasion, they become open to a variety of interpretations at a variety of stages in the life of the tradition. This issue will be the focus of our attention in the last two chapters.

Appendix: An Overview of the Basic Forms Used in the Psalter

1. *Hymns*

General Hymns: 8; 29; 33; 100; 103; 104; 111; 113; 114; 117; 135; 136; 145; 146; 147; 148; 149; 150.
Also: 78; 105.
Zion Hymns: 46; 48; 76; 87; 122.
Kingship Hymns: 47; 93; 96; 97; 98; 99.

2. *Laments*

Individual Laments: 3; 5; 6; 7; 12; 13; 17; 22; 25; 26; 28; 31; 35; 36; 38; 39; 42–3; 51; 54; 55; 56; 57; 59; 61; 63; 64; 69; 70; 71; 86; 88; 102; 109; 120; 130; 140; 141; 142; 143.
Communal Laments: 44; 60; 74; 77; 79; 80; 82; 83; 85; 90; 94; 106; 108; 123; 126; 137.

3. *Miscellaneous Forms*

Royal Psalms: 2; 18; 20; 21; 45; 72; 89; 101; 110; 132; 144.
Individual Thanksgivings: 9–10; 30; 32; 34; 40; 41; 92; 107; 116; 138.
Communal Thanksgivings: 65; 66; 67; 68; 118; 124.
Individual Psalms of Confidence: 4; 11; 16; 23; 27; 62; 84; 91; 121; 131.
Communal Psalms of Confidence: 115; 125; 129; 133.
Liturgies: 15; 24; 134.
Prophetic Exhortations: 14; 50; 52; 53; 58; 75; 81; 95.
Didactic Psalms: 1; 19; 37; 49; 73; 112; 119; 127; 128; 139.

11

The Psalter: Hymn-Book, Prayer-Book, or Anthology?

A. Looking at the Psalter as a Whole

The previous two chapters focused on the psalms as individual poems, with a particular 'setting-in-life' or a 'setting-in-liturgy'—either that of the public Temple liturgy, or the private lives of individuals. They have a different orientation from other Old Testament poems which are more integrated with narrative, and so have a 'setting-in-literature'.

Rather than concentrating on individual psalms, these final chapters will examine the Psalter as a whole, and will draw together the life/liturgy-centred approach with the literary one. An understanding of the Psalter as a composite work of literary worth in the end involves both approaches.

The 'life/liturgy' approach would see the primary influence upon the compilation of the Psalter as liturgical: it is a hymn-book, or a prayer-book. This has much to commend it: since the beginning of the twentieth century, the predominant view of scholars (in the main from Germany and Scandinavia) has been that the compilation of the Psalter was shaped by its liturgical use in the second Temple.

Such a view is suggested by the Hebrew heading to the entire Psalter found in several ancient manuscripts—*seper t^ehillîm*, 'the book of praises'—a title to which we have already made reference (e.g. Ch. 10, p. 209). The Greek titles are *Psalmoi* (a translation of the Hebrew word *mizmôr*, meaning 'hymn', a heading for over a third of the psalms) and *psaltérion* (possibly a translation from the

Hebrew n–b–l, meaning 'stringed instrument': hence the word Psalter refers to songs accompanied by a stringed instrument). The Greek and the Hebrew both imply clear liturgical use.

The idea that the Psalter was also a prayer-book is a modification of this approach, albeit with slightly less evidence. It appeals to another less common title for the psalms—*seper t^{e}pillôt*, 'the book of prayers'—taken from Ps. 72: 20: 'The prayers of David, the son of Jesse, are ended.' The word *t^{e}pillâ* is also found in the headings to Pss. 17, 86, 90, 102, and 142; the word is from the root p–l–l, meaning to pray (in terms of request or lament).

This, then is the traditional approach, and one which is well substantiated by the evidence of ongoing liturgical use, both public and private, within both the Jewish and Christian tradition. But there is another way of understanding the shape of the Psalter. This approach has been popularized in the main by American scholars over the last twenty years or so. It involves a literary, rather than liturgical, emphasis: instead of looking at the way the psalms were collected through the influence of worship, as part of an organic, dynamic process, this approach looks at the Psalter from its endpoint—from its final, 'received' shape. The emphasis is hence more upon the Psalter as 'canonical literature'; it is to be read as an intricately woven anthology of poems, brought together in many subtle but deliberate ways, predominantly for didactic, theological purposes. The emphasis is more holistic than the traditional one: the Psalter is to be read as a whole, rather than sung or prayed as smaller parts of that whole. Furthermore, the concern is not so much with a 'setting-in-life', be it that of second Temple liturgy and prayers, or later Jewish and Christian tradition, as with the 'setting-in-literature', observing the patterns and structures within the collection in its final stage.

This approach is also associated with several Continental scholars, such as J. Reindl and K. Seybold and P. Auffret; American contributors include B. S. Childs, G. H. Wilson, W. Brueggemann, and J. C. McCann. The collectors and editors responsible for the shaping of the Psalter are no longer seen to be Temple priests or Levitical singers, but rather scribes, part of Israel's broader wisdom tradition. Instead of being concerned with liturgical issues, they are seen to be more concerned with teaching, based upon a certain

'Torah-piety', and they shaped the collection as a whole in a more intellectual and theological way to this end. The text and the readers are the focus of attention, rather than the context and the earlier users.

A few illustrations of this approach should make the point clear. Working on smaller collections within the Psalter, a French scholar, P. Auffret, has shown how Psalms 15–24, 120–34, and 135–8 each have inner structural connections, and each collection forms a balanced chiasmus. For example, in the collection Pss. 15–24, Pss. 15 and 24 focus on the blessings of keeping the Torah, as also does the mid-point psalm, Ps. 19; Pss. 16 and 23 are balanced as psalms of trust; Pss. 17 and 22 as laments; and Pss. 18 and 20–1 as royal psalms. (See *La Sagesse a bâti sa maison* (1982).) The unity imposed upon the collection is as much literary and theological as it is liturgical.

A German scholar, K. Seybold, assesses Pss. 120–34 (a collection known as 'the Psalms of Ascents') and proposes that these psalms were composed away from Jerusalem, in outlying rural sanctuaries. As a collection, these psalms have been heavily redacted by editors, who inserted the several Zion/Temple motifs at the beginnings and endings of various compositions. In this way they could be adapted for pilgrims going up to Jerusalem. The collection is hence a coherent whole, with a Zion ideology superimposed. (See *Die Wallfahrtpsalmen* (1978).) In this case, the literary/theological and the liturgical aspects are part of the same process.

In *The Psalms of the Sons of Korah* (1982), M. D. Goulder takes the fourth book of the Psalter (Pss. 90–106) and proposes that this is another self-contained collection, adapted so that one psalm could be read each night and morning at the eight-day autumnal Festival of Tabernacles. Although much of the theory is again hypothetical, this is another study which illustrates how the liturgical and literary concerns of the editors overlap.

J. C. McCann, writing a chapter in a seminal book in this area, *The Shape and Shaping of the Psalter* (1993), looks at the third book in the Psalter (Pss. 73–89) and again finds a purposeful structure: prayers of lament alternate with hymns of hope throughout the entire collection, with the alternation often occurring in one composite psalm. McCann claims this pattern has been superimposed on the collection by one who was wrestling with the unanswered questions about theodicy after the experience of the exile and return.

Other scholars have found a superimposed unity not so much in overarching structures in collections as in smaller linkages between one psalm and its neighbour: the best example is that of catch-words, which frequently occur at the end of one psalm and the beginning of another, forming a system known as 'concatenation'. An American scholar, J. P. Brennan, has appropriated this within the whole of the fifth book of the Psalter (Pss. 107–50), as well as in a smaller collection of Pss. 1–10. For example, Pss. 7: 17; 8: 1; and 9: 2–3, each on the praise of God's majesty, suggest the use of con-catenation.

Two German scholars, C. Barth and W. Zimmerli, have also adapted the system of concatenation. Barth has worked on Book One (Pss. 1–41) and found word-pairs and sequences of word-patterns occurring repeatedly throughout this collection, again suggesting a coherent superimposed unity. Zimmerli has focused on twenty pairs of psalms which are believed to have such close literary relations as to be termed 'twin psalms' ('Zwillings-psalmen'). For example, Pss. 9–10, 20–1, 42–3, 50–1, 65–6, 105–6, 111–12, and 135–6 are seen to have been linked together as part of a deliberate editorial process, each being full of doublets and catch-words, and have been intentionally set side by side as a com-mentary of one on the other.

The two most significant works in this area to date (and it must again be noted that this process of reading the Psalter as a whole is still very much in its earliest stage, the most influential works having been published since the mid-1980s) are by W. Bruegge-mann and G. H. Wilson. These are important because each scholar looks at the Psalter in its entirety, rather than working with a smaller collection.

Wilson, in *The Editing of the Hebrew Psalter* (1985), sets his thesis in context by noting how the same editorial activity is evident in other hymnic collections from the ancient Near East (for example, as early as Sumerian hymnic literature in the third millennium BCE in Mesopotamia and as late as in Qumran hymnody in the second century BCE). Wilson proposes that Books One to Three of the

Psalter (i.e. Pss. 1–41, 42–72, 73–89) have many explicit indicators of the same editorial arranging, whilst Books Four and Five (Pss. 90–106, 107–50) have less evidence of this. He notes how Pss. 2, 72, and 89, all 'royal psalms', are set at the 'seams' of Books One to Three, and each gives prominence to and expresses confidence in the covenant between God and the Davidic king; the preponderance of psalms headed 'to David' within these three books further bears witness to this royal promise in one way or another. However, Ps. 89 ends with a cry of dereliction:

> How long, O Lord? Wilt thou hide thyself for ever?
> Lord, where is thy steadfast love of old,
> which by thy faithfulness thou didst swear to David?

> (Ps. 89: 49)

This suggests the dissolution of the monarchy, as the covenant with David has been broken. Hence Book Four (Pss. 90–106) is a response to this tension: the emphasis instead is now on God as King—an everlasting reign which cannot be broken. Book Five (Pss. 107–50) follows this theme by exhorting reliance and trust in God alone: the paean of praise in Pss. 145–50 is to God's eternal kingship.

Wilson concludes that whilst the time-conditioned royal themes predominate in the first eighty-nine psalms, more general didactic themes are evident in Pss. 90–150. The psalms which come at the 'seams' of Books Four and Five (i.e. Pss. 90–1, 106, 145) could be termed wisdom psalms. Wilson suggests that the overall theological-literary editorial activity of the entire Psalter is thus due to the work of the 'wise' incorporating Books One to Three with Books Four and Five. Although in some ways this study concentrates too much on specific psalms (not least those supposedly at the 'seams' of the books), it offers many refreshing insights concerning the shaping of the Psalter.

W. Brueggemann builds upon Wilson's thesis by making further comments on the first and last psalms—those which 'frame' the entire Psalter. In an article entitled 'Bounded by Obedience and Praise: The Psalms as Canon', he notes that the Psalter moves from the wisdom-type theme of obedience to the Torah (Ps. 1) towards the hymnic expression of praise which focuses on God alone (Ps.

150). However, this movement is not one uninterrupted progression of thought: the other 148 psalms move through various
stages of lament and complaint. Psalm 73 (at the mid-point), with
its theme of the transience of life, is a clear protest at the sim-
plicities of faith which may be couched either in an unthinking
'Torah-piety' or in superficial 'hymnic praise'. Brueggemann's
observations are similar to those of Wilson: the concern for keeping
the law and the didactic overtones again suggest this to have been
the editing and collecting work of the 'wise', rather than Temple
singers.

We are thus able to see two different but complementary
approaches in understanding the Psalter as a whole. The more
traditional liturgical emphasis cannot simply be set aside in favour
of recent studies, for even those emphasizing literary concerns (for
example, Goulder and Seybold) have had to give due weight to the
way the worship of the community has helped to shape a large part
of the collections of the Psalter. But the literary emphasis undoubtedly offers significant insights. In this sense, the Psalter
should be seen not only in a liturgical light as a hymn/prayer-book
but also from a literary perspective as an anthology of religious
poetry. And whether one credits the final editorial activity to the
work of the Temple priests (taking the hymn/prayer-book model as
paramount) or to the work of the wise (taking the poetic anthology
model as most important), one is still left with the impression that
the Temple personnel of the late restoration period worked with
great exactitude in compiling the various smaller collections into
larger units. This interconnecting process was as much influenced
by liturgical concerns as it was by literary ones.

In the assessment of the Psalter which follows, both approaches
will be used. In this chapter we shall consider the process of compilation, giving due attention primarily to the liturgical factors,
while in the last chapter, we shall examine from a more literary and
theological perspective the ways in which the final 'whole' can then
be interpreted and used.

B. From Smaller Collections to the Five Books of Psalms

It is possible to ascertain collections in the Psalter by categorizing them according to the same superscriptions which head the different psalms. The two largest collections in the Psalter are Pss. 3–41 and 42–89.

Psalms 3–41 lacks an obvious systematic order, being almost entirely made up of psalms whose titles associate the contents with David. The exceptions are Ps. 10 (which, on account of its broken acrostic form, is the second part of Ps. 9) and Ps. 33 (which may be a later addition, although it has close links with Ps. 32: for example, see 32: 11 and 33: 1, which are exhortations to the 'righteous' and 'upright'). The fact that in the Greek Pss. 9–10 are united, and Ps. 33 gains a Davidic heading, suggests that Pss. 3–41 was a self-contained collection by the time of the Greek edition of the Psalter in the second century BCE. As a collection, it comprises mainly individual laments. Exceptions include a few hymns (8, 19, 29, 33) and Temple liturgies (15, 24). Several psalms with Davidic headings fall into smaller groupings on account of their similar contents: these include Pss. 3–5 (laments against enemy oppression), Pss. 18, 20–1 (psalms with royal concerns), Pss. 26–8 (laments of one unjustly accused), and Pss. 38–41 (laments of ill-health).

Psalms 42–89 is the second largest collection, itself a composite work of smaller collections. The evidence suggests that it evolved independently of Pss. 3–41. In contrast to the first Davidic collection, this work has preserved a particular characteristic of a different name for 'God'. Whereas in Pss. 3–41 there are over two hundred and seventy references to God as 'Yahweh' (= 'the Lord', the particular Israelite title) and under fifty instances of 'Elohim' (a more general, universal title), in Pss. 42–83 there are just over forty references to Yahweh, and over two hundred and forty instances of Elohim. (Pss. 84–9 by contrast is similar to Pss. 3–41: there are thirty-one occurrences of Yahweh and only seven of Elohim; hence Pss. 42–83 is often called the 'Elohistic Psalter' within the collection overall.) This distinctive feature is particularly evident when comparing two pairs of duplicate psalms: in Ps. 14, the word 'Yahweh' is always used (vv. 2, 4, 7) whilst in the parallel psalm, Ps.

53, the word 'Elohim' prevails (vv. 2, 4, 6). In Ps. 40: 13–17, 'Yahweh' is used (except for v. 17*b*) whilst in Ps. 70, 'Elohim' prevails (except for vv. 1*b* and 5*b*). And even where parallels occur outside the psalms, as in Ps. 50: 7/Exod. 20: 2 and Ps. 68: 1, 7, 8/Num. 10: 35 and Judg. 5: 4–5, in the psalms 'Yahweh' is changed to 'Elohim'. The collectors clearly had their own reasons for limiting the use of the more particular Israelite term for God, preferring 'Elohim' instead.

This so-called 'Elohistic Psalter' (Pss. 42–83) comprises at least three smaller collections. These include another 'Davidic' collection, in Pss. 51–72. (The concluding verse, 'The prayers of David, the son of Jesse, are ended', probably referred to this collection, not the earlier Davidic collection as well.) There are also two other collections, with ascriptions not to David, but to guilds of Temple singers: one is to the 'sons of Korah' in Pss. 42–9, and another to 'Asaph' in Pss. 50, 73–83. That Pss. 84–9 is an appendix is further evident in the addition of more Korahite psalms in 84–5, 87–8— psalms which by contrast still overall preserve the name 'Yahweh'. The Korahite psalms are mainly preoccupied with the theme of God's protective presence in Jerusalem—a pre-exilic theme, the subject of the attention of the eighth- and seventh-century prophets such as Micah, Isaiah, and Jeremiah. The Asaphite psalms by contrast contain a number of references to the tribes of the northern kingdom, and are more concerned with God's judgement, whether on Israel or on her enemies, with several instances of the use of oracular material and a greater use of the Exodus and settlement traditions. It could well be that, originally, the psalms of Korah came from the pre-exilic Jerusalem cult, whilst the psalms of Asaph came from prophetic circles in a northern provenance. The lack of evidence of the Korahite and Asaphite guilds of singers before the writing of the Chronicler (e.g. 'sons of Asaph'; 1 Chr. 25: 1 ff.; 2 Chr. 5: 12; 29: 13; 35: 15) suggests that the actual collecting-together of these psalms under their particular superscriptions was a post-exilic process.

Psalms 42–89 thus display a complex process of growth, with various smaller collections and other single psalms added to these collections as 'frames'. Fig. 1 illustrates this in diagrammatic form.

One other large collection is Pss. 120–34, with the heading 'Song of Ascents' as the superscription common to each. We have already

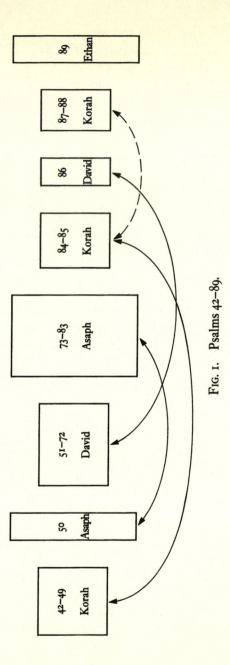

FIG. 1. Psalms 42–89.

referred to Seybold's thesis that these psalms could have been composed in outlying sanctuaries and were once peripheral to the Jerusalem cult, but were brought together in later times for use in second Temple liturgy. The term *šîr ha(la)-maʿalôt* (song of ascents) is difficult to determine: it could refer to the 'ascent' of pilgrims, going up to Jerusalem; or, more specifically, the 'going-up' of those returning from exile; or it could allude to the place where the psalms were sung, possibly the Temple steps; or to the 'graded rhythm' within each psalm; or to the idea of a 'series' or 'sequence' of songs, whereby the ending of one psalm is linked to the beginning of another. The first option is the most convincing. Their common theme is the exhortation to trust God: the words 'bless', 'keep', 'be gracious', and 'peace' occur throughout several psalms, thus suggesting that these psalms have been edited for use by pilgrims in the light of the Aaronic blessing in Num. 6: 24 ff.:

> The Lord bless you and keep you:
> The Lord make his face to shine upon you,
> and be gracious to you . . .

Within Pss. 90–150, three other collections are in evidence. A more scattered Davidic collection is found in Pss. 101, 103, 108–110, and 138–45: each psalm includes the same heading, 'to David'. In addition, two other collections are apparent, not so much on account of their superscriptions, as because of their shared themes: Pss. 93 and 95–9 form a unity in the theme of praise of Yahweh's kingship, and Pss. 104–6, 111–18, 135, and 146–50 (albeit another disparate collection) each contain several references to 'Hallel'— the word used for the praise of God, thus giving them the term 'Alleluia' ('Praise God') psalms.

Throughout the Psalter we find four comparable doxologies. All but one conclude various sets of collections. The first is found in Ps. 41: 13:

> Blessed be the LORD, the God of Israel,
> from everlasting to everlasting!   Amen and Amen.

The second occurs in Ps. 72: 18–19:

> Blessed be the LORD, the God of Israel,
> who alone does wondrous things.

> Blessed be his glorious name for ever;
> may his glory fill the earth!   Amen and Amen.

The third is in Ps. 89: 52:

> Blessed be the LORD for ever!
> Amen and Amen.

The fourth is Ps. 106: 48, occurring in the middle of a smaller collection:

> Blessed be the LORD, the God of Israel,
> from everlasting to everlasting!
> And let all the people say, 'Amen!'
> Praise the LORD!

This last doxology is also found in 1 Chr. 16: 36; it may indicate that the doxologies were fixed by the time of the Chronicler in about the fourth century BCE. The effect of the doxologies is to separate the Psalter into five books (although, as we have noted, the last one cuts across an existing collection). This creates the structure of the 'Five Books of the Psalms of David' rather like that of the 'Five Books of the Laws of Moses'. (It could also be that this fivefold structure enabled the psalms to be used in the synagogue lectionary alongside the readings of the law, but the evidence for this is inconclusive.)

The process of growth from individual psalms → collections → books → the entire Psalter, was inevitably a lengthy one. It is likely (as Wilson proposes) that the first three books evolved first; the psalms in this section almost all have headings (or multiple headings), reflecting a different process from that in Books Four and Five, where the greater proportion of psalms are without headings. It is also possible that the first edition of the Psalter began with Pss. 1 and 2 (added later to 3–41), and ended at Ps. 119. This would give the Psalter a wisdom/Torah introduction (Ps. 1) and conclusion (Ps. 119), thus illustrating its reflective/didactic use at that time. The addition of the Songs of Ascent (Pss. 120–34) and the inclusion of other Hallel psalms and Davidic psalms, with the creation of a doxology after Ps. 106, thus in time resulted in five clear books. This process is a complex one; it is illustrated in diagrammatic form in Fig. 2.

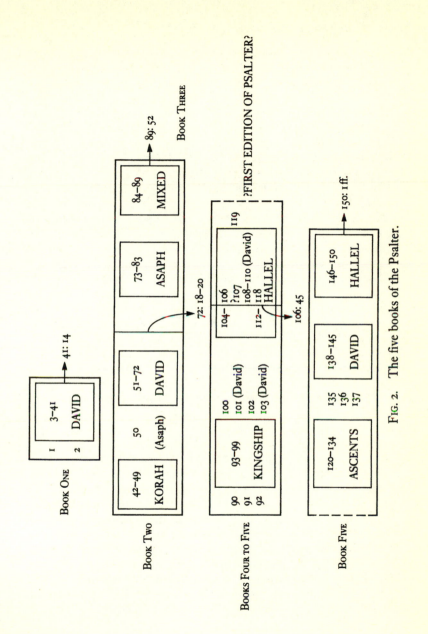

FIG. 2.   The five books of the Psalter.

One other important point needs to be made with regard to the way this complex process of compilation evolved. Many of the single psalms are also likely to be composite works; as the editors/compilers drew more psalms into the collections, it seems that they often added parts to existing psalms. We noted earlier that Ps. 19 is a composite psalm, with the first half on the theme of creation, and the second half on the theme of the law. Similarly, Ps. 108 is a reconstruction of Pss. 57: 1–11 and 60: 5–12. Psalms 18 and 144, and Pss. 115 and 135 also suggest this same process of borrowing and adaptation between one psalm and another. Furthermore, several individual laments may have been expanded in this same way: the endings of Ps. 22 (vv. 23–31) and 51 (vv. 18–19) suggest additions, concerned more with the affairs of rebuilding the community. Examples of this process abound. What was happening to the Psalter on the larger scale, in terms of various psalms being linked up, and other psalms being brought in to 'frame' the collections, would have happened also on the smaller scale, with individual psalms being similarly adapted at the same time and in the same way.

One final observation concerns the placing of the various psalmic forms within the Psalter as a whole. The previous chapter assessed all the main psalmic forms, from the two major forms of hymns and laments to the minor forms of royal psalms, thanksgivings, psalms of confidence, prophetic exhortations, and didactic psalms. The question arises: do these forms fit coherently into particular collections? Was this kind of classification recognized even from the earliest times?

Although the answer is less clear regarding the minor psalm forms, it is most certainly in the affirmative regarding the two major forms of hymn and lament. The laments of the individual occur almost entirely within the three Davidic collections—Pss. 3–41, 51–72, and 138–45. Elsewhere they are found mainly in insertion psalms such as Ps. 94 (which breaks up the collection of kingship hymns in 93, 95–9) and 102. The communal laments are also concentrated almost entirely in one collection—that of Asaph (Pss. 74, 77, 79, 80, 82, 83). By contrast, the hymns of praise occur mostly after Ps. 90. Hymns often conclude the collections: Ps. 100 follows Pss. 93, 95–9; Ps. 118 concludes the Hallel psalms; Ps. 134, the Songs of Ascents; and Ps. 145, the Davidic collection.

Hence it can be seen that the *individual* psalms cluster at the beginning of the Psalter, within Books One and Two; and the *corporate* psalms are found more towards the end of the Psalter, some in Book Three, but especially in Books Four and Five. Consequently, the *laments and prayers* are found predominantly in Books One to Three (Pss. 1–89), whilst the *hymns and praises* are found almost entirely within Books Four to Five (Pss. 90–150). We have already noted how these two forms, the $t^e hillim$ (hymns) and the $t^e pillôt$ (prayers) have been the two main forms by which the liturgical growth of the Psalter has been understood; hence it is no surprise to find a clear placing of these two forms (perhaps the psychological move from prayer to praise, a progression found also in many single psalms) within the Psalter as a whole.

C. The Superscriptions and the Psalms

All but twenty-four psalms have some sort of heading in the Hebrew. The LXX (Greek version) adds a heading to each psalm without one, with the exception of Pss. 1 and 2, and makes changes to several others: the variances between the Greek and Hebrew superscriptions show that this process was long and complex. The Greek often appears not to understand some of the Hebrew titles—not only the Davidic headings, but also the details concerning the music. For example, the rendering of 'Gittith', and the strange translation of 'to the choirmaster' as 'to eternity' (see below) may suggest that the superscriptions derive from an ancient (no longer understood) tradition. However, the fact that the LXX translators effected changes also shows that the headings were not entirely fixed or finalized by the second century BCE. Similarly, the fact that duplicate psalms such as 14 and 53 each have a different superscription shows that the headings do not relate only to content either.

The headings serve more as ascriptions than titles—that is, they ascribe a psalm to a particular collection. This is more in evidence in Books One to Three: as we have already noted, the last two books have far fewer superscriptions. Only occasionally do they describe the function of a psalm: exceptions include Ps. 100, 'A

Psalm for the thank-offering'; Ps. 92, 'A song for the Sabbath'; Ps. 30, 'A song at the dedication of the Temple'; Ps. 38, 'for the memorial offering'; and Ps. 102, 'A prayer of one afflicted, when he is faint and pours out his complaint before the LORD'. (It is noteworthy that no psalms are specifically assigned to particular festivals in the Hebrew; and even in the Greek, this is also rare: Ps. 29 is a notable exception—'for the Festival of Tabernacles'.)

The headings may be classified into three types: historical, personal, and liturgical.

(I) HISTORICAL HEADINGS

These all occur within the Davidic Collections (Pss. 3, 7, 18, 30, 34, 51, 52, 54, 56, 57, 59, 60, 63, 142: the LXX adds several more). Each title relates to an event in the life of David, and is thus the reverse of the process whereby psalms were inserted into narratives (see Ch. 7, pp. 157ff., concerning Hannah's Song, Jonah's Song, etc.). It is as if an interval were noted in the narratives concerning David in 1 and 2 Samuel, so that the addition of a psalm would have made good dramatic sense; but instead of inserting the psalm into the narrative (the only case where this did happen is 2 Sam. 22, which is a duplicate of Ps. 18) the superscriptions were added to a psalm whose contents suggested in some way the narrative in question.

For example, Ps. 3 (and Ps. 63) is seen (by way of its superscription, 'when David fled from Absalom his son') to fit into the narrative after 2 Sam. 16: 13; Ps. 54 ('when the Ziphites went and told Saul, "David is in hiding among us"') fits after 1 Sam. 23: 4; Pss. 34 and 56 ('when David feigned madness before Abimelech') fit after 2 Sam. 21: 10; and Ps. 51 ('when Nathan the prophet came to David, after he had gone in to Bathsheba') after 2 Sam. 12: 13 (there is also a catchword link in Ps. 51: 6 with 2 Sam. 12: 13). This process could, of course, work in reverse: the contents of a psalm could suggest a particular narrative. For example, the reference to God as 'refuge' in Pss. 57: 1 and 142: 5 suggests David 'in the cave', as in the heading; the reference to the 'dry and thirsty land' in Ps. 63: 1 suggests David 'in the wilderness of Judah', again in the heading; the reference to the 'insolent men' having risen against the suppliant in Ps. 54: 3 suggests the occasion of the Ziphites betraying David to

Saul. Perhaps it could be that both the narrative had to suggest a psalm, and the psalm had to suit the narrative.

M. D. Goulder (*The Prayers of David*, 1990) takes the view that the historical headings in Pss. 51–72 (the second Davidic collection) suggest that these psalms were actually written for David, by a close attendant, recording his sufferings during the last years of his life up to the succession of Solomon, and that a narrative agenda was offset by recitation of prayer. However, other evidence points to this being a separate tradition from the accounts in 1 and 2 Samuel: there are several discrepancies in the details. (For example, in Ps. 34, the Philistine king is Abimelech, whilst in 1 Sam. 21: 10 it is Achish; and in Ps. 56, David is supposedly captured, whilst in 2 Sam. 21 he goes to the Philistines on his own initiative.) It is more likely that, rather than suggesting Davidic authorship, the super-scriptions reflect a literary device (as part of a later process of theological interpretation of the psalms) from a much later period, when both the narrative (from 1–2 Samuel) and the relevant psalms within their 'Davidic collection' had become properly established within the community.

(II) PERSONAL HEADINGS

Connected with the above are the seventy-three psalms ascribed to King David. Is this the same sort of literary/theological device as seen in the more detailed historical headings? Certainly the Hebrew preposition *l*^{e} (translated 'to' David) has a variety of meanings: 'for' and 'of' and 'belonging to' are all equally possible. Thus the psalm could be dedicated to the memory of David, or associated with a tune or royal style from a Davidic tradition, or linked to the 'Davidic' guilds of singers. Certainly this is how the LXX understood it: one additional heading in the Greek (Ps. 71) ascribes the psalm not only to David but also to Jonadab, at the time of the exile, thus making it impossible to assume both headings were of historical worth.

There is no doubt (setting aside the LXX) that later Hebrew tradition assumed that the titles implied actual Davidic authorship: one of the Qumran Psalms Scrolls, 11 QPs^a 2: 4–5, 9–10, refers to David as the author of 3,600 psalms (*t^{e}hillîm*) and 450 songs (*šîrîm*).

So too in Rabbinic tradition, a Midrash on the Psalms (1: 2) clearly affirms David as the author of the Psalter in the same way that Moses was the author of the Law. Whether the titles were actually used in this way, and whether they should be read as such now, is a different issue: it is more appropriate to read the 'To David' headings as a means of seeing how different psalms are to be read *personally*: they address not only the life of one of the most important figures in Israel's history, but also the lives of any who choose to apply the psalm to their own situation. The 'life-centredness' of the psalms is again the point at issue here. It could be said that the psalms have been made specific so that, paradoxically, they can also become typical and general for use in other life-settings.

The same comments apply to the other psalms ascribed to particular personalities—for example, 'of Asaph', supposedly a contemporary of David (twelve psalms), and 'of Korah', a cultic official known at the time of Jehoshophat (eleven psalms). Other expressions include 'of Solomon' (two psalms—Ps. 72, whose contents might be associated with the wisdom of this king, and Ps. 127, whose first verse 'unless the Lord build the house' might suggest a link with Solomon's building of the Temple). The headings 'of Heman' and 'of Ethan' (Pss. 88 and 89) probably suggest musicians or wise men associated in different traditions with both David and Solomon. 'A prayer of Moses' (Ps. 90) may be understood by fitting various verses with events in the life of Moses—see 90: 1/Deut. 33: 27; 90: 10/Exod. 7: 7; 90: 13/Exod. 33: 12. A more problematic heading is 'to Jeduthun' (Pss. 39, 62, 77). According to the Chronicler, this was a musician associated with David and Solomon; however, the dual superscription in Pss. 39 and 62 ('to Jeduthun'; 'of David') and in Ps. 77 ('to Jeduthun'; 'of Asaph') as well as the Hebrew preposition *ʿal* (rather than *lᵉ*) might suggest that this is in fact a musical instrument rather than a person.

The fact that a good number of the psalms in question suggest historical situations and theological ideas long after the time of David and Solomon (for example, Ps. 89B must be exilic) would again suggest that these superscriptions are interpretative and are additions to the psalm. They are a means of understanding a psalm in a particular way in the hindsight of tradition; but they do not constrain us to read the psalm in that way alone.

(III) LITURGICAL HEADINGS

If the historical and personal headings enable us to read the psalms in one particular literary/theological way, then this group of superscriptions points towards the equally important liturgical use of the Psalter. The liturgical headings fall into four general categories: the type of psalm; the tune to accompany it; the instruments to be used; and the role of the choirmaster, possibly in leading antiphonally.

Of the *types* of liturgical psalms, the most common is the *mizmôr*. This occurs fifty-seven times, thirty-five of which are in psalms with Davidic headings. The Greek translates this as *psalmos*, meaning 'hymn', or 'song to music'. Another common term is *šîr* (once *šîrâ*), occurring twenty-nine times, thirteen of these alongside *mizmôr*. Again, this means 'song'. *Miktām* is used for Pss. 16 and 56–60; its root means 'hidden'. From this, one might surmise this was a psalm written on some sort of private inscription (see Isa. 38: 9), rather than being used for public recitation. *Maskîl* is a heading in seventeen psalms; its occurrence in Ps. 32: 8 suggests that it refers to the instructional value of a psalm. *Tᵉhillâ* (despite its use as a term for the heading of the entire Psalter) is found only in Ps. 145, and means, again, 'hymn'. *Tᵉpillâ* ('prayer') is found in Pss. 17, 86, 90, 102, and 142. *Šiggāyôn* is found in Ps. 7; its root suggests 'wail', 'howl': it could indicate a psalm of mourning, or lament.

Regarding the *tunes* of psalms, much is still uncertain. Relevant psalms include Pss. 8, 81, 84 (all ascribed to 'the Gittith'; one meaning is 'winepress'; hence this possibly refers to some vintage song). Psalms 57–9 and 75 are ascribed 'Do not destroy'—again, this may be some vintage tune. Pss. 45, 60, 69, and 80 are ascribed 'To the lilies' (or 'lilies of testimony'): these may be cue-words of a song, which in turn indicates a particular tune. Psalm 22 is headed 'On the hind of the dawn'; this may again refer to the words of a song whose tune is an accompaniment to the psalm. The same is the case for Ps. 56: 'To the dove on far-off Terebinths'. *ʿal-mût labēn* in Ps. 9 may indicate a male soprano, or another cue-word from a song; *ʿal-ʿalāmôt* in Ps. 46 may indicate the accompanying voices of women, or again may serve as a cue-word. In most cases above we may note the link between psalmody and 'secular' singing.

Concerning the *musical accompaniment* to various psalms, much is again surmise. The term $n^e g\hat{i}n\hat{o}t$ in Pss. 4, 6, 54, 55, 67, and 76 suggests some stringed instrument (see 1 Sam. 16: 16, 23). The term $\check{s}^e m\hat{i}n\hat{i}t$ in Pss. 6 and 12 may refer to an eight-stringed instrument, or even eight voices; $m\bar{a}h^a la\underline{t}$ in Pss. 53 and 88 may be a wind instrument (see 1 Kgs. 1: 40).

The term $la\, m^e na\underline{s}\underline{s}e'ah$ occurs fifty-five times. Certainly the LXX did not understand the meaning, translating this *eis to telos*—'for the end' or 'to eternity'. Its use in Ps. 18 but not in the duplicate psalm 1 Sam. 22 suggests it has to do with the performance of a psalm. One possible root is n–s–h—'to supervise', suggesting this is to be sung by the leader of the assembly—hence the translation 'To the choirmaster'. (Interestingly, the same Hebrew preposition l^e is used here, as in the 'To David' psalms: this indicates further that the Davidic psalms are more to do with use than with authorship, as with the acknowledgement 'To the choirmaster' in this case.) The ascription occurs almost entirely in Books One to Three (exceptions are Pss. 109, 139, and 140); thus in every case this is linked with the psalms of Davidic orientation.

Brief reference must be made to the term *Selāh* within this survey of the musical use of the psalms. The word is used seventy-one times in thirty-nine psalms. It never comes at the beginning of a verse, but always in the middle or at the end, and often after a refrain (for example, Pss. 24: 6, 10; 46: 7, 11; 52: 3, 5). It may relate to the root s–l–l, meaning 'to raise' (the hands? the eyes? the voice?). It may be associated with the root s–l–h, 'to bow down', or 'to prostrate oneself'—i.e., in worship. It may be linked with the Hebrew *sal*, meaning basket, or drum, indicating the beat or rhythm of a psalm. The most common interpretation is that taken up by the Greek, which translates *Selāh* as *diápsalma*, meaning pause; in this way *Selāh* indicates an interlude in the recitation or singing of a psalm.

In conclusion, this survey of the three types of headings to the psalms takes us back to the two different approaches to the Psalter outlined at the beginning of this chapter. The superscriptions give clear evidence both of the liturgical/cultic appropriation of the Psalter and of the theological/literary interpretation. Both complement each other; the combination of both types in the longer headings to psalms such as 22, 45, 46, 54, 56, 57, 58, 59, and 60 illustrates this point well.

D. From Pre-Exilic to Post-Exilic Temple Cult

It should now be clear that it is impossible to offer specific dates for any of the psalms. (On this issue, see also Ch. 8, pp. 186–9, on the psalmists as poets.) In individual cases, it is possible to conjecture settings based in part upon the contents and in part upon correspondences with external criteria. For example, it has already been proposed that the royal psalms were early (i.e., Pss. 2, 18, 20, 21, 45, 72, 89, 110, 132, 144: cf. Ch. 10, pp. 220–2), and that they suggest actual compositions from the time of the monarchy. They correspond well with the ideals of sacral kingship in the ancient Near East—the anointed one (Pss. 2: 2; 20: 6; 89: 20; 132: 10), adopted as the divine son (Pss. 2: 7; 89: 26), whose throne is like the throne of God (Ps. 45: 6), who also sits at the deity's right hand (Ps. 110: 1), whose reign is to subject nations under him (Pss. 2: 8ff.; 18: 43ff.; 144: 1–2, 10) and to bring in justice and order for his own people (Ps. 72: 1–4). These ideals have echoes in the court ideology in Mesopotamia and Egypt—both before and at the time of the Davidic monarchy.

For similar reasons some of the Zion hymns (Pss. 46, 48, 76, 84, 87, 122) also suggest an early date. They appear to borrow from early Canaanite mythology, concerning the deity's dwelling on a mountain (Pss. 48: 2), with rivers of healing flowing through the city (Ps. 46: 4), and the appearing of the deity to protect his people and judge the nations (Pss. 46: 6; 48: 8; 76: 8–9).

Similarly, a number of psalms which suggest a northern provenance (most of which are found in the Asaph collection) also contain mythological details about God in a heavenly council of divine beings (Ps. 82: 1, 6–7), and the older tribal traditions about land-possession (Ps. 83: 2ff.). Several Asaph psalms also contain prophetic oracles (Pss. 50: 5ff.; 81: 6ff.). It is more than likely that a good number of these psalms thus date from the pre-exilic period.

Four psalms speak of the desolation of the land (Ps. 79), the destruction of the sanctuary (Ps. 74), the end of the monarchy (Ps. 89: 38ff.), and the life of exile in Babylon (Ps. 137). The most obvious historical crisis behind each of these psalms is the time between 597 and 587 BCE.

Several psalms are preoccupied with the question of theodicy (that is, the prosperity of the wicked and the suffering of the righteous)—a question which is usually associated with wisdom concerns in the restoration period. Psalms 49 and 73, on the issue of the fate of the wicked and the vindication of the righteous, and Pss. 39 and 90, on the transience of life, all suggest this later period. Similarly late are psalms which reflect on the importance of ordering life through keeping the Torah (Pss. 1, 19, 119). Other later developments are found in the more spiritualized and internalized attitude to cultic ritual, whereby the offering of 'thanksgiving' is no longer that of sacrifice (as in Pss. 66: 13–15; 107: 22; 116: 17), but rather the inner attitude of heart (Pss. 26: 6–7; 69: 30–1).

It is likely, therefore, that the composition of biblical psalmody began as early as the monarchy and ended some time around the late Persian period. But the possibility of second-century Maccabean psalms (a view upheld by the majority of scholars at the beginning of the twentieth century) is now less compelling. There is evidence of Aramaic influence in the psalmic language, which could well suggest a date from the time of the Persian period onwards, but there is no convincing evidence of Greek influence in psalmody, which suggests a time before the Hellenistic period, from the latter part of the fourth century onwards. The fact that the LXX at least uses the same number and the same order of psalms indicates that the Hebrew text itself (albeit not the superscriptions) was in some final form by this time. Some of the findings at Qumran give us further evidence in this direction: psalms scrolls in Cave 4 reveal that Books One and Two of the Psalter were on the whole in the same form and order as in the Hebrew Psalter. The use of Ps. 79: 2–3 in 1 Macc. 17 may be another indication of the use of the Psalter in different Jewish communities by the time of the second century BCE.

We may therefore propose a *terminus a quo* for the composition of biblical psalmody from the time of the first Temple in the tenth century BCE (though some scholars would date Pss. 29 and 68, which appear to have several Canaanite borrowings, earlier) and the *terminus ad quem* for the actual composition of the latest psalms (although not necessarily the final arrangement) as before the Greek period at the end of the fourth century. These observations are summarized in Table 5. Again, a precise dating is impossible— not least in the cases of some of the larger groups of individual and communal psalms not listed. An observation from C. F. Barth (*Introduction to the Psalms*) is pertinent in this respect:

Kings, priests, and prophets, but, above all, unknown poets and singers, constantly contributed their gifts in this process. Of the Psalms more than any other book of the Old Testament it must be said that *all* Israel, the people of God 'from generation to generation' took part in its composition. (p. 4.)

During this period, a huge amount of theological adaptation must have taken place: psalms which were intended for individuals to use would have been appropriated by the community; psalms

TABLE 5. The composition of the psalms.

FIRST TEMPLE PERIOD 950–587 BCE	*Davidic Monarchy*: royal psalms (2, 18, 20, 21, 45, 72, 89, 110, 132, 144). *Solomonic Temple*: Zion hymns (46, 48, 76, 87, 122) and liturgies (15, 24) and other hymns (29, 68). *The Nation and the Land*: community psalms (65, 66, 67, 118) and individual psalms (7, 12, 23, 30, 40, 41, 51, 61, 140, 141). *The Ministry of the Prophets*: psalms with oracles (see royal psalms; also 50, 75, 81, 82, 95).
EXILE 587–520 BCE	*No Monarchy*: 'kingship' hymns (47, 93–9) and 'creation' hymns (19A, 104).

T<small>ABLE</small> 5 (*cont.*)

	No Temple: laments on Zion (Pss. 74, 77, 79, 137).
	No Nation: laments of the community (44, 60, 123, 126) and of the individual (13, 17, 22, 31, 35, 42–3, 54, 55, etc.).
	The Ministry of the Prophets: psalms of 'salvation-history' (78, 105, 107).
SECOND TEMPLE PERIOD 520–?323 BCE	*Theocracy*: adaptation of royal and kingship of God psalms.
	Second Temple: individual songs at temple (25, 84, 116, 138) and hymns of praise (8, 33, 100, 103, 111, 117, 135, 136, 145–50).
	Persian (then Greek) Rule: adaptation of earlier communal psalms for future hope.
	Decline of Prophecy: influence of wisdom and Torah piety (1, 19, 37, 49, 73, 112, 119, 127, 128, 129).

---

with royal connotations were now interpreted with a future hope for a coming ideal figure; and psalms which spoke of particular historical events, and of specific tribes and places, were understood as having instead a more general and universal application. All this was taking place before the Psalter received its final (canonical) form.

When this final stage of 'fixing' the tradition had happened, one might have thought that the process of adaptation was complete. Far from it: the surprising factor is that a great variety of further theological reinterpretation took place, not only in the Jewish tradition, but in the Christian tradition as well. This is as much a theological issue as it is a literary one. The issue of the reinterpretation of psalmody is complex, and provides the focus of attention in the final chapter.

12

The Interpretation of the Psalter

A. Different Translations of the Hebrew Psalter

The text of the final form of the Hebrew Psalter which is used in our English translations dates from copies made by a group of scholars known as the Masoretes (so called because they were responsible for consolidating the traditions behind the text of the Old Testament: these traditions were called *massorôt*). These were rabbis from Tiberias, Galilee, who worked in the ninth and tenth centuries CE—over a thousand years later than the time when the Psalter became canonical, as a fixed form within the Hebrew Scriptures. It goes without saying that the Hebrew text during this millennium must have undergone a process of change. One has only to compare duplicate psalms such as 14 and 53; 40: 12–16 and 70; 108 and 57: 7–11 along with 60: 5–12; and Ps. 18 and 2 Sam. 22, to find evidence of a number of variations which existed even in the same Hebrew texts.

The Masoretes were responsible for consolidating further the texts themselves, in terms of punctuation, vowel points, and accentuation. With respect to the psalms, a particular system was added to the whole of Psalms–Job–Proverbs, delineating lines of poetry by giving it a distinctive type of accenting (the *ṭe'amîm*, referred to in our discussion of metre in Chapter 3). Two manuscripts of the Masoretic Text (MT)—the Aleppo Codex (*c.*930 CE) and the Leningrad Codex (*c.*1008 CE)—form the basis of printed Hebrew editions today.

The LXX version of the Old Testament, from the second century BCE, is so called because of the number of seventy or so scholars from Alexandria, Egypt, alleged to have been employed to work on it. This version is understood either to be a reliable translation (so, A. Rahlfs), or a less precise interpretation (so, P. Kahle). As we have already noted, the LXX includes several literalisms in the psalmic superscriptions and also in the psalms themselves, suggesting some failure in understanding archaisms which had faded out of use. Nevertheless, the Greek version was used by the first (Greek-speaking) Christians, and most of the psalms quoted in the New Testament are taken from the LXX. Various other Greek editions of the Psalter appeared by the end of the second century CE: that of Aquila, closer to the Hebrew text; that of Theodotian, closer to the LXX; and that of Symmachus, considered to be best of the three. The main manuscript copies, all linked back to the LXX, are fourth-century and fifth-century: interestingly, this means that the earliest extant manuscript of the Psalter is not in Hebrew but in Greek. One Greek manuscript, Codex Vaticanus (B) lacks Pss. 105: 27–137: 6; but the other, Codex Sinaiticus (S) has the whole Psalter. A fifth-century manuscript, Codex Alexandrinus (A) is also significant, although this lacks Pss. 49: 20–79: 11.

The oldest Latin version is a translation of the Greek rather than the Hebrew, and dates from the second century CE. This was one of the several sources used by the great Latin scholar, Jerome, in the late third century, who made three different translations of the Psalter. Jerome's second translation, known as the Gallican Psalter, was incorporated into the Latin Bible known as the Vulgate (V), although his last translation is probably the best, being closest to the Hebrew Psalter.

Hence, by the end of the fourth century CE the Psalter existed in three major languages of the Orient. (We might also refer to another important Syriac version, called the *Peshitto* ('simple'), composed for Christians in the first century CE, using the pre-Masoretic, unvocalized Hebrew text.) Three observations are relevant for our own purposes.

First, one extra psalm (= Ps. 151) is found in variant forms in all the early Greek versions, as also in the Vulgate (and in Qumran). A psalm concerning David's slaying of Goliath, its difference from the canonical psalms may be seen in the following extract, translating from the LXX:

This Psalm is a genuine one of David, though supernumerary,
when he fought in single combat with Goliad.
I was small among my brothers,
and youngest in my father's house;
I tended my father's sheep.
My hands formed a [?] pipe,
and my fingers tuned a psaltery

.   .   .   .

My brothers were handsome and tall,
but the Lord did not take pleasure in them

.   .   .   .

I went forth to meet the Philistine,
but he cursed me by his idols.
But I drew his own sword, and beheaded him,
and took away reproach from the children of Israel.

The parallelism, though evident, is somewhat forced; and the
subject-matter is rather more specific—almost like narrative—in
comparison with the more typical poetic diction of the psalms. Its
claim to Davidic authorship is significant, for it shows how this was
a claim to authenticity, even after the five books of the Psalter
appear to have been fixed: the confession that it is 'supernumerary'
is further evidence of a fixed tradition. The addition of the psalm
means that the whole Psalter is now interpreted in the light of its
being 'of David', from beginning (Ps. 2) to end (Ps. 151).

Secondly, within all these different versions in different
languages, there is no evidence of a uniform system dividing one
psalm from another. Although the *contents* of the Psalter stay the
same, various combinations of psalm units are apparent. For
example, the LXX unites Pss. 9–10 and 114–15, but splits Pss. 116
and 147, still arriving at 150 psalms in all. But in other versions,
psalms with no headings are frequently combined with their neighbour: these include Pss. 1–2; 9–10; 42–3; 70–1; 93–4; 94–5; 104–5;
114–15; and 116–17. The result of splitting and uniting psalms is
that some manuscripts have only 148 psalms, whilst others, nearly
170. This feature is most significant in the light of our earlier
observations on more recent intertextual approaches to the Psalter,
which see one psalm in relation to others: this approach has older
precedents than one might imagine.

A final observation links back to our discussion in Chapter 2 on the dividing-line between prose and poetry. Different versions organize the poetry of the psalms in different ways: mostly line-forms are the key, but there are many variations of the cola, not least when faced with changes of syntax and sound between one language and another. Even in the Hebrew manuscripts, line-forms are presented not only by clusters of words, but also column by column; some versions run on continuously in prose form (as noted earlier, this includes the scroll 11 QPs at Qumran, and also psalmic texts from nearby Masada). The business of a consistent presentation of Hebrew poetry, from one language to another, is another age-old issue.

Yet in all three diversities, one clear feature stands out. The many variations are overall from one recension—in content, if not in number and order, a fixed form. The interpretations through translation may differ between tradition, culture, and language, but a normative text is beginning to emerge.

B. The Interpretation of Psalmody in Jewish Tradition

If the interpretations through translations differ, this is all the more the case when one looks at different commentaries on particular psalmic texts. This occurs not only in the Jewish traditions, but in the Christian traditions as well. Some of the Jewish interpretations of psalmody will be considered first.

(I) QUMRAN AND THE PSALTER

We noted above that the earliest manuscripts of the psalms in Hebrew date from the ninth century CE; in Latin, from the fourth century CE; and in Greek, from the second century CE. The findings at Qumran are important, for they give us access to *Hebrew* manuscripts some one thousand years earlier than the Masoretes. From 1947 onwards, over thirty texts of psalms (and commentaries on the psalms) have been found in eight caves on the shores of the Dead Sea. There are also numerous texts of Deuteronomy (about twenty-five in all), fragments of the text of Isaiah (at least eighteen), and of

Exodus (some fourteen), but by far the most extensive finds have been in the psalms.

Eighteen manuscripts were discovered in Cave 4. These have all been dated within the first two centuries BCE. An interesting feature in one scroll (4 QPs^a) is the combination of Pss. 38 and 71 as one psalm. Another scroll, 4 QPs^b, includes Pss. 91–118; although Pss. 104–11 are absent, the rest follow the Masoretic order.

The most significant finds have been in Cave 11. These were examined from 1956 onwards; according to J. A. Sanders, commenting on the five main scroll discoveries, they may be dated around the first century CE. 11 QPs^b contains many psalms in Books One to Three, and most of these follow the order of the MT. But 11 QPs^a is more problematic: mainly containing Books Four and Five of the Psalter, the order is entirely different from the MT. Psalms 106–8 and 110–17 are missing altogether; and thirteen psalms occur in a completely different sequence (Pss. 109, 118, 147, 146, 148, 119, 145, 139, 93, 133, 144, 140, 134). Psalm 145 is interspersed with a refrain after each verse: 'Blessed be God, and bless his name for ever.' The most consistent correspondence with the MT is in the Songs of Ascents (Pss. 120–34), where at least the first thirteen follow the same order. Another intriguing feature is the insertion of several other psalmic texts: 2 Sam. 23: 1–7 is included, as also is Ps. 151 (in a longer form A, and a fragment, B) and 154, 155, and Sir. 51: 13 ff. Editorial additions also include 'The Apostrophe to Zion', 'The Hymn to the Creator', and 'Davidic Compositions'.

Clearly this reflects a more flexible, open-ended use of the Psalter, and shows that within this community, as late as the first century CE, its final form was by no means fixed. Two alternatives are possible. Perhaps the findings are a liturgical collection, a separate tradition 'in honour of David' derived from an already fixed canon, but organizing material differently for the liturgical needs of the community. A biblical model for this would be 1 Chr. 16, which combines in a different order Pss. 105, 95, and 106 for its own liturgical (and theological) purposes. This is the view of P. Skehan. It stands in contrast to that of J. A. Sanders and G. H. Wilson, who conclude that the Qumran scrolls indicate that the Psalter was not finally established in any community until the beginning of the second century CE. Each community possessed its own collection, and that of the Qumran community is but one example of the different permutations.

Whichever view one holds, one factor is very clear: the canonical psalms, in whatever order and form they existed, have a certain distinctiveness, in style and in content, from their later imitations. We have already noted this with respect to Ps. 151. In Qumran, another scroll, 1 QH, is of the *Hôdayôt* (from the Hebrew ʾôdᵉkâ ʾadônây, 'I thank Thee Lord') which comprises thirty or so thanksgiving songs. Although they use parallelism in a similar way to the psalms of the MT, they are more a mosaic of deliberate borrowings from earlier psalms, with two dominant themes: the importance of salvation, and the acquisition of knowledge of God. Their theology is reflective, individualistic, and more overtly pious, as the following example shows:

> I thank Thee, O Lord,
>> for Thou hast redeemed my soul from the Pit,
> and from the hell of Abaddon
>> Thou hast raised me up to everlasting height.
>
> I walk on limitless ground,
> and I know there is hope for him
>> whom Thou hast shaped from dust
>> for the everlasting Council.
> Thou hast cleansed a perverse spirit of great sin
>> that it may stand with the host of Holy Ones
> and that it may enter into community
>> with the congregation of the Sons of Heaven.
> Thou hast allotted to man an everlasting destiny
>> amidst the spirits of knowledge,
> that he may praise Thy Name in a common rejoicing
>> and recount Thy marvels before all Thy works.
>> G. Vermes, 'The Thanksgiving Hymns' (1 QH iii. 5),
>> in *The Dead Sea Scrolls in English* (p. 173)

One final observation is important, for it shows some continuity between the Jewish readings of the psalms and those of Christian commentators. This concerns a recurrent theme of interpreting the psalms firstly in a *prophetic* spirit, and secondly as if spoken by *David*. We have already made reference to 11 QPs naming David as the composer of 3,600 hymns and songs; this ends: 'All these he uttered *through prophecy* which was given him from before the Most High.' The *pešer* (meaning commentary) on particular psalms brings out this interpretation most clearly. 4 Q 171, on Ps. 37, for example, reveals that the community thought itself to be living 'in the last days', so that David's words are prophecies now fulfilled in the 'community of the poor'. To illustrate:

'The wicked borrows and does not repay, but the righteous is generous and gives. Truly, those whom He [blesses shall possess] the land, but those whom He curses [shall be cut off].' (37: 21–2)

Interpreted, this concerns the congregation of the Poor, who [shall possess] the whole world as an inheritance. They shall possess the High Mountain of Israel [for ever], and shall enjoy [everlasting] delights in His sanctuary. [But those who] shall be cut off, they are the violent [of the nations and] the wicked of Israel: they shall be cut off and blotted out for ever. ('Commentary on Psalms' (4 Q 171), in Vermes, *The Dead Sea Scrolls*, 291–3.)

This Davidic/prophetic interpretation is a key emphasis in all early Judaeo-Christian readings of the Psalter from the time of Qumran onwards, as will be seen in the following two sections.

(II) THE PSALTER IN EARLY RABBINIC WRITINGS

The issue of the order (and hence the open-endedness) of the Psalter is not as prevalent in other Jewish traditions as it is in Qumran; usually the text appears to be like that of the MT. Nevertheless, there is evidence of free adaptation for liturgical purposes: a Rabbinic text *Berakhôt* 9*b*–10*a* reveals that the number of psalms is not 150, but 147, by the conjoining of Pss. 1–2, 114–15, and 117–18, probably for more convenient lectionary readings. And just as the Qumran texts reveal other additional material alongside the canonical psalms, so too other Jewish traditions by the second century CE reveal that the Psalter is interpreted and used alongside other liturgical material: examples include the 'Prayer of 18 Benedictions' and the Shema (from Deut. 6 and 11).

Furthermore, just as the *Hôdayôt* psalms at Qumran showed a derivation from a much older established tradition of psalmody, other collections of later psalms outside Qumran confirm these observations. The eighteen 'psalms of Solomon' are psalms in Greek and Syriac (the Hebrew original has never been found) and probably date from the first century BCE on account of the various references to the struggle against the Romans. Their use of parallelism, their conscious imitation of early psalmic formulas, yet also their preoccupation with more eschatological issues (not least, a coming deliverer) and their more explicitly individualistic concerns show them to be later copies of the earlier psalms:

> See Lord, and raise up for them their king,
> > the son of David, to rule over your servant Israel
> > in the time known to you, O God.
>
> Undergird him with the strength to destroy the unrighteous rulers
> > to purge Jerusalem from gentiles
> > who trample her destruction;
> > in wisdom and in righteousness to drive out
> > the sinners from the inheritance;
> to smash the arrogance of sinners like a potter's jar;
> To shatter all their substance with an iron rod;
> to destroy the unlawful nations with the word of his mouth;
> At his warning the nations will flee from his presence;
> > and he will condemn sinners
> > by the thoughts of their hearts.
>
> > ('Psalms of Solomon' 17: 21–5, in J. H. Charlesworth (ed.),
> > *The Old Testament Pseudepigrapha*, ii. 667.)

The other two features noted from the use of the Psalter in Qumran, namely the belief in overall Davidic authorship of the psalms, and a bias towards a contemporary prophetic interpretation, are also in evidence. A Rabbinic text, Pes. 117a, reads:

A harp was suspended above the bed of David. When midnight came the north wind blew on it and it produced music of its own accord. Immediately David arose and occupied himself with the Torah.

The greatest Rabbinic commentary on the psalms, *Midrash T*ᵉ*hillîm* (which was compiled somewhat later, between the third and thirteenth centuries CE) has exactly the same emphasis. First, the psalms are given a Davidic orientation as part of their *historical* exegesis; and second, they are given a prophetic orientation, as prayers now fulfilled in the life of the present community, as part of the *contemporary* exegesis. For example, in the *midraš* (meaning 'interpretation') on Ps. 2, a verse is taken as of David's time, and related to other verses from the law and prophets to give it a historical orientation. The fulfilment theme follows: the promises once made to the king (vv. 7, 8) are now to be fulfilled in the life of the people (they, like the king, are adopted 'sons of God') yet await ultimate fulfilment through a coming Messiah. In this way the psalms are not only prayers of David; they are prophecies from David.

C. The Interpretation of Psalmody in Christian Tradition

It is no surprise to find the theme of 'David the prophet' occurring frequently in the use of the psalms by the first Jewish Christians. The New Testament bears ample witness to this mode of interpretation. In fact, the Psalter is used more than any other book for a prophetic purpose (Isaiah, Deuteronomy, and Exodus are also used very frequently, but well over a third of the 360 OT references are from Psalms). In the following example from Acts 2: 25 ff., the context is a speech of Peter, establishing that the resurrection of Christ was foretold in the Hebrew Scriptures. The passage starts with a quotation from Ps. 16: 8–11:

> For thou wilt not abandon my soul to Hades,
> nor let thy Holy One see corruption . . .

It is assumed that these are David's words (Acts 2: 25—'for David says . . .'). The passage continues (vv. 30 ff.):

Being therefore a prophet, and knowing that God had sworn with an oath to him that he would send one of his descendants upon his throne [here this is a quotation from Ps. 132: 11], he foresaw and spoke of the resurrection of the Christ, that he was not abandoned to Hades, nor did his flesh see corruption. This Jesus God raised up, and of that we all are witnesses.

This passage illustrates well the continuity within the Jewish and Christian interpretation of psalmody. First, the unequivocal attribution to Davidic authorship, seen also in the Qumran scrolls and in Rabbinic tradition: the psalms are prayers composed by David in 1000 BCE; in this way, they have a potential for personal and corporate appropriation. Second, the unmistakable prophetic emphasis, like that we have seen in *pešer* on Ps. 37 at Qumran, and in the *Midrash Tᵉhillîm* on Ps. 2. The psalms possess a certain promissory element, and because the interpreters (from Jewish and Christian traditions alike) believed they were living in the 'last days', they also believed that the promises to David were about to be fulfilled—for example, promises about the breaking-in of a new kingdom of God's rule on earth, promises of inheriting the land, of defeat of the enemies, of victory through suffering, of blessing after perseverance in keeping God's law.

The obvious point of discontinuity between the earlier Jewish and the later Christian interpretations of psalmody is that the latter, without fail, are 'inclined Christwards'. In other words, David, the royal figure whose life encompassed both suffering and victory, both defeat and success, is but a type, prefiguring Christ. The constant use of Ps. 110: 1 is a good illustration of this: found in Mark 12: 35–7 (also in Matt. 22: 41–6 and Luke 20: 41–4), and in Acts 2: 34–5, Heb. 1: 13; 10: 12–13, this was originally a psalm inviting the king to ascend to his throne. Through an oracle, God promises him victory:

> The LORD says to my lord:
> 'Sit at my right hand,
>   till I make your enemies your footstool'

This is now seen to be God's conferment of victory on Christ, the anointed one, the Messiah, whose reign transcends that of David. At least three moves take place in the use of verses from royal psalms in this way. First, the psalm is no longer fundamentally about David, but about Christ: hence its *past* orientation changes. Second, the psalm is no longer about David's God, but about Christ, who is God: hence the *present* orientation changes. Third, the prophetic promises are fulfilled not by David, but by Christ: hence the *future* orientation also changes.

We may illustrate these three modes of interpretation further. First, that the past orientation has changed: the psalms are now *prayers of Christ.* The Gospel writers show in some detail how the psalms were indeed prayers of Christ, not least in the last day of his life: Matt. 26: 24 (Luke 24: 25) takes up Ps. 41: 9 at the Last Supper; Mark 14: 26 (Matt. 26: 30) implies the singing of some of the Passover Hallel (from Pss. 113–15) before the ascent to Olivet; Mark 14: 34 (Matt. 26: 38) refers to Ps. 42: 3, 11–43: 5 as part of the prayer in the Garden of Gethsemane; and on the cross, John 19: 28 ('I thirst') takes up expressions of suffering found, for example, in Pss. 22: 15 and 69: 21; Mark 15: 34 (Matt. 27: 46) is the cry of dereliction ('My God, My God, why have you forsaken me?') found in Ps. 22: 1; and Luke 23: 46 is the cry of commitment found in Ps. 31: 5: 'Into thy hand I commit my spirit.' (From prayers such as these, a further implication is that Jesus Christ, who prayed the psalms before us, also in some mysterious way prays them with us; as we enter into the mystery of Jesus' suffering through the psalms, so he enters into ours.) The Gospels thus provide us with an example of one type of Christian use of the psalms: they are only secondarily 'psalms of David'; they are primarily 'psalms of Christ'.

The second mode of interpretation is that the present orientation has changed. These are also *prayers to Christ.* He is 'the LORD' referred to in Ps. 110: 1—in a paradoxical sense, the giver of the promises once made to David as well as the recipient of them. In this way, the metaphorical language used to describe the God of Israel in the psalms now becomes transferred to Christ himself. He is the King, the Judge, the Redeemer of his people, the Deliverer, the Protector, the Teacher; and when the psalmists address God as their Rock, Fortress, Shepherd, Way, Truth, and Life—these now become focused towards Christ. One example from the psalms may be found in the use of Pss. 42–3. Contrasting images of water (thirsting, and drowning) are particularly vivid in the first half of the psalm. The suppliant appeals first to God who, in metaphorical terms, quenches thirst in a dry and parched land (vv. 1–3): this makes an ideal focus for Christian interpretation, for Jesus Christ, according to John, is the 'living water' (John 4: 13–15; 7: 37). The same suppliant speaks later to God who sets his steadfast love on him, even when 'the thunder of the cataracts' and 'waves and billows' threaten (vv. 7–8). A Christian interpretation, using the story of Jesus according to Mark 4: 35–41, would recall that during

the storm on the lake, Jesus rebukes the wind and says to the sea,
'Peace, be still.' This represents a typological approach to the
psalms, in that it moves from the metaphorical imagery in the
poetry to the literal fulfilment of the metaphor in the narratives in
the Gospel stories.

The third mode of interpretation is that the future orientation
has also changed. The psalms are now *prophecies about Christ*. The
promises to David are indeed fulfilled in these 'the latter days'.
This prophetic emphasis is achieved by taking two dominant
themes in the psalms, and using them as reflections on what was
achieved through Jesus' life and death.

The first theme is that of *royal victory*, and is usually found in the
hymnic forms. This theme anticipates the bringing in of the Kingdom (Kingship) of God. As well as the kingship hymns, the royal
psalms become the obvious focus of attention in this respect, and
Pss. 2, 110, and 118 in particular are used in this way. The royal
decree in Ps. 2: 7 'You are my son, this day have I begotten you'
becomes part of a different sort of decree spoken both at the
baptism and transfiguration of Christ: 'This is my Beloved Son,
with whom I am well pleased.' We have already referred to the use
of Ps. 110: in confrontation with the Pharisees, Ps. 110: 1 ('The
LORD says to my lord, sit at my right hand . . .') is used to show
that Christ is the speaker, whose royal, God-given authority
surpasses that of David. The most graphic example is found in Ps.
118, in part implying a thanksgiving song to be offered by the king
after some national victory. When Jesus enters Jerusalem on what
later became known as Palm Sunday, the Gospel writers use this
psalm to depict Christ as the coming deliverer, anointed by God,
leading his own victory procession:

> Hosanna to the Son of David!
>> Blessed is he who comes in the name of the LORD!
>
> The stone which the builders rejected
>> has become the head of the corner.
> This is the LORD'S doing;
>> it is marvellous in our eyes.
>
> Blessed be he who enters in the name of the LORD!
>
> (Matt. 21: 9; Ps. 118: 22, 26)

In this way, the early Christians found a mode of explaining not only that Jesus fulfilled the promises in the psalms, but also that the psalms interpreted properly who Jesus was—the promised deliverer, the heavenly King, the anointed one—the Messiah.

Not only was this prophetic emphasis achieved by reference to the psalms of royal victory; a second theme is found in another group of psalms, mainly lament in form, whose main concern is that of *human suffering and despair*. A number of psalms used in this way in the Passion narratives in the Gospels have already been pointed out. The most important include Pss. 22 and 69. Together these become reflections not only on the words of Jesus, but also on the way in which his suffering was apparently foretold. The references to the mockery of the onlookers at the crucifixion, the casting of lots for Christ's robe, and the offering of vinegar for drink are all supported by references from these two psalms (Pss. 22: 7, 8, 18 and 69: 21; cf. Matt. 27: 39, 43 and John 19: 24, also Matt. 27: 34). The most evocative examples are the cries of anguish from the cross, taking up the prayers of distress in the psalms, and hence showing Christ identifying with the pain of humankind, and sharing and bearing the depths of human suffering. In this way the psalms of 'royal victory' and the psalms of 'human suffering' necessarily complement one another: Jesus achieves a kingdom not through power of military victory for his people but through the pain of suffering with his people. (We may also refer here to the way in which similar poetry in the prophets was used along the same lines: the 'songs from the royal court' in Isa. 9 and Isa. 11 are used in the Christian tradition to take up the 'royal victory' theme, and the Songs of the Servant in Isa. 42, and 53 in particular, are used to serve as part of the suffering theme.)

The Christianizing of the psalms meant that by the second century CE, psalmody became a central part of the liturgy of the Church. The psalms enabled the early Church to recall its roots in the more ancient traditions of Judaism; yet also they gave the Church a fixed text whereby a distinctive Christian adaptation could be furthered. Hence the Psalter became the hymn-book of the Church. At the end of the second century, Tertullian speaks of the Sunday vigil service, where the psalms are interspersed with prayers, preaching, and blessings. By the fourth century, John

Chrysostom speaks of the vigils of the Church 'with David first, last and midst—in funeral solemnities, in convents of virgins, in the desert, man in communion with God, and David first, last and midst'. By the sixth century, the Canonical Hours of Prayer, taken by the Western Church from the East, refers to eight daily offices, with the psalms central in each. The *Primer* of the Middle Ages, a book of prayer for the laity, similarly keeps the psalms at the centre of its offices. And poets throughout the ages, as diverse as Herbert, Wesley, Watts, Wyatt, Vaughan, Milton, Lyte, Keble, and Tate and Brady, have all brought new patterns of psalmody into hymnody. Whether in the formal offices and liturgies, or in less structured homilies and devotions, or represented through art, sculpture, architecture, and music, the psalms have become the formative influence as hymn-book and prayer-book in the Christian as well as in the Jewish tradition.

In the light of our observations at the beginning of this chapter, reference must also be made to the complementary theological/ literary reading of the poetry of the psalms. This too has always been a significant part of the Christian tradition. Scholars and commentators from as early as the time of Origen (180–254 CE) and including Augustine (354–430) and Aquinas (1225–74) have contributed much on an allegorical and typological Christianized reading of the psalms, looking at them not only in terms of prayers and prophecies, but also as poems with a profound theological content. At the time of the Reformation, both Luther (who wrote commentaries and works on the psalms between 1513 and 1533) and Calvin (who in 1557 also published a sizeable commentary on the psalms) similarly viewed the psalms in a specifically theological light—interpreting them in typological and allegorical terms.

We may conclude that within both the Christian and Jewish traditions, there are two fundamental ways of appropriating the psalms: one is for liturgical use, and the other, for a literary/ theological understanding. More than any other biblical book, the Psalter sustains both a unity and a diversity: in the main, this is the result of the nature of the poetry. This issue of unity and diversity should provide an appropriate summary for an overall grasp of the theology of the psalms.

D. Towards a Theological Interpretation of the Psalter

The previous chapter on the history of the development of psalmody from the pre-exilic to the post-exilic cult gives a good indication of the diversity of theologies contained within the Psalter. Several vast cultural changes are evident: the movement from monarchy to theocracy; the change from the influence of prophecy (at the royal court) to the influence of 'the wise' and the scribes of the law; and the growing questions of theodicy, represented in the change in the people from nationhood to vassaldom. True, the human responses at times of sickness, death, loss of friends, slander, persecution, exile, good or bad harvest, and military defeat or victory would have been a constant, and the expressions of faith or despair, couched in the traditional language of the cult, similarly provided a continuity; but the vast changes in the world-views of the psalmists inevitably resulted in various paradoxical beliefs about the nature of God and his supposed relationship with the created order. These paradoxical beliefs might be classified under six broad headings.

First, the Psalter upholds on the one hand a belief in the *God of Israel*, yet on the other hand, a trust in the *God of all nations*. This tension is between what might be termed nationalism and universalism, or exclusivism and inclusivism, and is found usually in specific types of psalms. The royal psalms, the Zion hymns, and the historical psalms all testify to the more nationalistic concerns: Pss. 2, 18 (royal psalms), 46, 48 (Zion hymns), and 78 and 105 (historical psalms) are all good examples. There is a good deal of patriotic pride in these psalms ('Ask of me, and I will make the nations your heritage, and the ends of the earth your possession . . .' (Ps. 2: 8); 'the city of God, which God establishes for ever . . .' (Ps. 48: 8))—a pride which has often created difficulties of appropriation when set within other, non-Jewish cultural contexts. This approach is interestingly offset within the Psalter itself, in psalms which speak of God's cosmic rule, and of his concern for all creation and hence for all nations. The kingship psalms (e.g. Pss. 47 and 93) and the hymns of praise (e.g. Pss. 8 and 104) are good examples of this more open-ended and universal view of God as Creator of all peoples:

O LORD, our Lord,
How majestic is thy name in all the earth!

(Ps. 8: 1, 9)

O LORD, how manifold are thy works!
In wisdom hast thou made them all;
the earth is full of thy creatures.

(Ps. 104: 24)

A second example of paradox is found on the one hand in psalms which speak of the *God of the powerful*—in other words, the kings, priests, and prophets—and on the other hand in psalms which trust in the *God of the powerless*—the oppressed, the downtrodden, and the isolated, and those termed frequently in the psalms 'the poor and needy' and 'the saints' and 'the righteous'. Again the royal psalms (e.g. 45, 72, 110) are examples of the first category; and the communal and individual laments and the wisdom psalms (i.e. often the later post-exilic psalms) bear witness to the second type (e.g. Pss. 86, 109, 140, 37). This second emphasis, with its theological concern with the God who stands for justice for the oppressed, is highly relevant in the contemporary concerns for justice expressed in liberation theology and feminist theology. If this concern for freedom and justice is set alongside that for warfare and power, it may be seen as another expression of the tension between the exclusivist and inclusivist views of the nature of God, this time expressed within the community of Israel.

A third paradox is found in the different emphases on what 'pleases' God: some psalmists put the greater store on *God and cultic worship*, whilst others give priority to *God and inner devotion*. Quite clearly these are differences in emphasis, and need not be diametrically opposed. However, within the royal psalms and liturgies, the assumed context for praise and prayer is through ritual, sacrifice, processions, and festal occasions (e.g. Pss. 68, 118, 132). By contrast, the individual laments and thanksgivings and the wisdom psalms put greater store on integrity of the heart, on inner piety and trust, on social concerns, and on ethical obedience. Relevant psalms include Pss. 26, 32, 51, and 139, where the approach to God is portrayed in more personal and immediate terms. Neither view of God need exclude the other; Pss. 15 and 24, for example, combine both together. Nevertheless, each emphasis is apt to lead to a different view of God and his closeness or distance from the world of the suppliant.

A fourth more complex example of paradoxical diversity is found in the psalms relating to a *God of judgement* and others which speak of a *God of salvation*. These are expressed with regard to the fate of the community and of the individual. The judgement motif is mostly found in the lament form, where the experience of distress is seen as permitted, if not caused, by God, and where the judgement is either accepted as deserved (in which case, the lament form also includes some confession of sin) or fought against as undeserved (in which case, the psalm includes a long protest of innocence). Psalms 74, 77, and 89 all testify to the judgement of God; the confessions and protests interestingly mix in each. The motif of God as one who saves and redeems is the common theme of the thanksgivings (e.g. Ps. 40) and hymns (e.g. Ps. 100). Extracts from Pss. 74 and 100 make the contrasting theologies all too clear:

> O God, why dost thou cast us off for ever?
>> Why does thy anger smoke against the sheep of thy pasture?
>
> Arise, O God, plead thy cause;
>> remember how the impious scoff at thee all day!
>
>> (Ps. 74: 1, 22)

> Know that the LORD is God!
>> It is he that made us, and we are his;
>> we are his people, and the sheep of his pasture.
>
> For the LORD is good;
>> his steadfast love endures for ever,
>> and his faithfulness to all generations.
>
>> (Ps. 100: 3, 5)

A fifth aspect of diverse theologies is found in psalms which speak of the *God of the living* and others which acknowledge him also as the *God of the dead*. The former view is predominant; rarely is there an expression of faith which trusts in God beyond the grave. On this account, blessings and rewards are to be found in this life alone; and as a consequence, the plight of the righteous suffering and of the wicked prospering is all the more poignant and distressing. The result is seen in the vindictive curses found in many laments and wisdom psalms, which cry out for justice to be done, and to be seen to be done, during the present generation. Psalms which evince this theme among the laments are Pss. 109 and 137 and, among the wisdom psalms, Ps. 37. By contrast, a few psalms appear to move beyond this earth-bound belief: God's power extends beyond the grave, for he can indeed 'redeem' from 'the pit'. Here are two contrasting examples:

> I am reckoned among those who go down to the Pit;
> > I am a man who has no strength,
> like one forsaken among the dead,
> > like the slain that lie in the grave,
> like those whom thou dost remember no more,
> > for they are cut off from thy hand.
>
> Is thy steadfast love declared in the grave,
> > or thy faithfulness in Abaddon?
>
> (Ps. 88: 4–5, 11)

> But God will ransom my soul from the power of Sheol,
> > for he will receive me.
>
> (Ps. 49: 15)

The sixth and final paradox links back to the first. Just as a tension is evident between God's care for 'the nation' yet also for 'the nations', so too a tension exists between the *God of the individual* and the *God of the community*. We have already discussed the extent to which this tension has preoccupied psalmic studies over this century (see Ch. 8), for it is clear that within the Psalter, both concerns are apparent. The God of warfare, of the affairs of the royal court, and of the official Temple cult (seen e.g. in Pss. 44, 66, 121) can be very different from the God of personal and domestic affairs (compare Pss. 3, 4, 42–3, 54, 55). Official theology and private devotion are indeed complementary, but they each focus on different attributes of God and of his activity in the world. The 'Davidic' titles help in part to bridge this gap, for they unite together the two concerns of the public (royal) figure with the personal (human) details, but nevertheless, in terms of different emphases of belief in God, that these are contrasting beliefs is irrefutable.

E. Unity and Diversity in the Psalter

It is of course possible to minimize the various paradoxes and diverse theologies of the separate psalms, and to focus instead on a unifying theology of the entire Psalter. This takes us back to the issues of intertextual readings of the psalms which were discussed at the beginning of Chapter 11. A résumé of the various scholarly contributions should make this point clear.

One unifying theological approach could be to read the entire Psalter in terms of *God's covenant with David*, inaugurated (Pss. 1–72), broken (Pss. 73–89), and restored (Pss. 90–150). This is explored in the works of J. H. Walton and G. H. Wilson. A different way of expressing the same point would be to see the theology essentially about the *everlasting kingship of God*, first expressed in earthly terms, through the reigning king, and developed in the later psalms in terms of God's heavenly rule. This is basically the view of B. S. Childs. It is also shared by H.-J. Kraus, but made more specific (and somewhat more political) by linking it to the worship of *God as king of the city of Zion*: here, the movement of thought within the Psalter would be from expressions of God's presence in the earthly city, to the affirmation of his presence more universally in the whole of creation. A more basic yet nevertheless profound view of a unified theology is that the Psalter as a whole is a variable but consistent *witness to the distinctive monotheistic faith of Israel*: this view is proposed by J. Day (see *Psalms*, pp. 123–5).

Other unifying approaches might take a more literary standpoint. These would include C. Westermann's view that the Psalter's unity is in its movement *from lament* (basically found in Books One to Three) *towards praise* (expressed mainly in Books Four and Five) and also W. Brueggemann's proposal that the Psalter's unity is its movement *from the Torah-Psalms*, which affirm a relationship with God through obedience to the law (Ps. 1), *to the Hymns*, which live in that relationship, expressing it in terms of praise of God (Ps. 150).

Another way suggests a more pragmatic approach to the Psalter's theology. According to G. T. Sheppard, its unity lies in its being a *didactic guide to righteousness*; similarly, K. Seybold understands the theology of the Psalter to cohere in its being a *reflective guide to prayer and right living*.

Together, these several proposals, none of which excludes another, witness to the need to hold together a theology of the Psalter which may have several unifying factors, yet which also comprises several very diverse paradoxical parts. The watchwords are 'unity in diversity' and 'diversity in unity'.

In brief, the Psalter has not arisen out of any self-conscious creation of systematic doctrine; it has emerged from the experiences of life and of liturgy, and has been shaped dynamically by the various literary and theological concerns of the collectors and editors: hence its theological tensions, and its paradoxical views of life and God. Yet this factor is vital for our own interpretation of the psalms, for it offers us an excellent example of 'theology in process'. This means that any contemporary reader, similarly shaped by diverse experiences of life and of liturgy, may also discover in the poetry concerns, both literary and theological, which have as much meaning now as then.

Conclusion: Theology and Poetry

Throughout this study we have referred several times to the three different yet interrelated processes which have influenced the composition and transmission of biblical verse. The most significant is a *setting-in-liturgy*—mainly at the Temple but also at less formal, public, cultic occasions. Important too is a *setting-in-life*, whereby ordinary human experiences (corporate and individual) were ordered and expressed through the poetic medium. Equally critical is the *setting-in-literature*, where the theological concerns of the editors have given us a fixed text and a coherent framework in which to effect our own interpretation. All of these three processes—liturgical, personal, and literary—are complementary ways of enabling the reader to appreciate ancient Semitic verse. To use again the analogy of the 'score' and the 'performance', biblical poetry has still the power to perform by way of a creative discourse between the text and reader.

To speak of a creative discourse immediately implies a concern with the meaning of biblical poetry 'now' as well as 'then'. Although the importance of a contemporary appreciation of biblical poetry has been constantly underlined, the emphasis necessarily has been more on understanding ancient poetry as it was 'then' rather than as it is 'now'. This was the priority in Part I, which assessed the various ways in which we might determine ancient poetry from a prose form; it was similarly a predominant concern in Part II, which examined the ways in which ancient verse functions differently when it is contextualized by a narrative framework; and it was also the primary purpose of Part III, which discussed the performative qualities of ancient verse in its liturgical setting. On this account, by way of conclusion, it is important to redress the balance and return to an issue which was raised in the first chapter—that biblical poetry needs to be appreciated in terms of its contemporary significance as well as understood as an ancient text.

In actual fact, we have seen repeatedly how our appreciation of the text *only* as ancient literature 'then' is constantly restricted, because so many aspects of biblical poetry defy too much certitude. There is so much we do not (and cannot) know; the permutations seem to be infinite. First, we still cannot be sure of the boundary lines between prose and poetry. Secondly, we still do not possess an accurate, reliable knowledge of the rules of Hebrew metre. Thirdly, parallelism *per se* still does not seem to be the only criterion which creates good Semitic verse. Fourthly, even where there is some adherence to traditional poetic forms, these are by no means consistently appropriated, either within the Psalter or outside it. Fifthly, even though a good deal of the language of Semitic poetry is typical and formulaic, drawing in the main from a store of liturgical conventions, much of it is metaphorical and ambiguous, and again defies over-definition. And sixthly, even though the liturgical influence on biblical poetry is very much evident, any precise knowledge of the cultic (or non-cultic) setting will always evade us. We may conclude that any attempt to have a satisfactory and complete understanding of Semitic poetry as it might have been 'then' is somewhat self-defeating.

And so it is necessary to apply the observations which were offered in Chapter 1. Biblical verse is elusive and open-ended; it adheres to some (known) poetic conventions, yet it also reflects much original and creative freedom of its own. Its diction is full of ambiguity of meaning. As with all poetry, but perhaps especially in this case, the concealing/revealing aspect of biblical verse means that any interpretation involves as much the power of imaginative insight as any so-called 'objective' analysis. On this account, contemporary meaning and a creative discourse between the text and the reader are not only possible but also desirable. Biblical verse communicates to us not only through our mind but also through our imagination. To use a striking phrase of G. Bachelard: 'the image has touched the depths before it stirs the surface' (*The Poetics of Space*, quoted in Cox and Theillgaard, *Mutative Metaphors in Psychotherapy*).

All poetry has a certain power to become what T. S. Eliot calls that 'raid on the inarticulate': ancient biblical poetry particularly so. It reveals the limits of a purely deductive approach, and possesses a capacity by way of metaphor and allusion to stir our memories and our emotions. We are reminded of something more than we can evoke by ourselves, and this brings into our consciousness an awareness of a more profound reality, older than the present order of things. In a poem entitled 'Rising Damp' (1982), Ursula Fanthorpe expresses this most evocatively:

> It is the other rivers that lie
> Lower, that touch us only in dreams
> That never surface. We feel their tug
> as a dowser's rod bends to the source below.
>
> (quoted in Cox and Theillgaard,
> *Mutative Metaphors*, 151)

On this issue we are not only speaking about the way we read biblical poetry, but also about the way in which we need to participate in all types of theological discourse. The language of theology needs the poetic medium for much of its expression, for poetry, with its power of allusion, reminds us of the more hidden and mysterious truths which theology seeks to express. Poetry is a form which illustrates our need for a sense of balance in our study of theology: on the one hand, good poetry still testifies to the need to be properly analytical in our pursuit of knowledge, but on the other, it illustrates the importance of being open to the possibility of mystery and ambiguity in our pursuit of meaning. Perhaps to learn the art of reading biblical poetry is but a precursor to learning the art of 'doing' theology at all.

BIBLIOGRAPHY

General

Ackroyd, P. R., *Doors of Perception: A Guide to Reading the Psalms* (London, 1978).
Alonso Schökel, L., *A Manual of Hebrew Poetics* (Rome, 1988).
Alter, R., *The Art of Biblical Poetry* (New York, 1985).
Anderson, A. A., *The Book of Psalms (1-72)* (Grand Rapids and London, 1972).
—— , *The Book of Psalms (73-150)* (Grand Rapids and London, 1972).
Barth, C. F., *Introduction to the Psalms* (Oxford, 1966).
Day, J., *Psalms* (Sheffield, 1990).
Follis, E. R. (ed.), *Directions in Biblical Hebrew Poetry* (Sheffield, 1987).
Gray, G. B., *The Forms of Hebrew Poetry* (New York, 1915; reprint 1972).
Gunkel, H., *The Psalms* (Philadelphia, 1967).
Keel, O., *The Symbolism of the Biblical World: Ancient Near Eastern Iconography and the Book of Psalms* (New York, 1978).
Kraus, H.-J., *Theology of the Psalms* (Minneapolis, 1986).
—— , *Psalms 1-59* (Minneapolis, 1988).
—— , *Psalms 60-150* (Minneapolis, 1989).
Kugel, J. L., *The Idea of Biblical Poetry* (New Haven, Conn., 1981).
Miller, P. D., *Interpreting the Psalms* (Philadelphia, 1986).
Mowinckel, S., *The Psalms in Israel's Worship*, i and ii (Oxford, 1962).
Oesterley, W. O. E., *The Psalms* (London, 1939).
Petersen, D. L. and Richards, K. L., *Interpreting Biblical Poetry* (Minneapolis, 1992).
Robinson, T. H., *The Poetry of the Old Testament* (London, 1947).
Rodd, C. S. *Psalms 1-72* (London, 1963).
—— , *Psalms 73-150* (London, 1964).
Sabourin, L., *The Psalms: Their Origin and Meaning* (New York, 1974).
Seybold, K., *Introducing the Psalms* (Edinburgh, 1990).
Simpson, D. C. (ed.), *The Psalmists* (London, 1926).
Watson, W. G. E., *Classical Hebrew Poetry: A Guide to its Techniques* (Sheffield, 1984).
Weiser, A., *The Psalms: A Commentary* (London, 1962).

Westermann, C., *The Psalms: Structure, Content and Message* (Minneapolis, 1980).

Wilson, G. H., *The Editing of the Hebrew Psalter* (Chico, Calif., 1985).

Young, F., *The Art of Performance* (London, 1990).

Poets, Poems, and Performances

Eliot, T. S., *On Poetry and Poets* (London, 1957).

Keble, J., *The Psalter in English Verse* (London, 1839).

—— , *Lectures on Poetry* (Oxford, 1912).

Lewis, C. S., *Reflections on the Psalms* (London, 1961).

—— , 'The Birth of Language', in *Poems* (ed. W. Hooper) (New York and London, 1964), 10–11.

—— , 'The Language of Religion', in id., *Christian Reflections* (Glasgow, 1967; 1981, pb), 164 ff.

Lowth, R., *Isaiah: A New Translation with a Preliminary Dissertation* (London, 1778).

—— , *Lectures on the Sacred Poetry of the Hebrews* (London, 1839).

Russell, P. A. and Winterbottom, M. (eds.), *Ancient Literary Criticism* (Oxford, 1972).

Poetry and Prose

Berlin, A., *Poetics and Interpretation of Biblical Narrative* (Sheffield, 1983).

Carmi, T. (ed.), *The Penguin Book of Hebrew Verse* (Harmondsworth, 1981).

Clements, R. E., *The Prayers of the Bible* (London, 1985).

Collins, T., *Line-Forms in Hebrew Poetry* (Rome, 1978).

Craigie, P. C., 'The Poetry of Ugarit and Israel', *TB* 22 (1971), 3–31.

—— , 'The Problem of Parallel Word-Pairs in Ugaritic and Hebrew Poetry', *Semitics* 5 (1977), 48–58.

Dahood, M., *Psalms 1–50*, (New York, 1966).

—— , *Psalms 51–100*, (New York, 1968).

—— , *Psalms 101–150*, (New York, 1970).

Fisher, L. R. (ed.), *Ras Shamra Parallels*, i, *Analecta Orientalia* 49 (Rome, 1972).

Gordon, C., *Ugaritic Textbook* (Rome, 1965).

Gottwald, N. K., 'Hebrew Poetry', in G. Buttrick *et al.* (eds.), *IDB* (Nashville, 1962), iii. 829–38.

Greenberg, M., *Biblical Prose Prayer as a Window to the Popular Religion of Ancient Israel* (Berkeley, Calif., and Los Angeles, 1983).

Gunn, D. M. and Fewell, D., *Narrative in the Hebrew Bible* (Oxford, 1993).

Herdner, A., *Corpus des tablettes en cunéiformes alphabétiques* (Paris, 1963).

Korpel, M. C. A. and de Moor, J. C., 'Fundamentals of Ugaritic and Hebrew Poetry', *UF* 18 (1986), 173–212.

Mellor, E. B., 'The Poetry and Prose of the Old Testament', in id. (ed.), *The Making of the Old Testament* (Cambridge, 1932), 53–7.

Steinberg, M., *The Poetics of Biblical Narrative* (Bloomington, Ind., 1987).

van de Meer, W. and de Moor, J. C. (eds.), *The Structural Analysis of Biblical and Canaanite Poetry* (Sheffield, 1988).

Metre

Barnes, W. E., 'Hebrew Metre and the Text of the Psalms', *JTS* 33 (1932), 374–82.

Culley, R. B., 'Metrical Analysis of Classical Hebrew Poetry', in J. W. Wevers and D. B. Radford (eds.), *Essays on the Ancient Semitic World* (Toronto, 1970), 12–28.

Dahood, M., *Psalms 1–50* (New York, 1966).

—— , *Psalms 51–100* (New York, 1968).

—— , *Psalms 101–150* (New York, 1970).

Eaton, J., 'Music's Place in Worship: A Contribution from the Psalms', *OTS* 23 (1983), 85–107.

Freedman, D. N., *Pottery, Poetry and Prophecy* (Winona Lake, Ind., 1980).

Haik-Vantoura, S., *The Music of the Bible Revealed* (San Francisco, Calif., 1991).

Kosmala, H., 'Form and Structure in Ancient Hebrew Poetry: A New Approach', *VT* 14 (1964), 423–45.

Loretz, O., 'Psalmenstudien (III)', *UF* 6 (1974), 175–210.

O'Connor, M., *Hebrew Verse Structure* (Winona Lake, Ind., 1980).

Robertson, A., *The Interpretation of Plainchant* (London, 1937).

—— , *Music of the Catholic Church* (London, 1961).

Sendrey, A., *Music in Ancient Israel* (London, 1969).

Stuart, D. K., *Studies in Early Hebrew Meter* (Missoula, Mont., 1976).

Werner, E., *The Sacred Bridge: The Interdependence of Liturgy and Music in Synagogue and Church during the First Millennium* (London, 1959).

Zim, R., *English Metrical Psalms: Poetry as Prose and Prayer 1535–1601* (Cambridge, 1987).

Parallelism

Berlin, A., *The Dynamics of Biblical Parallelism* (Bloomington, Ind., 1985).

Boling, R. G., '"Synonymous" Parallelism in the Psalms', *JSS* 5 (1960), 221–55.

Burney, C. F., *The Poetry of Our Lord: An Examination of the Formal Elements of Hebrew Poetry in the Discourses of Jesus Christ* (Oxford, 1925).

Geller, S. A., *Parallelism in Early Biblical Poetry* (Missoula, Mont., 1979).

Gerhardsson, B., *The Origins of the Gospel Traditions* (Philadelphia, 1979).

Greenstein, E. L., 'How Does Parallelism Mean?' in S. A. Geller, E. L. Greenstein, and A. Berlin (eds.), *A Sense of Text: The Art of Language in the Study of Biblical Literature* (Winona Lake, Ind., 1983), 41–70.

Landy, F., 'Poetics and Parallelism: Some Comments on James Kugel's *The Idea of Biblical Poetry*', *JSOT* 28 (1984), 61–87.

Miller, P. D. Jr., 'Synonymous-Sequential Parallelism in the Psalms', *Bib.* 61 (1980), 256–60.

——, 'Meter, Parallelism and Tropes: The Search for Poetic Style', *JSOT* 28 (1984), 99–106.

Petitpierre, R., *Poems of Jesus*, i and ii (Leighton Buzzard, 1965).

Riesenfeld, H., *The Gospel Tradition and its Beginnings* (London, 1957).

Poetry outside the Psalter

Blenkinsopp, J., *Wisdom and Law in the Old Testament* (Oxford, 1989).

Cross, F. M. and Freedman, D. N. (eds.), *Studies in Ancient Yahwistic Poetry* (Missoula, Mont., 1975).

Freedman, D. N., 'Early Israelite History in the Light of Early Israelite Poetry', in H. Goedicke and J. M. M. Roberts (eds.), *Unity and Diversity: Essays in the History, Literature and Religion of the Ancient Near East* (Baltimore, 1975), 3–35.

Gervitz, S., *Patterns in the Early Poetry of Israel* (Chicago, 1963).

Gunkel, H., 'Die israelitische Literatur', *Die Kultur der Gegenwart*, herausg. P. Hinneberg (I/VII: Berlin, 1906, 1925²), 23–112.

Kselman, J. S., 'The Recovery of Poetic Fragments from the Pentateuchal Priestly Source', *JBL* 97 (1978), 161–73.

Oesterley, W. O. E., *Ancient Hebrew Poems* (London, 1938).

Sawyer, J. F. A., *Prophecy and the Biblical Prophets* (Oxford, 1993).

Watts, J. W., *Psalm and Story: Insert Hymns in Hebrew Narrative* (Sheffield, 1992).

The Psalmists as Poets

Albertz, R., *Persönliche Frömmigkeit und offizielle Religion* (Stuttgart, 1978).

Anderson, A. A., 'Psalm Study between 1955 and 1969', *BQ* 23 (1969–70), 155–64.

Anderson, G. W., '"Sicut Cervus": Evidence in the Psalter of Private Devotion in Ancient Israel', *VT* 30 (1980), 388–97.

Bellinger, W. H., *Psalmody and Prophecy* (Sheffield, 1984).

Beyerlin, W., *Die Rettung der Bedrängten in den Feindpsalmen des Einzelnen* (Göttingen, 1970).

Briggs, C. A. and E. G., *The Book of Psalms 1-50*, (Edinburgh, 1906).

—— , *The Book of Psalms 51-150*, (Edinburgh, 1907).

Brueggemann, W., 'Psalms and the Life of Faith: A Suggested Typology of Function', *JSOT* 17 (1980), 3–32.

Causse, A., *Les plus vieux chants de la Bible* (Paris, 1926).

Cheyne, T. K., *The Psalter* (London, 1904).

Childs, B. S., 'Reflections on the Modern Interpretation of the Psalms', in F. M. Cross, W. E. Lanke, and D. M. Miller (eds.), *Magnalia Dei: The Mighty Acts of God* (New York, 1976), 377–88.

Clines, D. J. A., 'Psalm Research since 1955, i. The Psalms and the Cult', *TB* 18 (1967), 103–16.

—— , 'Psalm Research since 1955, ii. The Literary Genres', *TB* 20 (1969), 109–25.

Croft, S. J. L., *The Identity of the Individual in the Psalms* (Sheffield, 1987).

Delekat, L., *Asylie und Schutzorakel am Zionheiligtum. Eine Untersuchung zu den privaten Feindpsalmen* (Leiden, 1967).

Drijvers, P., *Les Psaumes: Genres littéraires et thèmes doctrinaux* (Paris, 1958).

Driver, S. R., *Studies in the Psalms* (London, 1915).

Duhm, B., *Die Psalmen* (Tübingen, 1899).

Eaton, J., *The Psalms* (London, 1967).

Gunkel, H., *Die Psalmen übersetzt und erklärt* (Göttingen, 1926).

—— , and Begrich, J., *Einleitung in die Psalmen* (Göttingen, 1933).

Hauret, C., 'Les Psaumes: Études récentes, état de la question', in J. J. Weber (ed.), *Où sont les études bibliques?* (Paris, 1968), 67–84.

Herder, J. G., *The Spirit of Hebrew Poetry* (Burlington, Vt., 1833).

James, F., *Thirty Psalmists: A Study of the Personalities of the Psalter* (New York, 1938).

Johnson, A. R., 'The Psalms', in H. H. Rowley (ed.), *The Old Testament and Modern Study* (Oxford, 1951), 162–209.

——, *The Cultic Prophet and Israel's Psalmody* (Cardiff, 1979).

Keel, O., *Feinde und Gottesleugner: Studien zum Frage der Widersacher in den Individualpsalmen* (Stuttgart, 1969).

Kirkpatrick, A. F., *The Book of Psalms* (Cambridge, 1902).

de Langhe, R. (ed.), *Le Psautier: Ses origines. Ses problèmes littéraires. Son influence* (Louvain, 1962).

Mowinckel, S., *Psalmenstudien*, vi. *Die Psalmendichter* (Kristiania, 1924).

Murphy, R. E., 'Psalms', *JBC* (New York, 1968), 529–76.

Oesterley, W. O. E., *Ancient Hebrew Poems* (London, 1938).

Prothero, R. E., *The Psalms in Human Life* (London, 1909).

Robinson, T. H., 'The Methods of Higher Criticism', in A. S. Peake (ed.), *The People and the Book* (Oxford, 1925), 151–82.

Schmidt, W. H., *Das Gebet der Angeklagten im Alten Testament* (Giessen, 1928).

Seybold, K., *Das Gebet der Kranken im Alten Testament* (Stuttgart, 1973).

Szörenyi, A., *Psalmen und Kult im Alten Testament. Zur Formgeschichte der Psalmen* (Budapest, 1961).

Tournay, R. J., *Seeing and Hearing God with the Psalms* (Sheffield, 1991).

Wellhausen, J., *Prolegomena to the History of Israel*, ET, revised from the German edn. of 1878 (Gloucester, Mass., 1957).

——, *Polychrome Bible on the Book of Psalms in a New Translation* (London, 1898).

Westermann, C., *Praise and Lament in the Psalms* (Edinburgh, 1981).

The Psalms as Poems

Aejmelaeus, A., *The Traditional Prayer in the Psalms* (Berlin, 1986).

Buss, M., 'The Study of Forms', in J. H. Hayes (ed.), *Old Testament Form Criticism* (San Antonio, Calif., 1974), 1–56.

——, 'The Idea of Sitz im Leben: History and Critique', *ZAW* 90 (1978), 157–70.

Ceresko, A. R., 'The Sage in the Psalms', in L. G. Perdue, *The Sage in Israel and the Ancient Near East* (Eisenbrauns, 1990), 217–30.

Culley, R. B., *Oral Formulaic Language in the Biblical Psalms* (Toronto, 1967).

Gerstenberger, E., 'Psalms', in J. H. Hayes (ed.), *Old Testament Form Criticism* (San Antonio, Calif., 1974), 178–223.

—, *Psalms, Part I, With an Introduction to Cultic Poetry* (Grand Rapids, 1988).

Hempel, J., 'Psalms, Book of', *IDB* iii (New York, 1962), 942–58.

Herzog, A., 'Psalms, Book of', *EJ* xiii (Jerusalem, 1972), 1303–34.

Limburg, J., 'Book of Psalms', in D. N. Freedman (ed.), *ABD* iv (New York, 1992), 522–36.

Lipinski, E. and Saint-Arnaud, I., 'Psaumes', *SDB* suppl. 9 (Paris, 1979), 1–214.

McCullough, W. S., 'Psalms: Introduction', *IBC* iv (New York, 1955), 3–17.

Mowinckel, S., 'Zur Sprache der biblischen Psalmen', *ThLZ* 81 (1956), 199–202.

Raabe, P. R., *Psalm Structures: A Study of Psalms with Refrains* (Sheffield, 1990).

Tsevat, M., *A Study of the Language of the Biblical Psalms* (SBLMS 9: Philadelphia, 1955).

Watters, W. R., *Formula Criticism and the Poetry of the Old Testament* (Berlin, 1976).

Wevers, J. W. M., 'A Study of the Form Criticism of Individual Complaint Psalms', *VT* 6 (1956), 80–96.

Whitley, C. F., 'Some Aspects of Hebrew Poetic Diction', *UF* 7 (1975), 493–502.

Widengren, G., *The Accadian and Hebrew Psalms of Lamentation as Religious Documents* (Stockholm, 1928; Uppsala, 1937).

The Psalter

Alden, R. L., 'Chiastic Psalms (I): A Study in the Mechanics of Semitic Poetry in Psalms 1–50', *JETS* 17 (1974), 11–28.

—, 'Chiastic Psalms (II): A Study in the Mechanics of Semitic Poetry in Psalms 51–100', *JETS* 19 (1976), 191–200.

Auffret, P., *La Sagesse a bâti sa maison: Études de structures littéraires dans l'Ancien Testament et spécialement dans les psaumes* (Göttingen, 1982).

Brennan, J. P., 'Some Hidden Harmonies in the Fifth Book of Psalms', in R. F. McNamara (ed.), *Essays in Honour of J. P. Brennan* (Rochester, NY, 1976), 124 ff.

Brueggemann, W., 'Bounded by Obedience and Praise: The Psalms as Canon', *JSOT* 50 (1991), 63–92.

Childs, B. S., *Introduction to the Old Testament as Scripture* (Philadelphia, 1985).

Goldingay, J., 'Repetition and Variation in the Psalms', *JQR* 68 (1978), 146–51.

——, 'The Dynamic Cycle of Praise and Prayer in the Psalms', *JSOT* 20 (1981), 85–90.

Goulder, M. D., 'The Fourth Book of the Psalter', *JTS* 26 (1975), 269–89.

——, *The Psalms of the Sons of Korah: A Study in the Psalter* (Sheffield, 1982).

——, *The Prayers of David (Psalms 51–72): Studies in the Psalter II* (Sheffield, 1990).

McCann, J. C., 'The Psalms as Instruction', *Interp.* 46 (1992), 117–28.

—— (ed.), *The Shape and Shaping of the Psalter* (Sheffield, 1993).

Mays, J. L., 'The Place of the Torah-Psalms in the Psalter', *JBL* 106 (1987), 3–12.

Seybold, K., *Die Wallfahrtpsalmen: Studien zur Entstehungsgeschichte von Psalmen 120–134* (Neukirchen, 1978).

Walton, J. H., 'Royal Psalms at Seams of the Psalter', *JSOT* 35 (1986), 85–94.

——, 'Psalms: A Cantata About the Davidic Covenant', *JTS* 34 (1991), 21–31.

Watke, B. K., 'A Canonical Process Approach to the Psalms', in J. S. and P. D. Feinberg (eds.), *Tradition and Testament* (Chicago, 1981), 3 ff.

Wilson, G. H., 'Evidence of Editorial Divisions in the Hebrew Psalter', *VT* 34 (1984), 337–52.

——, 'The Use of "Untitled" Psalms in the Hebrew Psalter', *ZAW* 97 (1985), 404–13.

——, 'The Shape of the Book of Psalms', *Interp.* 46 (1992), 129–42.

Zimmerli, W., 'Zwillingspsalmen', in J. Schreiner (ed.), *Wort, Lied und Gottesspruch: Beiträge zu Psalmen und Propheten* (Würzburg, 1972), 105–13.

The Interpretation of the Psalter

Anderson, G. W., 'Israel's Creed: Sung, not Signed', *SJTh* 16 (1963), 277–85.

Berlin, A., *Biblical Poetry through Medieval Jewish Eyes* (Winona Lake, Ind., 1991).

Bratcher, R. G. and Reyburn, W. D., *A Translator's Handbook on the Book of Psalms* (New York, 1991).

Broyles, C. C., *The Conflict of Faith and Experience in the Psalms* (Sheffield, 1989).

Charlesworth, J. H. (ed.), *The Old Testament Pseudepigrapha* ii, New York, 1985.

Gunn, G. S., *God in the Psalms* (Edinburgh, 1956).

Holm-Nielsen, S., 'The Importance of Late Jewish Psalmody for the Understanding of Old Testament Psalmodic Tradition', *StTh* 14 (1960), 1–53.

Kugel, J. L., 'Topics in the History of the Spirituality of the Psalms', in A. Green (ed.), *Jewish Spirituality from the Bible through the Middle Ages* (New York, 1986).

Murphy, R. E., 'The Faith of the Psalmists', *Interp.* 34 (1980), 229–39.

Raabe, P. R., 'Deliberate Ambiguity in the Psalter', *JBL* 110 (1991), 213–27.

Ringgren, H., *The Faith of the Psalmists* (Philadelphia, 1963).

Sanders, J. A., *The Psalms Scroll of Qumran Cave 11* (Oxford, 1962).

Sheppard, G. T., 'Theology and the Book of Psalms', *Interp.* 46 (1992), 143–55.

Vermes, G., *The Dead Sea Scrolls in English* (London, 1962; 1990[3]).

Conclusion

Alonso Schökel, L., *The Inspired Word: Scripture in the Light of Language and Literature* (New York, 1965).

Barfield, O., *Poetic Diction* (London, 1952).

Barr, J., *The Semantics of Biblical Language* (London, 1961).

Coulson, J., *Religion and Imagination* (Oxford, 1981).

Cox, M. and Theillgaard, A., *Mutative Metaphors in Psychotherapy: The Aeolian Mode* (London, 1987).

Daiches, C., *God and the Poets* (Oxford, 1984).

Easthope, A., *Poetry as Discourse* (London, 1983).

Fanthorpe, U., *Standing To: Poems* (Plymouth, 1982).

Frye, N., *The Great Code* (London, 1982).

Gardner, H., *Religion and Literature* (London, 1971).

Lewis, C. S., 'The Language of Religion', in id., *Christian Reflections* (Glasgow, 1967; 1981, pb), 164 ff.

Merton, T., *On the Psalms* (London, 1957; repr. 1977).

Prickett, S., *Words and the Word: Language, Poetics and Biblical Interpretation* (Cambridge, 1986).

Ramsey, I., *Religious Language* (London, 1957).

——, *Models and Mystery* (Oxford, 1964).

Soskice, J. M., *Metaphor and Religious Language* (Oxford, 1987).

INDEX OF PASSAGES CITED

GENERAL INDEX

NB. Page references to tables are *italicized*.